CAMBRIDGE TEXTS
HISTORY OF POLITICAL

ALBERT VENN DICEY
Writings On Democracy And The Referendum

What are the limits to parliamentary sovereignty? When should the people be able to vote directly on issues? The constitutional theorist Albert Venn Dicey (1835–1922) was a cogent advocate of the referendum. While his enthusiasm for the institution was widely acknowledged in his own day, thereafter this dimension of his career has been largely neglected. This fall into obscurity is partly explained by the fact that Dicey never collected his writings on referendums into a single volume. Consequently, during the prolonged crisis over Brexit, the implications of Dicey's thought were unclear, despite his standing as a foundational figure in British constitutional law. This timely modern edition brings together Dicey's sophisticated and intricate writings on the referendum, and it covers his attempts to construct a credible theory of democracy on a new intellectual and institutional basis. An original scholarly introduction analyzes Dicey's thought in light of its contemporary context.

GREGORY CONTI is Assistant Professor of Politics at Princeton University. He is the author of *Parliament the Mirror of the Nation: Representation, Deliberation, and Democracy in Victorian Britain* (Cambridge University Press, 2019) as well as numerous articles about the history of liberalism, democratic theory, political representation, toleration, and freedom of speech.

CAMBRIDGE TEXTS IN THE HISTORY OF POLITICAL THOUGHT

General editor
QUENTIN SKINNER
Queen Mary University of London

Cambridge Texts in the History of Political Thought is firmly established as the major student series of texts in political theory. It aims to make available all the most important texts in the history of political thought, from ancient Greece to the twentieth century, from throughout the world and from every political tradition. All the familiar classic texts are included, but the series seeks at the same time to enlarge the conventional canon through a global scope and by incorporating an extensive range of less well-known works, many of them never before available in a modern English edition, and to present the history of political thought in a comparative, international context. Where possible, the texts are published in complete and unabridged form, and translations are specially commissioned for the series. However, where appropriate, especially for non-western texts, abridged or tightly focused and thematic collections are offered instead. Each volume contains a critical introduction together with chronologies, biographical sketches, a guide to further reading and any necessary glossaries and textual apparatus. Overall, the series aims to provide the reader with an outline of the entire evolution of international political thought.

For a list of titles published in the series, please see end of book

ALBERT VENN DICEY

Writings on Democracy and the Referendum

EDITED BY

GREGORY CONTI

Princeton University, New Jersey

Shaftesbury Road, Cambridge CB2 8EA, United Kingdom

One Liberty Plaza, 20th Floor, New York, NY 10006, USA

477 Williamstown Road, Port Melbourne, VIC 3207, Australia

314–321, 3rd Floor, Plot 3, Splendor Forum, Jasola District Centre,
New Delhi – 110025, India

103 Penang Road, #05–06/07, Visioncrest Commercial, Singapore 238467

Cambridge University Press is part of Cambridge University Press & Assessment,
a department of the University of Cambridge.

We share the University's mission to contribute to society through the pursuit of
education, learning and research at the highest international levels of excellence.

www.cambridge.org
Information on this title: www.cambridge.org/9781108845410

DOI: 10.1017/9781108955799

© Cambridge University Press & Assessment 2023

First published 2023

A catalogue record for this publication is available from the British Library.

A Cataloging-in-Publication data record for this book is available from the Library of Congress.

ISBN 978-1-108-84541-0 Hardback
ISBN 978-1-108-95817-2 Paperback

Contents

Acknowledgements   *page* vi

Introduction   viii

Chronology   xl

Note on the Texts   xliii

Bibliographical Note   xlvi

1 The Balance of Classes (1867)   3

2 Democracy in Switzerland (1890)   16

3 Ought the Referendum to Be Introduced into England? (1890)   53

4 The Defence of the Union (1892)   81

5 The Referendum (1894)   103

6 Will the Form of Parliamentary Government be Permanent? (1899) 112

7 The Referendum and Its Critics (1910)   127

8 The Parliament Act, 1911, and the Destruction of All
   Constitutional Safeguards (1912)   152

9 Development during the Last Thirty Years of New Constitutional
   Ideas (Extract from the Introduction to the Eighth Edition of
   Introduction to the Study of the Law of the Constitution, 1915)   171

Index   210

Acknowledgements

Belonging as I do to a generation for whom, as undergrads, the history of political thought as a field was almost synonymous with the "blue books," it is a real honor for me to contribute to this series. My first expression of gratitude must therefore go to Quentin Skinner for keeping the series going and for his kind words about the idea for this edition, and to Elizabeth Friend-Smith for her editorial guidance and her patience in waiting for the manuscript during the strange pandemic period. The anonymous readers of the proposal, for both this publisher and another, offered astute comments that helped me find the final shape of the collection; and the author of the clearance report on the full manuscript gave several important notes. Over the past few years, Anatole Grieu, Stephanie Conway, Jordan Rudinsky, Matthew Wilson, and especially Joseph Puchner have provided valuable research assistance. Stuart Jones, Charlotte Brewer, and Peter Gilliver lent me a hand in making sense of a particularly thorny and interesting passage. William Selinger and Annie Stilz read the introduction and offered helpful comments, and I appreciate the feedback I received on the introduction from audiences at NYU and Stanford. Many of my Princeton colleagues in political theory and adjacent fields have kindly read or listened to various iterations of my thoughts on Dicey; I thank them for their support and insight. I owe a special debt of gratitude to Melissa Lane for being the first to suggest that I undertake a collection of Dicey's writings on these themes. Librarians and archivists at several institutions have been extremely helpful. And it is my pleasure to acknowledge the previous editors and students of Dicey on whose outstanding work I have most relied: John Allison, Mark Walters, and above all Richard Cosgrove.

Finally, this edition is dedicated to Richard Tuck and Eric Nelson, for the example they have set me, and to the memory of Sungho Kimlee.

Introduction

Albert Venn Dicey is widely recognized as one of the most important of Anglophone constitutional lawyers. In particular, legal academics frequently read his landmark *Introduction to the Study of the Law of the Constitution* proleptically, by the standards of an analytic jurisprudence it supposedly established. Consequently, Dicey's politics are often ignored or, when considered, treated in a lamenting or caricaturish fashion. His constant attentiveness to public affairs, his curiosity about different regime-types, his assertion of his own values, his immersion in texts that we would now place within the field of political theory – these are seen as having prevented Dicey from reaching his appointed telos of apolitical constitutionalism and as tainting his legacy as a jurist. Historians of Victorian/Edwardian Britain come from a different angle, but likewise end up neglecting Dicey as a political theorist. For while they have been intrigued by Dicey's political activity, they usually treat him simply as a combatant in the party conflicts over Ireland, a perspective which encourages the presumption that his ideas were merely topical and thus beneath theoretical interest. Serious engagement with Dicey as a political thinker thus remains relatively rare, although encouraging signs of greater scholarly interest in this side of his work have appeared of late. This edition is meant as a contribution to the emerging understanding of Dicey as an important figure in political thought.

Such a reassessment is long overdue. For one thing, the conventional conceptions of Dicey have been misleading biographically. For Dicey, like so many of his generation, was extraordinarily prolific, making of steady intellectual work a spiritual substitute for the Evangelicalism of his ancestors in which he could no longer share. Though it is hard to quantify the

portions of his capacious corpus devoted to different subject areas, especially given that the Victorians operated with less firm boundaries between
the humanistic/social-scientific subjects than we have today, political
commentary and theorizing may very well have constituted the largest
area of his literary output. To be sure, Dicey was interested in putting the
academic study of law on a more professionalized footing and in demon-
strating that legal inquiry could be conducted with a healthy measure of
independence from contending political imperatives. But the development of his political ideas was not a departure from his true vocation of
espousing non-partisan analytic legal positivism. It was, rather, a core
component of his identity as a man of letters who sought to educate the
hyper-literate Victorian public about the major dilemmas of modern
society. It was not for nothing that his gravestone, beyond the customary
listing of professional affiliations and family ties, accorded him three
designations: "JURIST – POLITICAL PHILOSOPHER – PATRIOT."

That second appellation, if judged by the standards of his time and not
ours, indubitably fits Dicey. His was an age in which Tocqueville and Mill
stood at the summit of political philosophy – both of whom were concretely engaged in power politics, held public offices of note, commented
copiously on events in the periodical press, and wrote in a style that
(according to today's disciplinary distinctions) mixed sociology, political
science, philosophy, religion, law, literature, and history. Dicey followed
their example. His approach, which held across much of even his most
topical journalism, was to tease out the key principles underlying different
institutional dispensations, social trends, and bodies of thought; and his
advocacy of particular policies, while it could give way to passionate
declamation, generally sought both to tie his preferred measures back to
fundamental values and to weigh ineluctable tradeoffs. Scholars today
might therefore be inclined to call him, following Stefan Collini, a "committed observer" or "public moralist." He styled himself variously; in
addition to being a political philosopher, he was a "historical critic"
seeking to divine "what are likely to prove the permanent characteristics
of English democracy," a scrutinizer of "State system[s]," a diagnostician
of "states of opinion," and an expositor of the "spirit of institutions."[1]

---

[1] Dicey, "Democracy in England," *Nation* 30 (June 1880): 414–15; "Why Englishmen Are
not Alarmed at the Present Crisis," *Nation* 41(Oct. 1885): 340–1; "History of English
Philanthropy," *Nation*, 82 (Feb. 1906): 142–3; J.W.F. Allison, "Editor's Introduction," to
Dicey, *Lectures on Comparative Constitutionalism*, ed. J.W.F. Allison (Oxford, 2013).

In this multifaceted handling of cultural-political questions Dicey was of his epoch, which was a high-point for the influence and ability of bourgeois intellectuals. His lifetime broadly coincided with the shift from the highbrow press, dominated by the rationalistic but eclectic journals of general culture, to the academy as the centre of British intellectual life, and he was not alone in carrying the habits of mind forged in the former arena with him into the latter. (Even his friend Henry Sidgwick, presumed to be the progenitor of specialized academic moral philosophy, wrote tomes which would now fall into the camp of history or political sociology, and he penned numerous addresses and articles on public controversies.) Tellingly, both Dicey's first and last books, released sixty years apart, investigated the character and consequences of major historical institutions in a way that, he avowed, could not be cabined off as either strictly legal or political. More than to legal writers or judges, references to a kind of moral-political canon proliferate across Dicey's pages. Beyond the omnipresent Mill, his writing was littered with references to: great "geniuses" of political speculation such as Tocqueville, Burke, and Walter Bagehot; Enlightenment luminaries like Voltaire, Jean-Louis de Lolme, Bentham, and William Paley; contemporaneous social philosophers like Sidgwick and Herbert Spencer; romantics like Wordsworth (whom he read as a theorist of a salutary form of nationalism); fellow public moralists such as his cousins James Fitzjames and Leslie Stephen; Whig-liberal historians such as T.B. Macaulay and Henry Hallam; and a slew of then-cutting-edge social scientists such as James Russell Lowell, Moisei Ostrogorski, and his close friend James Bryce.

Even in the *Law of the Constitution* – a work which he framed as taking a legal angle on the constitution and which has so frequently been assimilated to today's notions of analytic jurisprudence – Dicey was unable, or rather hardly bothered, to prevent the spillover of political themes. Dicey's most famous book is predominantly devoted to showing how certain core principles of political theory (e.g. parliamentary sovereignty and the rule of law) are realized in the legal, cultural, and conventional underpinnings of the constitutional order. As the writer of the foreword to the first Russian edition perceived, the subject of the *Law of the Constitution* was nothing less than "a mode of life."[2]

---

[2] "Sir Paul Vinogradoff's Foreword to the Russian Edition (1891)," trans. Eric Myles, in Dicey, *Lectures Introductory to the Study of the Law of the Constitution*, ed. J.W.F. Allison (Oxford, 2013), 287.

We cannot, therefore, have an accurate understanding of Dicey's thinking – or really of the *mentalité* of Victorian letters more generally – if we neglect or rue the pervasively political character of his oeuvre. But there is also much to be gained substantively for political theory and the history of political thought by studying Dicey on these more accurate terms. For Dicey's was a fertile mind. He was a font of classifications and categories which remain useful. Some of these are descriptively ideal-typical, and reminiscent of Weber: for instance, he distinguished between parliamentary and non-parliamentary executives; between flexible and rigid constitutions, and between historical and non-historical ones; between the legal, civil, and military spirits of different regimes. Other dichotomies were more openly evaluative, as when he set natural partisan-ship (good) against party government (bad), or government by parliament (bad) against parliamentary government (good). Furthermore, his hunt for the essential properties of systems of government yielded results that one can test one's own assumptions against even now, as in his multi-pronged definition of federalism as: resting on a desire for "union" but not "unity"; inherently requiring the supremacy of the constitution, which in turn brought both an inevitable institutional correlate (judicial review) and an underlying cultural spirit (legalism); and producing both governmental weakness and political conservatism (187). Today, we can still ask profit-ably whether federal systems ineluctably exhibit these characteristics.

But what will be of greatest interest for most political theorists is that Dicey defended a vision of a legitimate and morally desirable political order, even if he did not do so with the systematicity of a *Leviathan* or *Social Contract*. From the 1880s onward, he set himself the task of describing (what he considered) a healthy liberal democracy and of assessing the threats to it which fellow holders of "democratic assump-tions" were inclined to overlook.[3] Intriguingly for twenty-first-century readers, Dicey was in several respects one of history's losers: many of the causes for which he fought failed, and many of what he regarded as pillars of a liberal polity have been fundamentally altered or fallen into the dustbin between his day and ours. And yet he was the first Anglophone thinker of note to appreciate what has become an absolutely central insti-tution of the modern age: the referendum. Consequently, if in some ways Dicey's thought testifies to the vastness of the gulf between the liberalism

---

[3] Dicey, "Democratic Assumptions [I–V]," 51–3 (1890–1): 397–8; 46–7; 497–8; 46–7; 83–4 respectively.

hegemonic as he came of age – what he called the "old liberal" worldview of "Benthamism" – and the liberalism of our world, in others he sounds more contemporary than do other eminent Victorians, and his democratic convictions were more pronounced than those of the liberal and liberal-conservative intelligentsia in which he circulated. In Dicey the old and the new, the past and the present, mingle in fascinating ways.

To comprehend Dicey's political vision, one of the first points to recognize is simply that his was a long life. He was born in 1835, shortly after the First Reform Act and still a couple years before Victoria's coronation, and he died after the Russian Revolution and World War I. The crucial decade of his life was the 1880s. His greatest literary success, the *Law of the Constitution*, which set the terms of British constitutional analysis for generations, came out in 1885 and was received as an instant classic. Shortly thereafter, the political contest which consumed much of Dicey's attention for the rest of his life was launched when Liberal Prime Minister William Gladstone announced the First Home Rule Bill, which would have granted considerable autonomy to Ireland and set up an Irish legislature and executive in Dublin while keeping Ireland within the United Kingdom; Dicey was from then on an implacable opponent of Home Rule (preferring even Irish independence to it) until the end of his days. Despite a congenital handicap, he lived (improbably, in his own mind) to 87; his correspondence over the last few decades of his life is full of reflections on the loss of friends and of predictions that he would imminently shuffle off his mortal coil. In his judgment, the Reform Act of 1832 had inaugurated political modernity in Britain. It constituted a "pacific revolution" that, in addition to transferring electoral power from the landed nobility to the commercial/industrial middle classes, had the more seismic effect of transforming the country's political culture from one averse to change and complacent about the blessings of its immemorial constitution to one that embraced consistent legislative innovation in the name of improvement. Hence Dicey, who was keenly interested in questions of periodization, saw his own life as coextensive with that of *modern* Britain.

Two notions prevail about the trajectory of Dicey's thought over his nearly nine decades, though they sit somewhat uneasily with one another. On the one hand, it is alleged that his ideas were fixed in amber as a young man and that he stubbornly refused to modify them as the world changed around him; on the other, he is charged with having frequently adjusted his views to serve partisan interests, especially regarding the Unionist fight against Irish Home Rule. Neither is accurate, and the truth, as usual, falls somewhere in-between. Dicey was, as he recognized, largely faithful to certain core tenets to which he had been committed by the 1860s, tenets which we would now call (partly due to Dicey's own influence) "liberal individualist"; it was precisely because he retained his confidence in these beliefs even as they lost their ascendancy over the British public that in the last third of his life he consistently spoke of having lived past his day. And yet his ideas did undergo revision, and in particular he came to rethink the institutional means available for realizing his values.

Dicey came to maturity in the "intellectual aristocracy" – that lofty stratum of familially interconnected members of the burgeoning knowledge-classes who did so much to set the tone of Victorian morals and letters – at Oxford, where he thrived in the discussion groups and politically charged sociability of "academic liberalism." These university liberals took inspiration from John Stuart Mill and also from now lesser-known prophets of the application of science to social questions such as Auguste Comte. At their zenith as young men in the late 1850s through the mid-1860s, they championed such causes as free trade, the extension of the franchise, national liberation movements abroad, nonsectarian education, the rationalization of administrative structures and reduction of government waste, and modernizing legal reform.

Dicey was an active presence in this milieu, and the culmination of this formative period for him came in the essay "The Balance of Classes." It was published as a chapter in the influential 1867 volume *Essays on Reform*, a series of arguments in favor of what would become the Second Reform Act; alongside another essay collection from the same year, *Questions for a Reformed Parliament*, this book stands as the best testament of the academic-liberal mindset. For our purposes Dicey's piece is important for two related reasons: first, because it set up Dicey on the most pro-democratic end of the liberal spectrum, and second, because it gave early expression to certain themes that would persist in his thinking.

"The Balance of Classes" was above all an attack on what Dicey (in agreement with Mill) regarded as the strongest plank of the anti-democratization platform: the theory of Parliament as "a mirror of every class" (4). While there were many variations on this theme, the core of the mirroring outlook was that the electoral system had to be engineered (by constructing constituencies with an eye to sociological conditions and applying appropriate qualifications for the vote) such that the major classes and interests in society would be present in the Commons in accordance with their "due" weight and importance (9). This approach opposed the notion that individual "persons" and their preferences were the appropriate objects of representation. Instead, the creation of a truly representative assembly required (depending on the author) securing sufficient seats for "organic interests" such as local communities, economic interests, class divisions, and religious groups and/or granting appropriate influence to valuable "social powers" such as experience, intellect, property, and education. To fail to take these elements into account was to commit a conceptual error: it was to proceed on the false notion that the "nation" was "a mere aggregation of millions . . . a homogeneous mass of units," rather than a community of communities.[4] But it was also to deny the country certain essential goods. For in a system of uniform universal suffrage, the majority (usually figured as manual labourers, but also potentially a grouping of a different sort, such as Catholics in Ireland) could impose its will unhindered. Such a situation threatened the rights of minorities, undermined parliamentary deliberation, and compromised stability by alienating marginalized sections of society from the political process. As is evident in the essay, Dicey's rebuttal to the class representation theory was multi-pronged. But the crux of his position was that there was no way to avoid arbitrariness in the attempt to sort citizens into relevant groups and assess their relative importance. Consequently, the only fair principle of parliamentary reform was what we might call sociologically agnostic egalitarian individualism.

In addition to this central thread, "Balance of Classes" contained in its short space a number of themes which would recur down the decades of Dicey's political writing. For one, he aligned his positions with an original liberal-radical tradition. The theory of class representation occupied a dominant position in mid-Victorian political culture; as Dicey acknowledged, it was avowed by self-declared liberals and conservatives alike. But like Burke appealing from the new to the old Whigs, Dicey called back to an "old Liberal" tradition, one that had formerly united "all democratic or radical Reformers," against more recent trends in liberalism with which he was less in sympathy (4). This would prove one of his favored rhetorical moves.

[4] W.R. Greg, "The Expected Reform Bill," *Edinburgh Review* 95 (1852): 213–80.

Dicey's identification with a more authentic liberalism was closely linked to one of the deepest dimensions of his thought: an allergy to the recognition in state institutions of class or sectional interest. In contrast to the political formations of the *ancien régime* – which provided separate representatives and embedded distinct privileges for numerous corporate bodies, estates, and orders – the modern state, Dicey held, strove for formal agnosticism toward the various substate allegiances and identities of citizens. For Dicey, this insistence on impartiality vis-à-vis the cleavages in civil society both inhered analytically in the ideal of equality before the law and was supported by pragmatic concerns for stability. "Incalculable evils," he wrote, followed from the "tendency to intensify differences" inherent in plans for class representation, for the members elected thereupon would see themselves as "special represen-tatives of a class" and hence "from their very position" inclined to "display and intensify class feeling" in its "most fanatical" forms (13). As was true of Victorian liberalism broadly, Dicey was fixated on class harmony as a necessary foundation for social progress and civic peace; more controversially, he would consistently locate the non-recognition in law and government of class differences as essential to such harmony.

The desire of the class-mirrorers to imprint a sociological image onto the electoral system struck Dicey, further, as objectionably essentialist. Democracy was characterized not by the effort to "stereotype" a notion of the nature of society and therefore to tilt the parliamentary playing-field in favor of certain outcomes (10), but by an open-ended conception of politics in which one accepted that through persuasion and voluntary mobilization a range of coalitions might come to power.

It is noteworthy that Dicey's antipathy to earmarking seats on a communitarian or corporatist basis extended to federalist versions of apportionment. "America," he averred, "is a standing warning ... against artificial schemes for insuring a definite amount of power to certain classes, since the whole theory of State Rights is nothing but a theory of class rights carried out on a larger scale" (13). While Dicey was not opposed to federalism in contexts in which it seemed to arise naturally out of historical conditions, he would be an implacable adver-sary of all measures to federalize the United Kingdom and the empire.

This mention of Dicey's attentiveness to trajectories of development dovetails with another feature of his political writing: its historicism. Dicey occasionally mocked what he considered an excessive reverence for history among his peers, which he judged an overweening swing of the pendulum in the direction contrary to Bentham's supposed indifference on that front. And he fretted that "the fashion of the day," which prescribed "one-sided devotion to the historical method," was inculcating a kind of relativism that was indistinguishable from complacent conservatism, for it was "leading the world to forget that ... to show how an opinion grew up is a different matter from proving its truth or falsehood."[5] And yet throughout his work he invoked the movement of history in favor of his conclusions, and he was not averse to deploying one of the key tools of the post-Constant/-Tocqueville liberal toolbox: the accusation of anachronism, of being behind or on the wrong side of history. Hence Dicey was not satisfied merely to charge class-representation schemes with being arbitrary and unfair; he also faulted them for hearkening back to the conditions of "the Middle Ages" and being unsuited to a "society like that of modern England" (13–14).

A final ingredient of Dicey's *Reform* tract that would persist beyond his academic-liberal period was a minimalist conception of democracy. For Dicey, democracy was simply that system of government in which "the greater number of citizens" was "ultimately supreme in the affairs of the State," in which "the greater number may be able to carry out their own wishes" over the objections of the "smaller number" (6). He would repeatedly enunciate this majoritarian-proceduralist view, which he took to be a simple extension of Bentham's philosophy; as he put it in a later work, "'Democracy' in its stricter and older sense ... means, not a state of society, but a form of government; namely, a constitution under which sovereign power is possessed by the numerical majority of the male citizens."[6] While Dicey was not altogether consistent in this respect, he generally resisted substantive definitions of democracy that equated it with a broad social ideal. The only values inherent in democracy were those necessary to justify and spell out the notions of political non-arbitrariness and majority consent touched on so far; democracy was therefore consistent with a variety of socioeconomic and cultural formations. Dicey was insistent on this point, against both socialists who wished positively to identify democracy with economic equality or state control of industry and conservatives who, "confused by the memories

---

[5] Dicey, "Sidgwick's Methods of Ethics [I]," *Nation* 22 (May 1876): 162–3; "The Weak Side of the Historical Method," *Nation* 24 (Apr. 1877): 217–18.
[6] Dicey, *Lectures on the Relation between Law and Public Opinion in England during the Nineteenth Century* (Indianapolis, 2008), 52.

of the Reign of Terror," were still associating "democratic government and revolutionary habits."[7] Dicey recognized that there were tricky questions to resolve about what a "majority will" entailed and how it could be discerned. But he belabored the message that "democracy [could] not be identified with any one kind of legislative opinion" and, conversely, that one could not be a democrat and reject majority decisions of fundamental political questions.[8] These convictions would slot in frictionlessly to his later argumentative arsenal in favor of the referendum.

Along with attempts to imbue the concept of democracy with broader social ideals, his 1867 advocacy contains hints of his enduring frustration with another side of the democratic ledger: a hard version of what today we call the theory of epistemic democracy. The supposition that majorities did not "fall into errors" was no part of his democratizing philosophy (9). Dicey distanced himself from extreme egalitarians who were inclined to assume the people were always right. Indeed, it was a common Diceyan refrain that in prior centuries a wider electorate would likely have led to a less "liberal" course of policy and fallen into major blunders that aristocratic government avoided. By contrast, Dicey highlighted that "the passing or the maintaining of good or wise laws" and the making of law "in conformity with the demands of public opinion" were irreducibly distinct ends, and that no guarantee of the coincidence of "wise" and "popular" government could be provided (173). Fortunately, there were measures available to render the people wiser, or at least to render their verdicts more deliberate. But at the end of the day, it was the mark of the true democrat to accept the judgments of majorities even when he fervently disagreed.

As the foregoing indicates, if Dicey was unsparing toward the "enthusiasts" who proclaimed that "the People will always govern rightly" and trumpeted such mantras as "*vox populi, vox Dei,*"[9] he was nevertheless keen to dispel the nightmare scenarios purveyed by antidemocrats. For instance, he dismissed the fear that democracies were especially liable to tyrannical action and denied the thesis that there was any tyranny peculiar to majority rule. Sensible exponents of democracy sought a

[7] Dicey, "An English View of American Conservatism [II]," *Nation* 30 (Apr. 1880): 282–3; "Another View of Lord Derby," *Nation* 36 (Jan. 1883): 31–3.
[8] *Law and Public Opinion*, 219.
[9] Dicey, "New Jacobinism and Old Morality," *Contemporary Review* 53 (1888): 475–502.

middle path: they steered clear of strong epistemic arguments which rested on implausible romanticizations of the wisdom and virtue of the people, left hostages to fortune, and could be gainsaid by inconvenient historical facts. But they also put forward reasons for cautious optimism about popular capacity, at least in a propitious institutional-cultural setting. Thus, he averred that while "of course, the majority is no infallible ruler," it was still the case that "belief in free government rests ultimately on the conviction that a people gains more by the experience, than it loses by the errors, of liberty" (9). Or in characteristic words from a couple of decades later: "This rule may be, and ... often is, unenlightened, dull, and (occasionally) oppressive. But no one who is really a democrat does not hold that on the whole it is best in a given state or nation that the will of the majority should be supreme."[10] A sober acceptance both of popular competence and of its limits was the appropriate concomitant of democratic commitment.

At just 32 years of age, then, Dicey had put in place the outlines of a vision within which he would continue to work. But it cannot be said that he had painted a full picture. Over the next decade-and-a-half he would churn out reams of journalism, practice law (without great success), and compose a couple of legal treatises. From the mid-1880s, however, he would elaborate both a diagnosis of the major problems of modern politics and a set of prescriptions for reforming the British political system to meet these challenges. For this reason, even if his thoughts were never systematized in a magnum opus, he has a claim to be ranked among the first truly modern democratic theorists in the English language. For unlike Bentham or Mill, Dicey observed institutions and conditions which remain fundamental to liberal societies today but which the former had not been able to appreciate. These included: a truly mass suffrage; the intensification of Irish nationalism; the bureaucratization of government and the growth of the civil service; centralized, disciplined parties with significant extra-parliamentary apparatuses, and the rise of direct action in uneasy conjunction with these parties; increasing executive control of parliamentary business; the laying of the foundations of the welfare state and greater government intervention into economic life; and, most of all, the referendum. For Dicey, these developments amounted to nothing less than a crisis of classical parliamentarism and Victorian liberalism.

---

[10] Dicey, "Americomania in English Politics," *Nation* 42 (Jan. 1886): 52–3.

In the mid-1880s, two causes, one political and one intellectual, spurred Dicey on to a sustained, if dispersed, endeavor to theorize liberal democracy that would occupy much of the rest of his life. The former was noted earlier: the Liberal party's conversion to Irish Home Rule in 1886. The second, more a process than a specific incident, was the considerable attention that Dicey began paying to Switzerland. While his well-documented horror at Home Rule was undoubtedly the lodestar of his political activity in the second half of his life, it is not true that it determined all his political thinking. Indeed, his interest in Switzerland – and his suspicion that its two most un-English features, the non-partisan executive and the referendum, might offer an alternative to British parliamentarism and party government that was superior for a democratic age – preceded Gladstone's commitment of the Liberal party to Home Rule.

In rebuffing Home Rule, Dicey has been alleged to have made a "conservative" turn, but this label is liable to be far too bluntly handled. From the mid-1880s onward, it is most appropriate to say that Dicey belonged to a category of disillusioned liberals, which included Sidgwick, who had come to harbor grave reservations about the Liberal party precisely because they saw it as having abandoned true liberal principles. Dicey tended to think of himself from then on as ideologically homeless, and he could identify in partisan terms only with the Liberal Unionists – the set of former Liberals who split over Home Rule and maintained a fraught alliance of necessity with Conservatives, toward whom Dicey never felt deep affection. Dicey did sometimes evoke "a rational Conservatism."[11] But this was in his mind little distinguishable from the Tocquevillian-Millian liberalism in which he had grown up, updated to be more mindful of threats to political stability, individual liberty, and the Empire that he judged had recently arisen. To equate Dicey with any deeper tradition of political-philosophical conservatism is thus liable to obscure more than it reveals, for few of the conventionally identified hallmarks of conservatism applied in his case. To give a few examples: he did not see prejudice as a source of imbedded wisdom; he did not treat the landed aristocracy as a specially beneficent political class; he was, depending on the day, either indifferent or hostile to organized religion;

---

[11] He hoped to "increase the power of rational Conservatism, for which I care much without increasing the power of the conservative party, for which I care nothing"; letter to Leo Maxse, 12 Oct. 1909, quoted in Richard Cosgrove, *The Rule of Law: Albert Venn Dicey, Victorian Jurist* (Chapel Hill, NC, 1980), 109.

and he saw the French Revolution as justified by the injustices of the *ancien régime*. Most of all, he despised "reaction" and the refusal to recognize "accomplished facts."[12] Chief among these *faits accomplis* was the arrival of democracy, and Dicey repeatedly chided conservatives for not embracing democracy with sufficient speed and sincerity. Indeed, Dicey's response to the pessimism that the Home Rule movement and other late-century trends inspired in him was to push further the democratic leanings of his salad days and to expose his countrymen to models of liberal-representative government alternative to the British parliamentary heritage. In other words, in his thirties, Dicey had believed that the sine qua non of political improvement was the defeat of the class-representationists and the melioration of the composition of the Commons, thereby ensuring a more democratic parliamentary system. In his fifties and beyond, however, he came to believe that "the sovereignty of the nation" within the framework of constitutional government required the techniques of extra-parliamentary democracy (208).

To grasp why Dicey made this switch, it is helpful to turn to the *Law of the Constitution*. The timing of Dicey's most famous work, which received its first edition in 1885, makes for a real irony in the history of political-legal letters. There is doubtless a patriotic aspect to the book – especially to his famous and not exactly impartial comparison between the English conception of the rule of law and French *droit administratif* – so it is perhaps pardonable that the *Law of the Constitution* has been persistently read as an unambiguous endorsement of contemporaneous English constitutional arrangements. This reading, however, is misleading. As mentioned above, *Law of the Constitution* was an effort to condense into a few principles the basic logic of a mass of law, conventional rules, and constitutional practices. The fact that it was primarily interpretive of the existing constitutional-legal situation and only secondarily or indirectly normative contributed to its being both universally acclaimed and enlisted for diametrically opposed political causes – including its citation by Gladstone a year later in justification of the Home Rule proposals to which Dicey would ardently object. Dicey was not, as has been claimed, a complacent worshipper of the Victorian status quo. He warned against seeing any constitutional setup as fixed in amber, and he poked fun at those who threw around the epithet "unconstitutional" as if its application

---

[12] E.g. "Walpole's History of England – The Conservative Opposition," *Nation* 31 (July 1880): 48–9; "Some Thoughts on French Affairs," *Nation* 46 (Apr. 1888): 405–6.

proved dispositive against a proposed reform. In truth, while the 1885 edition certainly conveyed a sense that the English Constitution had, all told, performed well, it made clear that this satisfactoriness rested on certain assumptions holding true. And in a key regard, Dicey was already becoming convinced that the requisite conditions were eroding. Along one of its principal axes, the *Law of the Constitution* illustrated well Hegel's dictum that the owl of Minerva flies at dusk.

Like all great books, the *Law of the Constitution* is ill-served by a quick summary. But its basic promise was that the British Constitution, for all its famous unwritten-ness, could nevertheless be understood in terms of three "guiding principles": parliamentary sovereignty, the rule of law, and constitutional conventions.[13] Dicey's treatments of the second and third of these themes are of tremendous significance, but for our purposes now what is important is his famous but oft-misunderstood analysis of the first principle.

Understandably, attention from constitutional lawyers has been focused on Dicey's formal definition, which focused on the reception of acts of Parliament by the judiciary:

> Parliamentary sovereignty may, looked at from its positive side, be thus described; any Act of Parliament, or any part of an Act of Parliament, which makes a new law, or repeals or modifies an existing law, will be obeyed by the Courts. The same principle, looked at from its negative side, may be thus stated; there is no person or body of persons who can, under the English constitution, make rules which override or derogate from an Act of Parliament, or which (to express the same thing in other words) will be enforced by the Courts in contravention of an Act of Parliament. (*LC* 36)

Importantly, though, this was only one of the concepts of sovereignty which the book supplied. For Dicey was careful to distinguish between two senses of sovereignty. The above, classical judicially focused formulation of the absoluteness of parliamentary sovereignty was, he insisted, true only from a legal point-of-view. Dicey was wary of the tendency for juridical notions to balloon and engulf the field of political-constitutional analysis. Just because, in the English system, the courts could not decline

---

[13] Dicey, *Lectures Introductory to the Study of the Law of the Constitution* (London, 1885), 34. Cited internally as *LC*.

to enforce a parliamentary statute did not mean there was nothing else to say about sovereignty. Quite the contrary: since everyone recognized that there were many policies which Parliament itself would never consider enacting and others which, if enacted, would provoke over-whelming resistance from the populace, it was necessary to accept that sovereignty had multiple meanings and avoid confounding them. For while "any expressions which attribute to Parliamentary electors a legal part in the process of law-making are quite inconsistent with the view *taken by the law*," they were nevertheless "not without *real meaning*" (*LC* 55). They simply pointed us to "a political, not a legal fact," namely, that

> that body is "politically" sovereign or supreme in a state the will of which is ultimately obeyed by the citizens of the state. In this sense of the word the electors of Great Britain may be said to be . . . the body in which sovereign power is vested. For, as things now stand, the will of the electorate and certainly of the electorate in combination with the Lords and the Crown is sure ultimately to prevail on all subjects to be determined by the British government . . . we may assert that the arrangements of the constitution are now such as to ensure that the will of the electors shall by regular and constitutional means always in the end assert itself as the predominant influence in the country.

This "political sense of the word 'sovereignty'," Dicey went on, was "fully as important as the legal sense or *more so*" (*LC* 67, my italics). To think that one could grasp (as he would call it regularly in later years) the "spirit" of the British constitutional order simply by noting that there was no authority which courts could invoke against Parliamentary statute was to succumb to a "fiction" (*LC* 65).

Right at the heart of his country's regime, then, there appeared to be a disconnect between two sovereignties. And yet it hardly troubled Dicey. Why did it not? The reason was that the mechanisms of representation worked to harmonize the two:

> Representative government presents a noteworthy peculiarity . . .
> The aim and effect of such government is to produce a coincidence, or at any rate diminish the divergence between the external and the internal limitations[14] on the exercise of sovereign power . . . Where a

---

[14] Dicey had picked up the terms of art "internal and external limits on legislative sovereignty" from his cousin Leslie Stephen's *Science of Ethics*. Dicey used *internal* to correspond to the wishes of Parliament itself about what to do and not do, and the *external* to what the subjects would and would not tolerate from their legal sovereigns.

Parliament really represents the people, the divergence between the
external and the internal limit to the exercise of sovereign power can
hardly arise, or if it arises must soon disappear ... To prevent the
divergence between the wishes of the sovereign and the wishes of
subjects is in short the effect, and the only certain effect, of bonâ fide
representative government ... The essential property of representative government is to produce coincidence between the wishes of
the sovereign and the wishes of the subjects; to make, in short, the
two limitations on the exercise of sovereignty absolutely coincident.
This, which is true in its measure of all real representative government, applies with special truth to the English House of Commons.
(*LC* 77–8)

The genius of effective representation was that the gap between the
formal armature underpinning the British state (legal Parliamentary
sovereignty) and the basic reality that in a democratizing society, one
with a literate, politicized public and modern communications, the
people felt themselves rightly to be in charge (political popular sovereignty) constituted more a conceptual curiosity than a practical problem.

Before proceeding further in our treatment of the development of
Dicey's thought, it is worth highlighting a few other important aspects of
his 1885 examination of sovereignty. First: Dicey is often associated, and
not without some justification, with classical Whiggery; the label accords
with the general sense that Dicey lived past his time, and he occasionally
applied it to himself. But he recognized that there was considerable
distance between a number of his ideas and those of Whiggism from
Burke to Macaulay, and on no front was this truer than in his reinter-
pretation of parliamentary sovereignty. For Whigs, the doctrine had
served as an alternative to both monarchical and popular sovereignty;
Burke and his ilk fashioned themselves no more friendly to democracy
than to the divine right of kings, and the point of asserting the absoluteness of parliamentary supremacy was to assure a considerable margin of
autonomy for parliament as a corporate body alike from crown and
populace. This understanding was, Dicey was cognizant, antithetical to
his own, on which the standing of Parliament as sovereign in law drew its
legitimacy ultimately from the legislature's perceived reliability in
tracking a political reality external to it – namely, the national will.
Indeed, in contrast to the Whig tendency to identify representative
regimes as those in which legislative assemblies were considered the only
institutions by which the general will could be expressed, Dicey had

already abandoned any such exclusive conceptions. Although in England the people's opinion could be legally expressed through Parliament alone, he cautioned that "this is not a necessary incident of representative government. In Switzerland no change can be introduced in the constitutions which has not been submitted for approval or disapproval to all male citizens who have attained their majority" (*LC* 55). Though Britons plumed themselves on having perfected representative government, representative government did not in fact require parliamentary supremacy as they had enshrined it in law. "This omnipotence of an elected assembly is not the result, or at any rate, the final result, of democratic progress or development, but the result of the peculiarities of English history."[15] In the service of a more democratic theory, he had transformed the dictum that only parliament could speak for the nation from an incontestable truth about the nature of sovereignty into a defeasible presumption.

Second, we can glimpse in these passages from the *Law of the Constitution* a change in the way that Dicey spoke about democracy. In the 1860s, as we saw, Dicey defended a more popular electoral settlement by appealing to moral first principles, or, perhaps more accurately, by attacking alternatives to democracy for violating certain fundamental values. From the mid-1880s (following the Third Reform Act which had expanded the suffrage yet again, and with the French Third Republic now well entrenched), however, he relied on a more historicist posture, one which stressed that Britain, the "Anglosphere," and much of Europe had irreversibly entered a democratic age. Like Tocqueville, he framed democracy as the necessary conclusion of a long historical trajectory; the task of the intellectually honest analyst was, correspondingly, to help readers judge how well certain institutions and practices suited democratic times.

At the very heart of a work which has all too commonly been depicted as a lodestar of analytic legal positivism or an apotheosis of Victorian complacency, there was thus already an attempt to set the shibboleth of parliamentary sovereignty within a background context that explained why it was politically tolerable, as well as a recognition that the British model was not the sole attractive model of representative government on offer. What Gladstone's adoption of Irish Home Rule in the following

[15] Dicey, "Introduction," to *Lectures on Comparative Constitutionalism*, 12.

year did to Dicey's thought was to put a large tear in the fabric of assumptions which had made British parliamentary arrangements seem an acceptable structure for liberal democracy. It did this more by confirming and accentuating preexisting worries than by sparking a whole new set of ideas. The battle against Home Rule that Dicey would wage, beginning the year after *Law of the Constitution* and lasting the rest of his life, was theoretically fruitful because he generalized from it to diagnose a crisis of representative assemblies and liberal values. Dicey of course opposed Home Rule on the substance, and with a striking vehemence. But what is of most interest here is that in the movement to implement Home Rule he believed he espied the metastasis of modern political pathologies.

What the Home Rule issue demonstrated, in Dicey's eyes, was the grave danger of *minority usurpation* on constitutional, foundational matters. In other words, it revealed the tenuousness if not outright falsity of the *harmonizing* view of representative government, the confidence that with elections conducted on a wide suffrage only those policies would become law which were clearly approved by the citizenry.

Although Gladstone's initial effort did not pass the Commons, Dicey treated the episode as exposing several grave perils of the parliamentary system, and this conviction only deepened as the struggle over Home Rule and against other "New Liberal" programs continued through his remaining decades. In particular, it alarmed Dicey (as it did many who would become Unionists) that Gladstone was prepared to wrangle his party behind a change that altered profoundly the relations between the constituent parts of the United Kingdom (and, as Dicey saw it, portended the ultimate federalization of the British state and the unraveling of the Empire) without having clearly campaigned on the issue. That the sizable majority of Liberal MPs followed their leader and the whip on a matter of such import despite lacking "the deliberate and undoubted sanction of the people of the United Kingdom" suggested that the government of Britain had de facto transformed into a party-plebiscitary operation wherein the very nature of the state was subject to the private whims of the premier (94).

Furthermore, since there was no reason to think that the issue, having been broached in the Commons and with the agitation for it showing no signs of abating, would be permanently dropped, every election that returned a Liberal majority would potentially precipitate a constitutional crisis. For given enough chances the Liberal "machine" would eventually manage to get a Home Rule bill through the Commons, as indeed happened again just seven years after Gladstone's first bill. Such an eventuality would require the Lords – an aristocratic chamber with discreditably one-sided Conservative biases – to reject the bill on behalf of a nation that had not been allowed to assent to or refuse it directly. This situation would set up rival claims to represent the popular will which would strain the machinery of government and lead to civic disorder. (This was indeed the scenario that brought about the considerable abridgment of the Lords' powers in the Parliament Act of 1911 which Dicey criticized in Chapter 8 here.) Hence the functional dispensation of public power in Britain would consist of a unicameral quasi-plebiscitary chamber in which, thanks to Britain's famously flexible constitution, no class of "fundamental law" was protected from hasty upending (94). Such reversals were all the more easily accomplished due to the fact that the two-party system was itself breaking down under the rise of splinter groups and sectional parties (as he judged the Irish Nationalists and nascent Labour), leading to dynamics of "logrolling" that gave undue leverage to extremist factions over the legislative agenda, and that the executive was gaining ever more dominance over the parliamentary agenda as the purview of government administration expanded and social conditions grew more complicated. When Dicey reflected on Parliament, he saw power-hungry operators buying off single-issue zealots in order to sustain fragile governing majorities, and "wirepullers" browbeating backbenchers to toe the party line with threats to oust them from their constituencies. And these tendencies were further aggravated by the truth – unpleasant, but one which candid democrats had to face – that a mass electorate was more apathetic than the restricted one of a bygone era and therefore could be less relied upon to push back against rash proposals from the parliamentary leadership ranks.

In brief, Home Rule confirmed Dicey in abandoning "the assumption ... made till recent times by every democrat and to a great extent admitted by persons who were not democrats that a fairly and properly elected Parliament must on all important matters represent the will of its electors."[16] Over the decades, on several vital issues (including especially the People's Budget and the proto-welfare state legislation

---

[16] Dicey, "Parliamentarism," in *Lectures on Comparative Constitutionalism*, 143.

under Asquith's Liberal government, which he bitterly reprobated), Dicey found disproven this premise of the old "reformers" that where "corruption or intimidation has not falsified the result of their votes" then a democratically elected legislature would "necessarily express the will of the electors or, at any rate, the majority of them."[17] "Real parliamentary government," it turned out, had vanished with the advent of democracy, and left in place a "vicious" form of party hegemony and legislative horse-trading that allowed minorities, often fanatical ones, to triumph over majority opinion on even the most critical issues.[18]

Confirming his fears on this front was the conduct of other democratic nations. Dicey asserted constantly that the bloom was off the rose of parliamentary bodies and that legislatures were embarked on a long secular decline. He was living, he believed, through what modern-day commentators would call a "crisis of representation." This was reflected, he argued, in the overwhelming tendency across the democratic world toward restricting the sphere in which the legislature could act autonomously. The simple fact was that Britain's own colonies were not following the British model – Dicey held that the Australian Constitution "embod[ied] the principle, though not the name, of the Swiss institution known as the referendum"[19] – and around the globe a wave of ever more elaborate written constitutions was taking an increasing number of issues out of the legislature's hands. Dicey was extremely attentive to developments in America, where a burst of revisions at the state level had led to new constitutions which were of much greater length and which included regulation of an array of topics unrelated to traditional questions of the distribution of offices and the ordering of public power. This phenomenon adapted the original bedrock principle of American constitutionalism that "no legislature can be entrusted with anything like unlimited power" for an age in which the low moral-intellectual quality of legislative personnel and disgust with party machines had driven confidence in assemblies to new lows (160).

The result of this transnational turn to limit legislatures, as Dicey saw, was either to empower the judiciary to strike down more laws as *ultra*

---

[17] Dicey, "Introduction," to *Lectures on Comparative Constitutionalism*, 14.
[18] Quoted in Yves Beigbeder, "Referendum," in *Max Planck Encyclopedia of Public International Law* (Oxford, 2011).
[19] Dicey, *Introduction to the Study of the Law of the Constitution*, sixth edition (London, 1902), note IX.

vires or to allow the population of a town or state to vote directly on certain issues. The referendum had already been written into more than one constitution, and was being debated and experimented with in a variety of formats elsewhere. In Belgium, Leopold II lobbied for a "royal referendum," according to which the king would have the "right to appeal to the referendum after the two Chambers have voted, in order that it may guide him in exercising his right of consent, and enable him effectually to quash the decision of the parliamentary majority."[20] Across the Channel, the Third Republic was carrying on the French heritage of constitutional supremacy, and the referendum, both in local and in national versions, was being promoted again, in the shadow of the plebiscites that had marked the Second Empire. That latter regime, moreover, was the emblem of another trend on which Dicey (and many of his contemporaries) dwelled, usually fretfully: that democracies were showing themselves more friendly to the personal rule of the executive than to traditional parliamentary practices. Dicey tracked these directions of travel assiduously, and concluded that there was no going back to that classical age of parliamentary government when "the moral authority of representative bodies" was at its zenith.[21]

The intra-parliamentary dynamics at play in the Home Rule crisis, then, demonstrated one pathway by which the democratic expectation of majority rule could be disappointed. But there was an extra-parliamentary form of minoritarian usurpation which Dicey feared as well. This was mob rule, the use of coercive tactics among small but determined mobilizations of citizens "to change or override the law by use of force, and to substitute the desires of a faction for the lawfully expressed commands of the nation."[22] Here as well, Dicey's anxieties predated Gladstone's adoption of Home Rule and were not limited to the behavior of agrarian and nationalist agitators in Ireland. For all that he praised the English "spirit of legality" (*LC* 277, 340), he had already for several years prior to the *Law of the Constitution* been expressing distress that this customary national virtue had been waning; "an inadequate sense of the sanctity of the law" had spread in "English society."[23] But Ireland powerfully aggravated

---

[20] Simon Deploige, *The Referendum in Switzerland*, trans. C.P. Trevelyan (London, 1898), xlvi. Leopold's advocacy was unsuccessful. Dicey was aware, as well, that a similar proposal for a monarchical referendum had found supporters in England (64).
[21] Dicey, "General Conclusions," in *Lectures on Comparative Constitutionalism*, 160.
[22] Dicey, "New Jacobinism," 492.
[23] Dicey, "The Prevalence of Lawlessness in England," *Nation* 37 (Aug. 1883): 95–6.

these antecedent worries. Dicey was among many once ardent, now skeptical liberals who saw the Land War, the rise of "boycotting" (a term coined in the Irish context), the leadership of Charles Parnell, and Fenian "physical force" tactics as rank criminality made even more blameworthy by donning the mantle of political causes. He and other disaffected liberals, like his cousin Fitzjames Stephen, consequently returned to themes at the very heart of early-modern social contract theory: that the state exists first and foremost to ensure order, preventing the violence that comes from individuals or groups acting on their own private judgments outside (as Locke called them) "settled standing rules, indifferent, and the same to all parties." For Dicey, the actual enforcement of the law, even against those who claimed to be acting on behalf of a righteous cause, was an essential part of "the equality of the law" which required "that men be treated even in the matter of punishment as equals." To waive the punishment of offenses out of respect for the nobility of purpose of the malefactors or out of sympathy with their political ends was to do nothing more than connive at wrongdoing; and since every crime involved the violation of the "freedom of the law-abiding citizen," to allow a class of crimes to persist through selective application of the state's police powers was to allow "the infliction of gross injustice on large bodies of men." "If the law gives rights opposed to public expediency, the law should be changed by lawful means. While the law exists justice demands its equal enforcement against all men," Dicey intoned. Anything else was "favouritism," "privilege," and "ruinous partiality."[24]

Yet if the particulars of Irish "lawlessness" were rarely far from Dicey's mind, his reading of the situation connected to a broader diagnosis of the prospects of modern politics. And here he confronted what looked like a tragic paradox regarding the standing of the law in democratic times, to wit, that from one angle the authority of the law was more sacrosanct in democracies than in other regimes, but from another it was more vulnerable. To begin with the sacrosanctity: in democracies alone was it the case that "obedience to the law" was required not only to respect the legal rights of others and ensure civic peace but also "as an act of loyalty to the sovereignty of the people," from whom the law originated.[25] For it was the peculiar genius of democracy that "the law"

---

[24] Dicey, "New Jacobinism," 492, 485; "The Home-Rule Movement – II, Its Weaknesses," *Nation* 42 (June 1886): 463–4.
[25] Dicey, "New Jacobinism,"493.

was "the voice of the nation" (90). These truths, which contained the essence and value of democracy itself for Dicey, all told in favor of a strict and "equal enforcement of law against every person, and against every class" as a core part of how democracies operated (90–1). One would have expected, accordingly, democracies to be severe in law enforcement, to suppress without compunction those who broke existent law in the name of a higher law, on the grounds that after all it was open to the latter to persuade their fellow citizens and have the law changed via legal channels by convincing a majority to back their cause. "The English democracy ... because it is a democracy, may, like the democracy of America, enforce with unflinching firmness laws which, representing the deliberate will of the people, are supported by the vast majority of the citizens of the United Kingdom."[26] Since the lifeblood of democracy was *counting* heads, democratic states would be the least inclined to tolerate *breaking* them.

And yet the reality, Dicey feared, was that democracies were prone to fall into the opposite extreme, a liability exposed not only in the Irish context but in happenings across the Christian world. Dicey put forward two reasons for this surprising finding. First, the average citizen of a modern civilized democracy had for a variety of reasons become highly susceptible to "sentimental" appeals. (Dicey penned a four-part series on "sentimental" trends in English political culture for the *Nation*.) Demagogues seized on this susceptibility. They manipulated the masses into showing mercy to offenders who professed to follow their consciences in the short run in a way that, in the long run, undermined the rule of law, for most people did not grasp the truth that, at the societal level, "love and justice" rightly considered were not opposed but mutually constitutive.[27] Second, when confronted with the determined resistance of a section of the community, democrats had difficulty standing behind even those laws for which support ran deep in the nation as a whole. For according to democratic sentiment

> law should on the whole correspond with public opinion; but when a large body of citizens not only are opposed to some law but question the moral right of the state to impose or maintain a given law, our honest democrat feels deeply perplexed how to act. He does not

[26] Dicey, *England's Case against Home Rule* (London, 1887), 282.
[27] Dicey, "New Jacobinism," 482.

know in effect how to deal with lawlessness which is based upon a
fundamental difference of public opinion ... Thus many
Englishmen have long felt a moral difficulty in resisting the claim
of a nationality to become an independent nation, even though the
concession of such a demand may threaten the ruin of a powerful
state and be opposed to the wishes of the majority of the citizens
thereof ... and in many other cases which will occur to any intelligent reader, English democrats entertain a considerable difficulty in
opposing claims with which they might possibly on grounds of
expediency or of common sense have no particular sympathy. The
perplexity of such men arises from the idea that, at any rate under a
democratic government, any law is unjust which is opposed to the
real or deliberate conviction of a large number of citizens.[28]

It was, consequently, a constant temptation for democratic governments to decline to enforce even essential and popular laws if a group of
citizens seemed earnestly to oppose them. By this route democracies
could slide into a culture of ill-considered antinomianism inconsistent
with the good working order of society: there was "current a notion (the
more dangerous because it is the perversion of a fine and noble idea) that
no man can be rightly punished or made to obey the law whose dis-
obedience arises from following the dictates of his conscience."
("Hence," he continued, "the difficulty of dealing with the martyrs of
the anti-vaccination craze." Concerns about oversolicitousness toward
resisters of vaccination endured throughout his career.[29]) Making
matters worse, these factors tending toward disorderliness both fed into
and were fed by another phenomenon: the deepening of party feeling.
With consensus hard to come by (as Dicey believed it would be, for the
fracturing of opinion was irreversible in modern societies that respected
free speech), and where deference toward strong sectional convictions
was a widespread if incorrect interpretation of the democratic credo,
then "the conviction [spreads] that persons who do not belong to this
political connection cannot count as part of the nation. Party becomes
everything, the Nation sinks to nothing" (107).

Such were some of the main elements of Dicey's somber analysis of
the challenges facing Britain and the "civilized" world. His response was,
at bottom, Tocquevillian: the problems of democracy could only be

---

[28] Dicey, "Introduction," to *Law of the Constitution*, eighth edition, xlii.
[29] Dicey, "The Tyranny of Minorities in England," *Nation* 34 (Mar. 1882): 248–9.

resolved by institutions which "fall[] in with the democratic belief and sentiment of the age" (148). The central prescription that Dicey offered was the referendum.

Dicey's embrace of the referendum was prompted by this view of the pathologies afflicting his and similar societies. He thought, certainly, that those who had a democratic self-conception could only with great contortions reject the referendum, for "to attack the referendum is to attack democratic government" itself (46); and his affection for the referendum resonated with his long-held democratic commitments. But he had not been brought to support the referendum by transcendental arguments about which institutions or procedures were inherent to democracy's essence. Unsurprisingly, then, much of his argumentation tracked the concerns just described: he presented the referendum as a cure for the maladies he identified. To these he also added other justifications, and ultimately arrived at what remains one of the fullest, most multifaceted articulations of the place of the referendum in the modern state. Importantly, his justification combined both democratic rationales (e.g. equal voting power, popular empowerment, majority rule) and liberal ones (the limited state, the preservation of law, the benefits of deliberation). In his apologias for the referendum Dicey emerges as a quintessential *liberal democrat* in the history of British political thought, both more comfortable with democracy than the famous liberals who came before and more wedded to a "classical liberal" worldview than radical democrats who came after.

Looking from the twenty-first century, we know what Dicey could only have predicted: that the referendum would become widespread and that it would be implemented in a great variety of ways and for a variety of purposes. The first thing to emphasize about Dicey on this subject was that, in contrast, he promoted only a particular instantiation of the referendum, and did so (with some slight fudging around the edges) unchangingly. He rejected other versions even as he followed their spread abroad during what must be considered the first major wave of direct-democratic devices in the modern age.

The Diceyan referendum was a (significant) modification of the Swiss institution, to which he self-consciously traced his inspiration; the fact that the referendum was in use in Switzerland, where democracy had "turned out a complete success," was ever-present in his advocacy (19). Concretely, Dicey proposed adapting one aspect of Swiss direct democracy – the mandatory constitutional referendum – to the British context. According to this reform, bills which touched on constitutional terrain, after having passed the two chambers of Parliament, would be submitted to the electorate for confirmation or refusal. (Dicey was not entirely consistent in demarcating this category. While certain core aspects of public law were always included, he sometimes stretched the notion of "fundamental institutions of the State" to areas of policy such as education and poor relief [69].) Legislation that altered the foundations of the state would become valid only after receiving the majority approval of the nation and, were a bill to garner only minority support at the referendum stage, would be considered failed just as if it had lost the vote within the Commons or Lords or been vetoed by the monarch.

It was crucial, Dicey held, to distinguish his recommendation from two superficially similar practices. The first was the initiative, by which a certain number of persons could force the preparation of a regular bill or constitutional amendment. Dicey was hostile to this mechanism and insisted that it was no "part of the Referendum" (61). For Dicey, the referendum was not to displace Parliament but to "add[] an additional safeguard" for when Parliament ventured onto areas of foundational import (61). He did not wish to "enable the electors to pass laws at their own will" and insisted that his desired "Referendum Act would . . . in no way diminish the need for obtaining for every Bill whatever the sanction of both Houses of Parliament and of the Crown. It would do nothing more than require for any Bill affecting the statutes scheduled in the Referendum Act the sanction, not only of Parliament, but also of the electorate" (143). In other words, Dicey countenanced no popularizing changes which *supplanted* the legislature, only those which *supplemented* it. Such a reform, in conjunction with a wide and fair suffrage for regular elections, fully realized popular sovereignty as Dicey conceived of it. Dicey illustrated why through one of his favorite analogies for understanding the referendum within the framework of democratic constitutionalism:

> The referendum is sometimes described, and for general purposes well described, as "the people's veto." This name is a good one; it reminds us that the main use of the referendum is to prevent the passing of any important Act which does not command the sanction of the electors. The expression "veto" reminds us also that those who advocate the introduction of the referendum into England in fact demand that the electors, who are now admittedly the political

sovereign of England, should be allowed to play the part in legislation which was really played, and with popular approval, by *e.g.* Queen Elizabeth at a time when the King or Queen of England was not indeed the absolute sovereign of the country, but was certainly the most important part of the sovereign power, namely Parliament. (203)

As in a monarchical epoch the sovereignty of His Majesty was made concrete by his "negative voice," the appropriate way to express the people's sovereignty in a democratic epoch was to "secur[e] to the citizens that share in legislation which in England used to belong to the Crown" (48). Hence the referendum could be said to crown democracy in a way that was more than mere metaphor, for constitutionally speaking it made of the people what kings had been previously. And just as, in England at least, monarchs had ruled alongside Parliament, so the introduction of the people's veto did not end but merely modified representative government. Whatever one may think of Dicey's particular evaluation of the benefits of this institution, it is thus indisputable that he saw early and clearly a major feature of the twentieth- and twenty-first centuries: that liberal states would tend to be defined by a combination of direct popular input with more traditional representative institutions.

If Dicey stressed that his notion of the referendum was "purely" negative (208) and hence not kindred with the initiative enacted in Switzerland and fiercely championed by American progressives, he was even more adamant that his plan not be conflated with the *plébiscite*. As a young man Dicey had detested the French Second Empire which the "despot" Louis-Napoleon Bonaparte had installed after his coup toppled the Second Republic, a government on which the young Dicey had looked with hope. Notoriously, both the coup and the formal transformation of the Republic into the Empire had been ratified by plebiscite, as would be the series of changes that amounted to the creation of the "Liberal Empire" in 1870, just before the regime fell in the debacle of the Franco-Prussian War; as a result, the direct consultation of the people was seen as a keystone of Caesarism. Since the Second Empire was the *bête noire* of British liberals and was regarded as the antiparliamentary state-form par excellence, it cast a shadow over the advocacy of direct-democracy mechanisms.

Dicey shared this extreme distaste for the Caesarist "appel au peuple." To him, the plebiscite was marked by adhockery, contempt for legality, and the absence of real choice. As he grasped it, the distinguishing features of the plebiscite were that it occurred at the whim of the executive and that the question was framed at its discretion, so that the setting of the agenda was ripe for manipulation; no regular legal forms limited the Bonapartist government's purview in holding, or declining to hold, a popular vote. Moreover, as the plebiscite was often called soon after critical events had taken place, voters were confronted with either having to accept a just-established dispensation or launching the country into an unspecified state of disruption. These were hardly circumstances propitious for genuine public deliberation, and there was neither adequate time for debate nor security that all sides of the issue could be aired. Finally, parliament was sidelined: the Caesarist plebiscite was based on the presumptions of the people's confidence in the personal executive and of the identity of will between them. A true referendum such as his proposal would create, Dicey claimed, was directly contrary on all these fronts. It was "a regular, normal, peaceful proceeding" characterized by the elimination of executive discretion and the respect for legally binding process (58); whatever the ambitions of the sitting government, a referendum would take place when and only when the conditions laid out above had been met. Moreover, holding the referendum on a bill only once it had passed both Houses accomplished two crucial goods. First, it forced the people to render judgment on the "distinct, definite, clearly stated" text of the bill itself (61), reducing problems of agenda-setting and bias in the formation of the question; second, it ensured ample parliamentary deliberation preceding the referendum, which provided the public a suitable opportunity and structure in which to form a "rational decision" (57). Unlike the Imperial plebiscite, which rested on channeling the popular will through affirmations of a charismatic leader, Dicey's referendum was intended to create a new kind of popular-parliamentary composite sovereign which we might call Crown-and-People-in-Parliament, one defined by legality and the curtailment of executive control.

From the referendum conceived in this manner as popular veto and "constitutional safeguard" (152), Dicey expected a stunning range of benefits to flow. So variegated were the advantages which he attributed to it that we must content ourselves with glancing at a few key themes. A principal goal of Dicey in the selections presented here was to convince his contemporaries that Britain would profit along a number of dimensions by implementing the referendum; the logic underlying some of these propitious forecasts was rather elaborate, and the reader will have to judge for herself how convincing he is in showing the positive consequences of and the important values served by the referendum.

To begin, Dicey stressed the referendum as guaranteeing *true majority rule*, against the forces of minority usurpation afore-described, thereby achieving democracy's promise of equal political input. Further, the process of appealing to the people on constitutional questions and leaving the decision to a "genuine" majority reaffirmed (what were for Dicey) basic democratic values such as political equality and devotion to the common good above sectional interests and subnational attachments; it constituted "an institution which is in absolute harmony with the democratic principles or sentiment of the day" (108). Not only did "the referendum place[] the nation above parties or factions" as a matter of constitutional design, but this institutional innovation had positive knock-on effects on political culture. For one, the knowledge that "the nation's destiny must be referred to a more august tribunal than the House of Commons, or even than Parliament" would help accustom the population to place the public interest over private or partial interests, and it would generate the right kind of patriotism (110). This public-spiritedness would be furthered by the positive deliberative environment engendered by a well-constructed referendal procedure. For such a procedure would separate out party preference and personal qualities from the content of the constitutional issue in question and confront the public with the clear question, *would this revision to the basic structure of the polity leave the nation better- or worse-off?* Such moments were educative, "promot[ing] . . . among the electors a kind of intellectual honesty" and stimulating habits of "rational" judgment on policy (209).

The referendum's revival of "the authority of the nation" and its edificatory potential were targeted at a particular enemy in Dicey's mind: excessive partisanship (110). Dicey spent considerable energy delineating between a mild, healthy form of party identification and a full-blown "party system," the latter of which he judged a degenerate type of representative democracy (146). What was invaluable about the referendum was that it would prevent "parties, factions, and sections" from remaking the foundations of the state via hijinks in the legislature independent of "the deliberate sanction of the people" (79, 75), thereby providing an institutional brake on the potentially runaway power of party. Seen from this angle, the referendum served the conventional liberal objective of erecting checks and balances. It was also a way of introducing a distinction central to modern constitutionalism but famously absent in the British constitutional heritage – that between fundamental and ordinary law. Importantly, it insulated the former from "transient" or "corrupt" legislative majorities *without* establishing judicial review. (Dicey was skeptical of the latter and decidedly did not want it imported into his home country, although he recognized its necessity in federal systems.) By dampening polarization and party fervor, the presence of the referendum, standing as it did for the supremacy of the nation within the political order, would generate improvements in the "working and in the morality . . . of the Constitution" (149).

The referendum made clear exactly where the majority stood on an issue in a way that general elections, which intrinsically involved the jumbling of persons and platforms and events, never could. This clarity of popular verdict was the source of another significant benefit. It contributed to stability by "lend[ing] moral strength to law," for in democratic epochs only indubitable demonstrations of majority (dis) approval could quell the dispersive and discordant forces that partial associations and group loyalties exerted (48). Dicey endorsed the referendum in considerable part because he held to this majority-revelatory logic of civic concord.

These are some of the main planks of his advocacy, but Dicey piled reason upon reason and expectation upon expectation in favor of his cherished scheme. In conclusion, though, one additional point deserves to be highlighted, both for its importance to him and for its counter-intuitive quality to readers today.

Referendums are now often associated with "populism" and presumed to appeal principally to anti-establishment/anti-elitist movements. But for Dicey the referendum had nothing of this flavor. He believed adam-antly in the need for popular decision where fundamental questions of the nature of the state were concerned and to that degree fancied himself an egalitarian and popular-sovereigntist. Yet he was also a creature of the establishment if ever there was one, and he certainly possessed an "elitist" streak. For Dicey, the everyday tasks of governance were rightly the province of training and expertise. Much of his allergy to party govern-ment derived from his frustration that it led to constant administrative turnover and to the placement of amateurs in important roles; service to party, rather than intellectual fitness for the post, was the primary qualifi-cation in this system. The referendum appealed to him as an instrument for breaking this deplorable modus operandi. Drawing again from the Swiss case, where the referendum appeared to exist in harmony with a non- or cross-partisan executive in which able ministers served for long periods, Dicey predicted that administrative continuity and the evidence-driven, "businesslike" dispatch of public concerns went hand-in-hand with the appeal to the people: "The Referendum would certainly facilitate the continuous employment in successive Cabinets of men who, whilst holding a particular office, such as that of the Chancellorship, acted rather as experts than as men who shared the political opinions held by their colleagues" (149). As Dicey recognized, the transformation of executive power which he desired involved rejecting a central plank of the cabinet system as it had evolved in Britain: "with ideas of business the notion of the collective responsibility of the executive is inconsistent" (34).

Alongside, indeed bolstering, his enthusiasm for the introduction of an element of direct democracy was thus the inspiring but unattainable ideal of the objective, non-partisan, expert-driven conduct of normal public affairs. Secure in the knowledge that they would have a chance to weigh in on the great existential matters affecting the constitution, citizens would be willing to leave ordinary matters of regulation and administration to competent technocrats regardless of party affiliation. In this way, he presaged, a great goal of nineteenth-century political theory, and one especially close to the hearts of his old band of university liberals – of reconciling "brains" and "numbers," expertise and majority will – would finally be accomplished. And in conjunction with its contribution to constitutional stability and public order, the manner in which the referendum would foster appropriate deference to sound administrators was tantamount to achieving another reconciliation. By the referendum, "true conservatism" and "true democracy" would be brought into union (94), the former considered less in a party-political sense than as the expression of the people's natural attachment, when not goaded to extremism by unrestrained party competition, to existing customs and institutions and its distaste for revolutionary innovations.

Doubtless many readers today, even those who generally look kindly on referendums, will find Dicey's hopes for the device unduly optimistic. But in fairness to Dicey, he insisted that there was no truth about the worth of an institution apart from the "spirit" in which it was worked. With the referendum, Dicey was hoping to salvage as much of classical liberal parliamentarism as was possible, while honoring and adapting to the values embedded in the long historical trajectory toward democratization, and he thought his fellow citizens could comprehend this motivation and operate and appreciate his innovation accordingly. Of course, we cannot view the referendum in precisely the same way now, for we do not occupy the same historical juncture. It should not be overlooked, though, that several of the desiderata which Dicey awaited from the referendum are still widely longed for by present-day liberal democrats, and his apprehensions about the fates of liberalism and representative government in his time find more than a few echoes in the public discourse of the first quarter of the twenty-first century.

The last years of Dicey's life coincided with the writings of two younger Germans better known to political theorists now than Dicey is: Max Weber and Carl Schmitt. On the diagnostic side, in analyzing how and why liberalism appeared to be receding and what the predominant features of a mass-democratic nation-state were likely to be, the trio shared a great deal. But unlike Schmitt, Dicey wanted not to get beyond liberalism but to preserve as much of its mid-Victorian practice and ethos as he could through a referendal-representative system that we might think of as a kind of mixed regime for a democratic age. And in contrast to Weber, Dicey could not embrace the Caesaristic and personalistic element in mass politics, nor could he accept that deeply conflictual party struggle was fated to course through the public life of modern states. Whose interpretation of democracy is most compelling? Whose expectations for the shape of political life going forward have proven most clear-sighted? These questions cannot be answered without interrogating to the very core our own sense of politics and history.

Chronology

1835   Born (4 February) in Leicestershire, third son of Thomas
        Edward and Anne Mary Dicey. He suffers from birth with a
        muscular disability which will make writing, among other
        activities, difficult all his life. Through his parents he is
        connected to both the Whig press and the highest echelons of
        the Evangelical elite.
1848   "The Springtime of the Peoples": revolutions break out
        across the Continent. Like many in his generation, Dicey
        would credit these events for waking him up to "conscious
        existence."
1851   In France, Louis-Napoleon Bonaparte carries out a coup
        (2 December) after the National Assembly fails to amend the
        one-term limit on the presidency. A plebiscite ratifying the
        coup follows a few weeks later, and soon after the constitution
        of the Second Empire is ratified by plebiscite as well.
1854–8 Undergraduate at Balliol College, Oxford.
1860   Elected a fellow of Trinity College, Oxford.
        Publishes his first book, *The Privy Council*, a work of
        historical institutionalism, after it wins the Arnold
        Prize Essay.
        The US Civil War begins. Dicey is a strong supporter of the
        Union from the outset.
1861–82 Lives in London, practicing law and writing legal tracts as
        well as political-social commentary for the press, most
        importantly as a regular contributor to the *Nation*.

1867   Passage of the Second Reform Act, significantly extending
        the suffrage to the working classes. Dicey supports this
        measure enthusiastically, contributing an article to *Essays on
        Reform.*

1870   Tours the USA with his friend James Bryce. The trip has a
        formative impact on both men, confirming Dicey's
        Americophilia and planting the seed of Bryce's *American
        Commonwealth.*

1872   Marries Elinor Mary Bonham-Carter, daughter of a Whig
        MP who had died when she was an infant.

1874   Switzerland enacts, via referendum, a revision to its
        constitution. This document will be a touchstone for much of
        Dicey's subsequent political thinking.

1882   Elected Vinerian Professor of English Law at Oxford.

1884   Passage of the Third Reform Act, again considerably
        expanding the electoral rolls. While roughly 40 percent of
        adult men still lack the vote and plural voting persists, Dicey
        along with others sees the Act as cementing democracy in
        the UK.

1885   Publishes the first edition of the *Introduction to the Study of
        the Law of the Constitution* (this and only this edition is
        formally entitled *Lectures Introductory to the Study of the Law
        of the Constitution*). It will go through seven more editions in
        Dicey's lifetime.

1886   Gladstone introduces the First Home Rule Bill. It fails in the
        Commons. The Liberal Unionist party, with which Dicey
        will long identify, is formed in reaction.
        Dicey's long and heated antagonism to Home Rule receives
        its first book-length salvo with *England's Case against Home
        Rule.*

1893   Gladstone introduces the Second Home Rule Bill. It passes
        the Commons but is rejected by the Lords.

1896   Publication of *A Digest of the Law of England with Reference to
        the Conflict of Laws*, the greatest of Dicey's strictly legal
        tracts. It elaborates general principles of, and seeks to codify,
        private international law.

1898   Appointed Principal of the Working Men's College in
        London, an establishment founded in the 1850s by Christian
        Socialists to provide education for working male adults.

1905   Publication of *Lectures on the Relation between Law and Public Opinion in England during the Nineteenth Century*, which does much to popularize such lasting notions as the clash between individualism and collectivism. It is based on lectures given at Harvard Law School the previous decade.

1911   The controversy over the "People's Budget" which had been raging since 1909 culminates in the Parliament Act, which ends the Lords' veto over finance bills completely and, for all other matters, converts it into a "suspensive" veto whereby bills passed by the Commons in three successive sessions become law even over the Lords' opposition.

1914   The Third Home Rule Bill is passed via the Parliament Act but its implementation is suspended due to the outbreak of World War I.

1915   The eighth and final edition of the *Law of the Constitution* is published.

1920   Publication of Dicey's last book, a co-authored historical-legal-political study of the 1707 Anglo-Scottish Union. Amidst the Anglo-Irish War, the Fourth Home Rule Act passes, establishing Northern Ireland and Southern Ireland as separate Home Rule jurisdictions within the United Kingdom.

1922   Dies (7 April) in Oxford.
The Irish Free State is established (5 December).

Note on the Texts

The selections for this volume appeared in a variety of outlets and formats – thereby providing a window onto the world of letters in the late nineteenth and early twentieth centuries. Five were released in those characteristic products of the Victorian "higher journalism," the great "reviews [which] governed intelligent conversation" and served as the "principal vehicle of expression" for the interlocking literary, political, and scientific elites.[1] One came out in the sort of organ that would do so much to displace the periodicals just mentioned: an academic journal. And three are taken from stand-alone books, two being chapters from multi-author collections and one an excerpt from the final edition of Dicey's most famous work. Some inkling of Dicey's range as a writer can therefore be gained from this volume.

Chapter 1 was the fourth chapter of the collection *Essays on Reform* (London: Macmillan & Co., 1867, 67–84).

Chapter 2 was published in *The Edinburgh Review* 171 (Jan. 1890): 113–45.

Chapter 3 was published a few months later in *The Contemporary Review* 57 (Apr. 1890): 489–511.

Chapter 4 also came out in *The Contemporary Review* 61 (Mar. 1892): 314–31.

Chapter 5 was the leading, and longest, of five articles by prominent politicians and commentators under the heading "The Referendum" in

---

[1] Christopher Kent, "Higher Journalism and the Mid-Victorian Clerisy," *Victorian Studies* 13 (1969): 181–98; Roland Hill, *Lord Acton* (New Haven, 2000), 109–11.

The National Review 23 (Mar. 1894): 65–80 (Dicey's entry runs until p. 72). The contributors did not all subscribe to Dicey's position.

Chapter 6 appeared in *The Harvard Law Review* 13 (June 1899): 67–79.

Chapter 7 was published in *The Quarterly Review* 212 (Apr. 1910): 538–62.

Chapter 8 was the fourth chapter of *Rights of Citizenship: A Survey of Safeguards for the People* (London: Frederick Warne & Co., 1912, 81–107), a collection of (negative) reflections on the condition of the constitution following the passage of the Parliament Act by Unionist and Conservative writers.

Chapter 9 was part (d) of the new introduction (book-length in itself) which Dicey wrote for the eighth edition of *Introduction to the Study of the Law of the Constitution* (London: Macmillan & Co., 1915, lviii–c).

Befitting their titular purpose as "reviews," the articles here presented as Chapters 2 and 7 appeared with the bibliographic information of the books being reviewed at their head. I have left these citations in place, even though this custom may look somewhat unusual for this series.

I have largely preserved the spelling and punctuation of the originals, even though they can sometimes look a little odd to modern eyes. I have made changes only where there was a clear typographical error, and not simply to bring the text into conformity with modern usage. As was customary, Dicey frequently quoted from foreign texts in the original language; the translations of those passages are my own.

I have taken a fairly active hand in supplying editorial notes. While there are some potential downsides to doing so – cluttering up the bottom of pages or in explaining points that are "obvious" to those well versed in nineteenth-century history – these seemed risks worth running in order to render Dicey's material as accessible as possible to non-expert readers today. For Dicey's style was forged in the aforementioned "great monthly journals of general culture, that unrivalled stage upon which so many of the intellectual and literary dramas of mid-Victorian life were acted out," and this medium may make "his writings a little too full of topical references for the ease of the uninstructed modern reader."[2] Essays in this distinctive genre – which should rank along with the novels and the advances in the natural sciences as hallmarks of the

---

[2] Stefan Collini, *Arnold* (Oxford, 1988), 22.

intellectual greatness of the period and which nothing in our contemporary public debate can rival – not only came chock-full of references to current events and personalities, but also were characterized by an allusiveness that assumed a command of a wealth of historical, political, and literary sources and facts which are certainly not top of mind for a twenty-first-century audience. I have aimed to illuminate this material in the notes without weighing down the primary texts overly much. My own editorial notes are designated in Arabic numericals; notes by Dicey himself in the original are designated by Roman numerals.

It should be stressed, however, that the generic conventions that informed Dicey's writing are all things considered a strength. As these texts were meant to engage an educated public rather than to impress specialists in a narrow academic field, they are energetic, jargon-free, and fluid. And even though Dicey cultivated a self-image of dispassion and had something of a drier prose, the polemical pugnacity and directness of Victorian intellectual jousts – scandalizing to modern elite conceptions of civility and mutual respect – occasionally come through, even if other members of his circles such as James Fitzjames Stephen or Matthew Arnold tended to be more obviously cutting and unsparing in controversy. In sum, while three of these chapters were composed after Victoria's death and belong in several respects resolutely to the twentieth century, Dicey considered himself a "mid-Victorian" through his final years in the Roaring Twenties. For ill and (mostly) good, until the end his prose bore the hallmarks of the self-assured intelligentsia whose domination of the periodical press coincided with the prime of his life.

Bibliographical Note

Unfortunately, there is no authoritative edition of Dicey's oeuvre, and unlike many other Victorian men of letters (including, for example, his cousins James Fitzjames and Leslie Stephen) Dicey did not republish swathes of (what he judged the highlights of) his periodical and review writing as their own volumes. As a result, the study of Dicey requires a good deal of searching about. In my view, the bulk of Dicey's best short journalism was published in *The Nation*, and happily one can rely on the "Haskell Index" (*The Nation: Indexes of Titles and Contributors, v.1105*, by Daniel Haskell) at the New York Public Library. *The Wellesley Index to Victorian Periodicals* database (https://about.proquest.com/en/products-services/wellesley) is useful for identifying Dicey's contributions to other outlets. The bibliography compiled by Richard Cosgrove in *The Rule of Law: Albert Venn Dicey, Victorian Jurist* (London and Chapel Hill, NC, 1980) remains the best entrée into Dicey's many-sided sub-book-length output more broadly.

There are very good modern editions of Dicey's most prominent books. His *Digest of the Law of England with Reference to the Conflict of Laws* still forms the backbone of the standard textbook on private international law, *Dicey, Morris & Collins on the Conflict of Laws*, now in its fifteenth edition (London, 2012). J.W.F. Allison has done an inestimable service with his two volumes of the *Oxford Edition of Dicey* (Oxford, 2013). Volume I covers the *Law of the Constitution*, using the original 1885 edition as its main text but then carefully covering the additions and changes in the seven subsequent editions overseen by Dicey himself. Even more impressive as an editorial accomplishment is volume II, *Lectures on Comparative Constitutionalism*, which gathers essays, notes, and lectures on assorted constitutional and political topics. (Allison's *Comparative Constitutionalism* supersedes Dicey, *General Characteristics of English Constitutionalism: Six Unpublished Lectures*, ed. Peter Raina [Berne, 2009], in which some of this material had been previously printed.) The Liberty Fund has published good editions of both the *Lectures on the Relation between Law and Public Opinion in England during the Nineteenth Century* (ed. Richard VandeWetering: Indianapolis, 2008) and the *Law of the Constitution* (ed. Roger E. Michener: Indianapolis, 1982), although the critical apparatus of the latter cannot compete with that provided by Allison.

Befitting a figure who has become almost a stand-in for certain understandings of constitutionalism and the rule of law, the literature related to Dicey is sizable. Here I can simply flag some of the most illuminating and useful work.

On the life, I must again commend Cosgrove's *Rule of Law*, which after four decades is still a necessary touchstone for all serious engagement with Dicey. The more-or-less authorized biographical work is the *Memorials of Albert Venn Dicey, Being Chiefly Letters and Diaries*, ed. Robert Rait (London, 1925). And while ostensibly focused on Dicey's constitutional jurisprudence and theory of the common law, Mark Walters's *A.V. Dicey and the Common Law Constitutional Tradition: A Legal Turn of Mind* (Cambridge, 2020) is so ambitious and touches on so many facets of Dicey's life that it deserves mention as an account of the man and his times above and beyond its legal-academic contributions to understanding Dicey's legal thought. On the socioeconomic/professional milieu which Dicey inhabited, the best point of access is still Noel Annan, "The Intellectual Aristocracy," in *Studies in Social History*, ed. J.H. Plumb (London, 1955), 243–87.

The discussion of Dicey by academic public/constitutional lawyers is vast. For upwards of a century now, scholars have elaborated their understandings of the nature of the British Constitution and the meaning of the rule of law through examining – and not infrequently criticizing – Dicey. Among the most important of these engagements are: T.R.S. Allan, *The Sovereignty of Law: Freedom, Constitution, and Common Law* (Oxford, 2013); J.W.F. Allison, *The English Historical Constitution: Continuity, Change and European Effects* (Cambridge, 2007) and Allison's two chapters in *Handbook on the Rule of Law*, ed. Christopher May and Adam Winchester (Cheltenham, 2018); Tom Bingham, *The Rule of Law* (London, 2010); F.H. Lawson, "Dicey Revisited [I–II]," *Political Studies* 7 (1959): 109–26, 207–21; Ivor Jennings, *The Law and the Constitution*

(London, 1933); Martin Loughlin, *Public Law and Political Theory* (Oxford, 1992) and *Foundations of Public Law* (Oxford, 2010); Loughlin and Stephen Tierney, "The Shibboleth of Sovereignty," *Modern Law Review* 81 (2018): 989–1016; E.C.S. Wade, "Preface/Introduction" to Dicey, *Introduction to the Study of the Law of the Constitution*, ninth edition (London, 1939) and tenth edition (London, 1961). For sympathetic appreciations of Dicey's theory of the rule of law by libertarian- or small-state-leaning thinkers, see Lord Hewart, *New Despotism* (London, 1929), F.A. Hayek, *Constitution of Liberty* (Chicago, 2011), and Nadia Nedzel and Nicholas Capaldi, *The Anglo-American Conception of the Rule of Law* (London, 2019). And for Dicey's place in the formation of modern English legal education and legal self-conceptions, see David Sugarman, "Legal Theory, the Common Law Mind and the Making of the Textbook Tradition," in *Legal Theory and Common Law*, ed. William Twining (Oxford, 1986), 26–61.

There are several fine books on the political-intellectual culture of Victorian liberalism that accord Dicey an important role. Among these are: Stefan Collini, *Public Moralists: Political Thought and Intellectual Life in Britain, 1850–1930* (Cambridge, 1993); Christopher Harvie, *The Lights of Liberalism: University Liberals and the Challenge of Democracy 1860–86* (London, 1976). Julia Stapleton's *Liberalism, Democracy: Five Essays, 1862–91* (Bristol, 1997) reprints and analyzes Dicey's "Balance of Classes." Patrick Malcolmson's unpublished dissertation "Judicial Statesmanship and the Rule of Law: A Study of the Political and Legal Thought of A.V. Dicey" (Toronto, 1992) likewise examines Dicey as a liberal political thinker. Recently, Gregory Conti, *Parliament the Mirror of the Nation: Representation, Deliberation, and Democracy in Victorian Britain* (Cambridge, 2019) and William Selinger, *Parliamentarism: From Burke to Weber* (Cambridge, 2019) have taken up Dicey in the context of debates on parliamentary representation. On the clash between class representation and democratizing views in which Dicey participated, in particular, see Conti, "Plural Voting and Popular Government in Victorian Britain," in *People Power: Popular Sovereignty from Machiavelli to Modernity*, ed. Chris Barker and Robert Ingram (Manchester, 2022) and "Democracy Confronts Diversity: Descriptive Representation in Victorian Britain," *Political Theory* 47, no. 2 (2019): 230–57.

Dicey has often figured in scholarship on the "Irish Question." For notable treatments of Dicey's opposition to Home Rule, see Richard Bourke, *Peace in Ireland: The War of Ideas* (London, 2003); D. George

Boyce, "Moral Force Unionism: A.V. Dicey and Ireland, 1885–1922," in *From the United Irishmen to Twentieth-Century Unionism*, ed. Sabine Wichert (Dublin, 2004), 97–110; Tom Dunne, "La trahison des clercs: British Intellectuals and the First Home-Rule Crisis," *Irish Historical Studies* 23 (1982): 134–73; Christopher Harvie, "Ideology and Home Rule: James Bryce, A.V. Dicey and Ireland, 1880–1887," *English Historical Review* 91 (1976): 298–314; Hugh Tulloch, "A.V. Dicey and the Irish Question, 1870–1922," *Irish Jurist* 15 (1980): 137–65. For works that treat the political contest over Home Rule with an eye to the realm of ideas, see for example Eugenio Biagini, *British Democracy and Irish Nationalism, 1876–1906* (Cambridge, 2007) and Ian Cawood, *The Liberal Unionist Party: A History* (London, 2012).

Some studies, but not a great many, have attended to Dicey's views on the referendum. The cream of this crop includes: Vernon Bogdanor, "Dicey and the Reform of the Constitution," *Public Law* (1 Dec. 1985): 652–78; Bogdanor, *The People and the Party System: The Referendum and Electoral Reform in British Politics* (Cambridge, 1981); Bogdanor, "The Constitution and the Party System in the Twentieth Century," *Parliamentary Affairs* 57 (2004): 717–33; Kevin Manton, "British Unionism, the Constitution and the Referendum, c. 1907–14," *Historical Research* 85 (2012): 505–25; J. Meadowcroft and M.W. Taylor, "Liberalism and the Referendum in British Political Thought 1890–1914," *Twentieth Century British History* 1 (1990): 35–57; Mads Qvortrup, "A.V. Dicey: The Referendum as the People's Veto," *History of Political Thought* 20 (1999): 531–46; Rivka Weill, "Dicey Was Not Diceyan," *Cambridge Law Journal* 62 (2003): 474–93; Corinne Weston, *The House of Lords and Ideological Politics: Lord Salisbury's Referendal Theory and the Conservative Party, 1846–1922* (Philadelphia, 1995).

A spate of interesting books and articles has approached Dicey from angles germane to political thought. These include: Duncan Bell, "Beyond the Sovereign State: Isopolitan Citizenship, Race and Anglo-American Union," *Political Studies* 62 (2014): 418–34; D.A. Brühlmeier, "Dicey and the Swiss Constitution," *Public Law* (1985): 708–16; David Dyzenhaus, "Austin, Hobbes, and Dicey," *Canadian Journal of Law & Jurisprudence* 24 (2011): 409–30; Ian Fletcher, "'This Zeal for Lawlessness': A. V. Dicey, 'The Law of the Constitution,' and the Challenge of Popular Politics, 1885–1915," *History of Parliament* 16 (1997): 309–29; Jeffrey Goldsworthy, *The Sovereignty of Parliament: History and Philosophy* (Oxford, 1999); James Kirby, "A. V. Dicey and

English Constitutionalism," *History of European Ideas* 45 (2019): 33–46; Dylan Lino, "Albert Venn Dicey and the Constitutional Theory of Empire," *Oxford Journal of Legal Studies* 36 (2016): 751–80 and Lino "The Rule of Law and the Rule of Empire: A.V. Dicey in Imperial Context," *Modern Law Review* 81 (2018): 739–64; Haig Patapan, "The Author of Liberty: Dicey, Mill and the Shaping of English Constitutionalism," *Public Law Review* 8 (1997): 256–69; Jordan Rudinsky, "James Bryce and Parliamentary Sovereignty," *Modern Intellectual History* (forthcoming); Julia Stapleton, "Dicey and His Legacy," *History of Political Thought* 16 (1995): 234–56; Hugh Tulloch, "Changing British Attitudes towards the United States in the 1880s," *Historical Journal* 20 (1977): 825–40.

Finally, while Dicey's mixture of "historical criticism" (as he called it), academic legal scholarship, and public philosophy is hard to pursue in our more specialized age, his example does occasionally inspire imitations: see *Law and Opinion in Twentieth-Century Britain and Ireland*, ed. W. John Morgan and Stephen Livingstone (Houndmills, 2003).

I am sure other worthy works have slipped my mind; my apologies to those neglected.

Political
Writings

The Balance of Classes (1867)

"It is the principle of the English Constitution, that Parliament should be a mirror, — a representation of every class; not according to heads, not according to numbers, but according to everything which gives weight and importance in the world without; so that the various classes of this country may be heard, and their views expressed fairly in the House of Commons, without the possibility of any one class outnumbering or reducing to silence all the other classes in the kingdom."[i]

In these words Sir Hugh Cairns sums up that theory of representation, which makes it the end of Parliament to be the representative of classes.[1] This view is entertained by persons who differ in every other political opinion. It is the pet theory of so-called philosophic Liberals, and of most intelligent Conservatives. Nothing indeed can show its prevalence more clearly than the indignant criticism excited by the expressions of Mr. Gladstone, which seemed, though in all probability untruly, to intimate his adhesion to a totally different doctrine.[2] For it cannot be concealed that the theory of class representation is fundamentally opposed to the arguments, which, till recently, have been employed by

---

[1] Cairns was a Conservative politician who would later serve as Lord Chancellor. He was here objecting to the Liberal Reform Bill of 1866, not the more generous Conservative Bill that would eventually pass in 1867.

[2] William Gladstone, at this time Chancellor of the Exchequer in charge of stewarding the Liberal Reform Bill through the Commons, would go on to serve four terms as Prime Minister. Dicey is alluding to such comments as Gladstone's famous proclamation in 1864 that "every man who is not presumably incapacitated by some consideration of personal unfitness or of political danger, is morally entitled to come within the pale of the constitution."

[i] Speech, April, 1866, Hansard, vol. 182, p. 1463.

3

all democratic or radical Reformers. Of such men, Mr. Bright is the most eminent, as well as the most consistent leader;[3] and the idea which lies at the bottom of all his theories of Reform, is, that representation should be primarily a representation of persons—only in so far as it may be so accidentally, a representation of classes. It is because of his entertaining this belief, a belief shared by nearly all the old Liberal leaders,[4] that he is constantly reproached with the crudeness and unphilosophic character of his policy; and the fact becomes every day more apparent, that between persons who hold that the object of Reform is more nearly to represent classes, and those who cling to the opinion that its main end is gradually to give the full rights of citizens to all persons, there can be no ultimate agreement as to the course which ought to be pursued by Parliamentary Reformers. It is, therefore, of primary importance for all Liberals to make up their minds whether Parliament ought or ought not to aim at being, in the words of Sir Hugh Cairns, "a mirror of every class;" or whether it should aim to represent persons, and leave the representation of classes to take care of itself.

Before entering upon a discussion of the class theory of representation, and the arguments by which it is supported, it is well to clear away some misconceptions by which that discussion is confused. It is often, for example, asserted, that the most desirable kind of Reform is one which should admit the working classes to a share of influence, without changing the balance of power. Persons who use this language either do not understand what their words mean, or mean something which they do not wish their hearers to understand; for it is of the very essence of all Reform to change the balance of power. If the working classes gain influence, some other class must lose it; and if each class remains with no more political power than before, then there will have been no real Reform; and it is not to be supposed that either working men or any other class, will be satisfied with a measure, simply because it is entitled a Reform Bill, and because, while changing nothing, it professes to change everything. If, on the other hand, what is intended is, that the alteration to be desired is one which shall leave the rich as powerful as now, but effect some new

---

[3] John Bright was a radical-liberal MP; he was one of the most important advocates of expanding the suffrage and (especially) free trade.

[4] The difference between "the philosophic Liberals" of the mid-Victorian period and the "old Liberal leaders" of earlier in the century is neatly summed up in the contrast between Jeremy Bentham's democratic approach to the suffrage and his disciple J.S. Mill's more restrictive and inegalitarian recommendations.

distribution of power between the 10*l.* householders and the working men,[5] then the wish expressed for a Bill which does not change the balance of power, is doubly dishonest; since it does not express what it means, and seems to express what it does not mean. For the desire really felt is not that political power should remain unchanged, but that, within certain limits, it should be surreptitiously shifted in a particular direction.

It is again to be noted, that much which is often and honestly said about the effects of giving representatives according to numbers, is, strictly speaking, not argument, but rhetoric. It is constantly asserted, with more or less distinctness, that the enfranchisement of the masses is the disfranchisement of the rich.[6] Such an assertion is, however, nothing more than a rhetorical mode of saying that the influence of the rich will be unduly diminished by a wide extension of the franchise; for, as a matter of fact, no man is disfranchised by the enfranchisement of another. Take the most extreme case, and suppose universal suffrage established. In this case the wealthier classes might indeed be a minority, but they would be as far from disfranchisement as any other equal number of persons in the kingdom. Under the most unfavourable circumstances they would exercise a controlling influence by supporting that section of the people to which they were least opposed. But the influence of a minority is always considerable, and the influence of a rich minority could never be insignificant. If a proposal were made really to disenfranchise all possessors, say of a thousand a year, rich men would soon perceive the difference between being disfranchised and being in a minority. One partner of a numerous firm never dreams of stating that he has no vote because he may constantly be outvoted; and expressions which would be ridiculous applied to the transactions of private life do not gain additional force or accuracy from being applied to politics. The real question at issue is not one of disfranchisement, but of supremacy.

---

[5] The Representation of the People Act 1832, better known as the (First) Reform Act, took steps to replace the previously haphazard electoral rules with a more standard set of regulations; increased the overall number of citizens eligible to vote (to roughly one-in-five adult males); revised the map of electoral districts; and implemented measures to reduce corruption. One of its most famous provisions was the creation of a single "middle-class" franchise across all borough districts, which gave the vote to householders who paid a yearly rental of at least £10.

[6] It was common in Victorian debates to speak of disfranchisement in an extended sense, to indicate not only the formal withholding of the suffrage from an individual, but also more broadly to describe the position of belonging to a permanent minority group within a constituency.

Advocates of class representation desire such a political arrangement as would enable a minority, in virtue of their education, wealth, &c. to carry out their views, even though opposed to the sentiments of the majority of the people. Democrats, on the other hand, desire the gradual establishment of a constitutional system under which, in the case of a direct conflict of opinion between a greater and a smaller number of citizens, the greater number may be able to carry out their own wishes. There are arguments to be used in favour of either party; but the first requisite for weighing such arguments is to perceive clearly what is the point at issue. This point undoubtedly is, whether or not the greater number of the citizens ought to be made ultimately supreme in the affairs of the State.

The theory to which the passage quoted from Sir Hugh Cairns' speech gives expression may be summed up in the following propositions:—

(1) A nation consists of classes.
(2) Each of these may have, or may conceive themselves to have, conflicting interests.
(3) It is therefore desirable that each class should be duly represented.
(4) Since one of these classes greatly exceeds the others in number, it must not be represented in proportion to its numbers, because, if it were so, this class would be supreme.

This theory is supported by arguments which assume very various forms, but which may be reduced to a few heads.

It is, in the first place, urged that the nation is in reality an organization, of which classes are the essential parts; and much ingenuity is shown in the use of different metaphors, all of which aim at setting forth the idea that a nation does not primarily consist of the individuals who make it up. To most minds these attempts to distinguish between the nation and the individuals to be found in it, will appear as idle and unsatisfactory as the Aristotelian discussions about the natural priority of the individual or the State. And without going into political metaphysics, ordinary writers may be allowed to point out that though individuals may be considered as members of different classes, it is as individuals that they either suffer or inflict wrong, and that their individual interests can by no device whatever be merged in that of the class to which they belong. The assertion indeed of a most able writer that "John Smith *quâ* John Smith cannot be oppressed, but John Smith *quâ* artisan can," neatly sums up what will appear to most persons the exact opposite of a *reductio*

6

ad absurdum of the application of very doubtful metaphysics to the defence of a doubtful political dogma.

It is not, however, reasoning of a transcendental kind which has lent a weight to the theory of class representation. An argument of real force, urged by some speculators, is that the introduction into the legislative body of members belonging to different orders of the community would tend greatly to improve the character of the legislature. No candid critic can deny that there is some truth in this allegation. The remark, however, may be justly made that representation according to numbers is not inconsistent with the presence in Parliament of men belonging to different pursuits and professions. The first French Assembly, after the Revolution of 1848, was elected by universal suffrage, yet amongst its numerous faults this was not one, that it did not contain members from different sections of the nation. It must further be noticed that it is not, and never has been, a primary object of constitutional arrangements to get together the best possible Parliament in point of intellectual capacity. Indeed, it would be inconsistent with the idea of representative government to attempt to form a Parliament far superior in intelligence to the mass of the nation. There is no doubt that most country gentlemen were till recently, if they are not still, grossly ignorant of political economy, yet no one supposes that for the purposes of free government it would be desirable to exclude from Parliament every squire who could not understand the fallacies of Protection.

A remark of far more importance is, that this argument, whatever it is worth, points towards the direct representation of orders, and means that there ought to be representatives of, for example, the Church, law, medicine, the working classes, &c. seated in Parliament; and thus its value depends upon the answer given to a question hereafter to be considered, *i.e.* whether or not it be on the whole desirable that Parliament should consist of Members for orders. It will, however, be found that the demand for class representation gains its force almost exclusively from a single line of reasoning.

It is said that without class representation the interest of individuals will never be fairly protected. Each class (and the working classes may be considered in this respect neither better nor worse than the rest of the community) will always consider its own interest as supreme, and therefore if it be sovereign will oppress all other portions of the community; hence it is of infinite importance that no one class be sovereign. But representation of numbers would make the working classes sovereign, and thus, in denying to them representation according to numbers, statesmen deny them no more than is refused to every other class.

This argument admits of profuse and effective illustration. It is said, for example, that the working men, being in a majority, might throw all the burden of taxation on the shoulders of the rich, and expand all the proceeds of taxation on the enjoyments of the poor, or might establish laws for the protection of labour as oppressive as the laws which English gentlemen established for the protection of corn.[7]

The weakness of this argument is that the truth which it contains applies to all governments. The danger pointed to in the supremacy of numbers is a danger common to all supremacy. No distribution of representatives, no cunning device of political theorists, can prevent the existence in every State of some person or body of persons who can if they choose act contrary to the interests of the rest of the community.

But if it be alleged that tyranny is specially to be feared where numbers are supreme, there seems to be little proof for the allegation. In all countries the majority must be a fluctuating, unknown, indefinite body, which has neither the will nor the power to act with systemic tyranny. In England especially, where classes are intermingled, and where it is absolutely impossible to draw a clearly marked line between the different divisions of the nation, — where, for instance, it is hard to say what are the limits of the so-called middle class, — it is highly improbable that the whole of the poor (and it is only when acting as a whole that they could in any case be supreme) would act together as one man in opposition to the wishes of all those who are not technically working men.

For the so-called working class is, like all others, notoriously broken into divisions; for example, of artisans and labourers. The legitimate influence—to use the words in their true sense—of the rich and the educated has immense weight with all who depend for their livelihood on their wages.[8] It is, indeed, a more reasonable fear that a widely extended

---

[7] The Corn Laws were a set of tariffs and limits on the importation of grain. They were repealed in 1846, marking a major victory for free trade.

[8] "Legitimate influence" was a sort of term of art in the Victorian era, meant to distinguish appropriate deference to those of high social status, large property and wealth, or great attainments from "illegitimate" activities such as bribery, intimidation, or treating.

suffrage may unduly increase the influence of landowners and capitalists, than that it will lead to the unexampled result of placing the multitude in permanent supremacy over the rich. There is, however, no use in blinking the fact that occasions might arise on which the majority of the nation might adopt a policy opposed to the judgment of the minority. But on such occasions, it is as likely as not that the majority might be in the right. The American Union was saved because the energy and decision of artisans and farmers overruled the hesitation and weakness of the merchants of New York.

But, of course, the majority is no infallible ruler. The working men of England might easily commit errors as great—they could not commit greater—as the mistakes committed by George III. and by Pitt.[9] If, however, the majority should fall into errors, it may still be well that the majority should rule. All belief in free government rests ultimately on the conviction that a people gains more by the experience, than it loses by the errors, of liberty, and it is difficult to perceive why a truth that holds good of individuals and of nations, should not apply equally to the majority of the individuals who constitute a nation.

Advocates of class representation have expended immense ingenuity in devising schemes for effecting an hypothetical balance of power, and the complexity of these devices has given an appearance of philosophic profundity to the theory which makes such devices necessary; for it is difficult for any one to believe that an object which needs thought and ingenuity for its attainment may, after all, not be worth attaining. But calm observers, though willing to give all due weight to the objections which may be urged against the representation of numbers, may yet be inclined to suspect that thinkers who advocate the establishment of a balance of power, entertain views open to greater difficulties than are the theories which these thinkers assail. It is, at any rate, worth while to remember that a scheme may be philosophic, even though it be simple, and though it command the support of Mr. Bright.

All schemes for effecting a so-called balance of classes are open to a primary charge of utter impracticability. Their object is to give "due" weight to each interest, but no standard exists by which the "due" weight may be measured. Mr. Disraeli is honestly convinced that the

---

[9] George III was king from 1760 to 1820. William Pitt the younger, a Tory, was his longest-serving Prime Minister, from 1783 to 1801 and again from 1804 to his death in 1806.

landed interest has not its due share of power.[10] Most other persons would think a diminution of the influence of the country gentleman essential to the establishment of a fair constitutional balance; but there exists no test by which to decide between the correctness of his Mr. Disraeli's views and the views of his opponents, unless principles be introduced which are fatal to the theory of the balance of power. Sir Hugh Cairns, with his usual acuteness, perceives this difficulty, and gets over it by the suggestion that each class should have the power in Parliament which it has in the world without. Unluckily, the very object of all sincere Reformers is to effect a change in the social and other influences of different portions of society. It is, therefore, idle to hope to satisfy the demand for Reform by creating a Parliament, the object of which is permanently to embody distinctions, with Reformers desire to diminish.[ii]

But even were it possible that persons of opposite views, such as Mr. Mill and Mr. Disraeli, could be brought to agree on the exact proportion of influence which ought to be retained by the landed, commercial, and working classes, under a future constitutional arrangement, such an agreement would be as worthless as it would be illusory; for in politics nothing is more certain than that it is impossible to predict how political and social forces will adjust themselves under a new Constitution. In 1832, no prophet could have foretold, as the result of the Reform Bill, that the practical supremacy of the middle classes would have been

---

[10] Benjamin Disraeli, Chancellor of the Exchequer at the time of this essay's publication and future Prime Minister, was an enigmatic Conservative Party leader. He played a significant role in reconstructing the party after the Repeal of the Corn Laws split it, and he would go on in 1867 to engineer the passage the Second Reform Act, which "dished the Whigs" by expanding the suffrage more widely than the 1866 Liberal bill would have done.

[ii] It is not in truth to be supposed that a skilled lawyer, well accustomed to practical life, intends deliberately to advocate any elaborate arrangement for a representation of different classes. He would, doubtless, be content with the existing state of things. What, however, he must be taken to urge is, that any change ought to have as its object the giving representation in accordance with the power of different classes out of Parliament. And the policy he proposes may be easily shown to be open to the objection that has been brought against it. The landowners or capitalists, for example, have immense influence in modern society. Landowners and capitalists ought, therefore, according to Sir Hugh Cairns, to have an immense share of the representation. If this share be given them they will indubitably have the power, which they are likely to use, of hindering changes which might affect their weight in society. Hence, deliberately to give to landowners and capitalists representation according to their influence is to perpetuate and, as it were, stereotype that influence.

found compatible with government through the nobility. Had it been deemed requisite to ascertain beforehand what would be the exact amount of weight given by the Reform Act to each section of society, Gatton and Old Sarum might still be sending up Members to Parliament,[11] whilst Commission after Commission was attempting to obtain information, which is absolutely essential if it be desirable to establish an elaborate balance of power, and yet is in its own nature unattainable.

Theoretical speculators easily perform in imagination feats which are found impossible by practical politicians, and various enthusiasts have sketched out, with more or less ingenuity and inconsistency, what should be the exact balance of power established in what one of their number has termed "the Constitution of the Future." Whoever wishes to see an excellent specimen of the speculations of the men who are called "thinkers," should read Professor Lorimer's book, in which this Constitution of the future is sketched out. It is instructive, at any rate, to observe that a Professor and a thinker, quite consistently with his theory, while giving votes to every man in proportion to his merits, gives only one vote to a simple citizen and ten votes to the happy possessor of ten thousand a year, who, indeed, would, under the Professor's scheme, as a general rule, have at least twenty votes.[iii] This is instructive, because it points to the conclusion that the principles laid down by Sir Hugh Cairns almost inevitably tend in practice, as they do in Professor Lorimer's theory, to the establishment of a Plutocracy. But even this theory does not fully exhibit one of the most important features of class representation.

This feature is the introduction into Parliament of the representative of orders. The ablest and most sagacious of the advocates of class representation distinctly contemplate this result, and, as before pointed out, one of the strongest arguments in favour of their theory is the advantage which it is supposed would accrue to the country from the presence in the legislature of the members of different classes or orders.

[11] Gatton and Old Sarum had been two of the most notorious of the "rotten boroughs" that had been common in the unreformed parliament. Rotten boroughs had tiny numbers of voters and were controlled by landowners or a wealthy patron.

[iii] Constitution of the Future, p. 174. [James Lorimer, *Constitutionalism of the Future, or Parliament the Mirror of the Nation* (Edinburgh, 1865). In addition to being a theorist of representation, Lorimer would go on to be an important philosopher of international law.]

It is indeed a boast of some able writers that, if they deny to the working classes representation in proportion to their numbers, they are willing to ensure the working classes the possession of a certain body of, say fifty or a hundred, special representatives of the masses. It is in truth so apparent that any theory of class representation must ultimately lead to the presence in Parliament of members specially delegated to represent such different classes, that it becomes a matter of importance in estimating that theory, to settle whether the presence of such members would be a national gain or loss. The presence in Parliament of fifty or a hundred working men, or at any rate distinct representatives of working men, would not, it must be owned, in all points of view be without advantage. But if these men sat as the special representatives of a class, the advantage which their presence might confer would be purchased by incalculable evils. It may be pointed out in passing, that representation by orders, after having been tried in all European countries, has been universally given up, and this fact of itself suggests that such representation has peculiar defects; but the special evil which at the present moment needs attention is that the proposed representation of orders threatens to introduce supremacy of numbers in its worst form. Let there, for example, be fifty special representatives of working men in Parliament, and these fifty men will inevitably become, not members, but tribunes.[12] Elected by a class numerically the greatest, they will soon claim and exert an authority beyond that given them by their numbers. On a question of peace or war, they would have it in their power to enter, on behalf of the mass of the nation, protests against the course adopted by the majority in Parliament, and such protests could not in practice go unheeded whatever might be the theory of the Constitution.

In this matter it is unnecessary to appeal to *à priori* reasoning. Irish and Scotch Members are from the necessity of the case representatives of a class, and do therefore exert a force out of all proportion to their numbers. Few governments would dare to legislate for Scotland or Ireland in the face of the united opposition of the Scotch or Irish Members. Any one who is unwilling to see the working classes legislate for the majority of the nation, as the Scotch Members legislate for Scotland, will prefer the direct supremacy of numbers to the indirect supremacy of a tribunate.

---

[12] Dicey is referring to the ancient Roman institution of the *tribunus plebis*. The tribunes acted as protectors and representatives of the plebeians as a class.

For class representatives have an inherent defect beyond that of exerting undue influence. From their very position they at once display and intensify class feeling. What the leaders of Convocation are to the body of the clergy,[13] that the specially elected leaders of the working men would be to the artisans. They would be the most fanatical, the most narrow of their class. Our county representatives, again, are a near approach to the representatives of a class; and the country gentlemen all but hooted down Mr. Mill because he tried to make them understand that a sick cow ought not to be valued at the price of a healthy animal.[14] America itself is a standing warning, not against the supremacy of numbers, but against artificial schemes for insuring a definite amount of power to certain classes, since the whole theory of State Rights is nothing but a theory of class rights carried out on a larger scale; and this theory till recently obtained such weight throughout America that most politicians were ready to attribute a sort of sacredness to the rights of States, just as enthusiasts for a balance of power are ready to see something sacred in the name of a class. For it is necessary to point out that, after all, there is nothing specially to be reverenced in orders or interests. Half the evils of modern England arise from the fundamental fault of class distinctions, and the fundamental fault of class representation is its tendency to intensify differences which it is an object of political Reform to remove.

In criticizing a theory of class representation, the words "classes," "orders," or "interests," must be constantly employed. The very employment, however, of these expressions gives an undue advantage to the view criticized. For it is, after all, to be suspected that the very basis on which this view rests is not firm enough to support the conclusions grounded upon it. This basis is the assumption that English society can be, for practical purposes, divided into classes or orders. Classes no doubt exist, but they are not of the distinct, clearly-marked, homogeneous kind which the class theory of representation requires. In a society such as that of the Middle Ages, where marked orders existed, representation by orders, with all its disadvantages, arose,

---

[13] Convocation here refers to the assembly of the Anglican clergy for the management of church affairs.

[14] Mill's first two speeches as a Member of Parliament (on 14 and 16 Feb. 1866) concerned the "Bill to Amend the Law Relating to Contagious or Infectious Diseases in Cattle and Other Animals."

as it were naturally, from the surrounding condition of civilization. In a society like that of modern England it is difficult to find the orders on which laboriously to build a scheme of class representation. Take, for example, a class frequently mentioned in political discussions, that of the 10*l.* householders. What, after all, is the real community of view or interest, which binds the members of the class together? They are of different politics; they pursue different professions; they belong, in many cases, to different religious bodies. Looked at in one point of view, they may be called a class; looked at in another, they are a disconnected mass of different small classes. Take, again, any class of Englishmen, from the highest to the lowest, and it will be found to mix, by imperceptible degrees, with the class below it. Who can say where the upper class ends, or where the middle class begins? Who, again, can draw a line which shall accurately divide working men from small tradesmen? Yet if there exist a class or order, it is the class of workmen. To those who see this class from without, and from a distance, it appears, no doubt, much more of a class or order than it really is; because its subdivisions escape notice. That these exist is granted even by Conservative speakers, who, like Sir Hugh Cairns, injure the force of their arguments by indulging in boasts of the Conservatism to be found among artisans. But let it be fairly granted that there is more class feeling among workmen than amongst the rest of the community. The reason is not far to seek. Treated as a class, they have fallen back upon their class feeling, and have devoted their energies to class interests. If it had not been for the Reform of 1832, the middle classes would form as distinct a body as the working men. A free extension of the franchise in 1867 will, in thirty years, make the artisans as little distinguishable from the rest of the nation as are the men whose fathers in 1832 almost overthrew the Constitution from which they were excluded.

Much indeed has been said and written by Professors and theorists as to the unphilosophic character of the Democratic view of Reform. This view is, however, as a fact, held by men who, whether they think rightly or wrongly, have as much right to the much abused name of "thinkers" as their opponents. The so-called unphilosophic and vulgar Radicalism, with which politicians are taunted, who desire, slowly but ultimately, to make the majority of the nation arbiter of the nation's destiny, rests upon two principles: the first, that on the whole each man is the best manager of his own affairs; the second, that citizens ought to be looked upon, primarily, as persons, secondarily only, as members of classes. Those who take this view need not be blind to the advantages which may be gained by the free representation in Parliament of different portions of society. But they hold that, as a matter of fact, such representation of classes has been obtained by gradually extending the suffrage to those personally fitted for its exercise, without measuring beforehand what might be the exact influence of such extension on the balance of power. It is, moreover, in the opinion of such radical Reformers, worth incurring some risk, to bring the mass of the nation within the bounds of the Constitution. The widest franchise any government is likely to propose, would, after all, stop far short of universal suffrage. The question, after all, therefore is, whether the risk (if risk it be) be not worth running. The theory of class representation rests, indeed, on the assumption that theorists can sketch out the future of the nation; but this is an assumption which history and experience emphatically contradict. It rests on the further assumption, that national progress is best attained by ingeniously balancing class against class, and selfish interest against selfish interest. This assumption is, indeed, expressed by Sir Hugh Cairns, in a form which, from its very vagueness, commands general assent. Most persons are captivated by the idea of Parliament being a mirror of the nation; but a speaker's meaning must be gathered as much at least from the circumstances under which he speaks, as from his mere words. The true interpretation of Sir Hugh Cairns' sentiments is to be found in the fact, that his speech was made in opposition to a proposal, not for universal suffrage, but for a very moderate extension of the franchise, and that his political friends have averred, that if Parliament is to be a perfect "mirror," it should represent, at least as fully as at present, the important class of landowners.

Democracy in Switzerland (1890)

1. *The Swiss Confederation.* By Sir Francis Ottiwell Adams, K.C.M.G., C.B.,
   late her Majesty's Envoy Extraordinary and Minister Plenipotentiary at
   Bern, and C.D. Cunningham, 8vo. London: 1889.
2. *Das Staatsrecht der Schweizerischen Eidgenossenschaft.* Bearbeitet von
   Dr. A. von Orelli. Aarau: 1875.

Switzerland is to Englishmen the best explored country and the least
known State of modern Europe.[1] Yet the commonwealth which is the
oldest of European republics and all but the youngest of European
democracies deserves the study of philosophic thinkers as much as any
empire, or realm, or republic of the civilised world.

Sir Francis Adams and Mr. C. D. Cunningham have supplied the
means by which to dispel English ignorance about Swiss politics.[2]
The design of their 'Swiss Confederation' may be fairly attributed to
the late Sir Francis Adams. The credit of its execution must be shared
between the two literary partners. To appreciative criticism falls the duty
(tinged by the recent death of Sir Francis Adams with sadness) of
impressing on the not over-receptive intellect of the intelligent reader

---

[1] By "best explored" Dicey is alluding to the fashion for Alpine mountaineering among
Victorian intellectuals, including notably his cousin Leslie Stephen. Dicey was himself too
infirm to participate in such activities.

[2] Adams was an author and diplomat who was British Ambassador to Switzerland from
1881 nearly until his death at the end of the decade; he had previously served in Japan and
written a history of that country. Dicey did not just commend the book, which is a
substantial work of historical and political-scientific scholarship, upon its release, but also
had a considerable role in shaping it: it was not for nothing that he (and James Bryce) are
thanked for "advice and assistance" in crafting the "constitutional and political chapters."

the importance of a book which may possibly not obtain immediately from the general public all the attention it merits.

For Adams's 'Swiss Confederation' lacks some qualities which insure literary success. It is not written to maintain any political dogma or paradox. It does not aim at giving anecdotes of Swiss life. It pretends to no special charm of style. The treatise has indeed been compared to a Blue Book; the comparison is apt and just, for Adams's 'Swiss Confederation' is written with the sole object of conveying in plain language to all persons whom it may concern the knowledge of plain facts. We should, however, ourselves prefer to describe the treatise as Adams's last memorandum on the affairs of Switzerland. It is a memorandum addressed not to the Foreign Office, but to the British nation, and thoughtful Englishmen will be the losers if they do not peruse it with care. For the memorandum displays, with a little of the dryness, all the merits—and they are great—which belong to the best official literature. It is written without bias. It aims wholly at giving information. It teems with facts. The facts it contains are gathered from life. Simplicity, freedom from affectation, and directness mark every line of a book which, because it is written by a man who is not thinking of himself, reflects all the best qualities of its author. Sir Francis was neither by disposition nor by training a theorist. He knew the world in which he moved and of which he wrote, and wrote therefore with his eye fixed upon the facts before him. He possessed great advantages for the acquisition of information. The representative of Great Britain to the Swiss Republic must always command respect, and, from the relation between the two countries, can never excite enmity. If there existed at any time difficulty in maintaining friendly intercourse between two States formed by nature for friendship, our late Minister was admirably fitted for making apparent to Switzerland the goodwill of England. Sound sense, kindliness, and intelligent sociability are qualities which aid not a little in the transaction of affairs. They are characteristics which, from the days of Herodotus down to those of Arthur Young, have well served inquirers into the condition of foreign countries. A stranger to Bern learnt more about the reality of Swiss politics from conversation with Sir Francis's friends at the Minister's dinner table than the most industrious of students could gain from days of labour in a library.

Adams's first-hand knowledge of Switzerland gives to his book a freshness and reality not always to be found in the writings of men who in profundity of thought and in the graces of style are his admitted superiors. In most respects it were gross injustice to our author to compare Adams's 'Swiss Confederation' with Maine's 'Popular Government.'[3] But it is the simple truth to assert that the late Minister at Bern displays in every word he writes about Switzerland a kind of knowledge not possessed by the most original and charming of English jurists. From a few facts known to him about Swiss institutions Sir Henry Maine drew far-reaching inferences, sometimes of great importance and always of great interest. But the author of 'Popular Government' writes of Swiss affairs as of a subject known to him from reading and from meditation. And a critic may justly say that, to Maine, Switzerland is rather too much the country of the Referendum. Adams, on the other hand, writes of Swiss politics as of things which he has, so to speak, touched and grasped. When he describes the Swiss Council of State he deals with no mere institution known to him by report. He has before his memory definite Swiss statesmen—Dubs, or Ruchonnet, or Droz—with whom he has transacted business or been on terms of intimacy. He knows the Council in the same way in which many of us know a college common room or a board of railway directors. Switzerland, in short, is to him a country where he has lived and which he knows so well that he realises how little he knows about it. 'Switzerland,' he has been heard to say, 'is the most difficult country in the world to understand. One canton differs as much from another as if each were a different country. I understand the Japanese'—Sir Francis had been Minister in Japan—'better than I do the Swiss.' Hence he supplies to his readers a kind of instruction not to be found in Maine's pages. We yield to no man in veneration for the thinker whose keen intellectual insight and beauty of literary expression revived English interest in the problems of jurisprudence. What we do assert is that at the basis of sound political speculation must lie first-hand knowledge of political facts and institutions, and that while Maine's inferences sometimes outrun the limits of his knowledge Sir Francis Adams has supplied just that kind of knowledge which would have been invaluable to such a

---

[3] Henry Maine, *Popular Government: Four Essays* (London, 1885). This book, perhaps the capstone of late-Victorian anti-democratic polemic, is frequently referenced by Dicey. Maine was one of the most influential legal scholars in nineteenth-century Britain, pioneering a historical and comparative approach to law, and he served an important term as "legislator of India," that is, the legal member of council in India. A "classical liberal" proponent of free market and the sanctity of contract, he came to oppose democracy virulently later in life.

thinker as Maine. No man, we may add, would have prized it more highly; for no man would have turned Adams's facts to such good account as the author of 'Ancient Law.'[4] Meanwhile the best service which a critic can render to his readers is to bring to the study of Sir Francis Adams's last memorandum something, if that be possible, of the open-eyed intelligence, which characterises the best work of Sir Henry Maine.

Democracy in Switzerland has turned out a complete success.

This is the all-important conclusion forced by Sir Francis Adams on the notice of Englishmen. Under very peculiar circumstances Swiss statesmanship has solved problems which perplex most European States. In Switzerland national defence is secured (as far as any small State can secure it) by the maintenance of a large, a cheap, and effective force which displays much of the discipline, and brings on the country none of the evils, of a standing army; every citizen is a soldier, and every soldier is a citizen.[i] National finances are prosperous and the country is not overburdened by a national debt;[ii] education has permeated every class, and Zürich has achieved results which may excite the envy of Birmingham or of Boston. Among a people traditionally disposed to lawlessness complete liberty has been made compatible with order, and theological animosities, which for centuries have been the special bane of the Confederacy, have been assuaged, or removed, by the healing influence of religious freedom and equality. The good fortune or the wisdom of the Swiss has accomplished other results which many nations have found, or find, all but impossible of

---

[4] Henry Maine, *Ancient Law: Its Connection with the Early History of Society, and Its Relation to Modern Ideas* (London, 1861). This book elaborated Maine's thesis, one of the most famous in Victorian social science, that "the movement of the progressive societies has hitherto been a movement from Status to Contract." This idea was closely related to his anti-democratic turn, for he believed that the progress of modern societies could be undone if the masses, who were hostile to individual autonomy and *laissez-faire*, were granted political power.

[i] Adams, chap. xi. pp. 140–61.

[ii] 'The public debt of the republic amounted, on January 1, 1889, to 30,572,000 francs [1,222,880*l*.], at 3½ per cent. The interest amounts to 1,070,020 francs [42,800*l*.], and the sinking fund to 699,000 francs [27,960 *l*.]. As a set-off against the debt there exists a so-called "Federal fortune," or property belonging to the State, valued at over 66,483,000 francs [2,659,320*l*.] (1888). The various cantons of Switzerland have their own local administrations and their own budgets of revenue and expenditure. Most of them have also public debts, but not of a large amount, and abundantly covered, in every instance, by cantonal property, chiefly in land. At the end of 1882 the aggregate debts of all the cantons amounted to about 12,000,000*l*.' (Statesman's Year-Book, 1889, p. 518.)

attainment. Small and often hostile States have been fused into a nation. The transition from a condition of feudal inequality, far more oppressive than the *ancien régime* of France, to the system of equal rights and equal laws, which befits a modern industrial society, has been accomplished without bringing on the country one tithe of the horrors which were the price of French emancipation from the tyranny of privilege, and without exposing Switzerland to those alternations between revolutionary violence and reactionary oppression which for a century have harassed the people of France. Switzerland has closed the era of revolution. Perils indeed impend over the Confederacy, but they spring from external causes; they are due to the certain power and possible unscrupulosity of the gigantic military States which are the curse of modern Europe.

A circumstance which enhances the impressiveness of the triumphs gained by popular government in Switzerland is that they are not due to any of the providential privileges (such as the possession of unlimited territory or the impossibility of foreign intervention) which have fostered the prosperity of the United States.

Every obstacle which taxes the resources of statesmanship has stood in the path of Swiss unity and of Swiss welfare.

Switzerland is among the least fertile of European lands; she is surrounded by hostile Powers. Her population is less than the population of Belgium, of the Netherlands, or of Sweden. In mere numbers Switzerland falls below Scotland or Ireland; for the Swiss amount to about 2,900,000 persons, whilst the population of Scotland is in round numbers 3,700,000, and of Ireland 5,100,000. Yet Switzerland, from a body of citizens less in number than the inhabitants of London or of Lancashire, is forced to support for the maintenance of national independence an army of 200,000 men; this force may be called petty if compared with the hosts of the German Empire or of the French Republic, but it is enormous if measured by the resources of the Confederacy.

Switzerland further, though a small country, contains all those sources of division which have dismembered greater States. The Swiss are from one point of view not so much a nation as a league of twenty-two nations. Not until historically recent times have they obtained a common national name. They possess no common language. German, French, and Italian are each in official use, and the public recognition of three tongues recalls the danger that the attractions of race or speech may detach some of its members from the Confederation and draw them towards one of the large neighbouring nations.

Diversities of race have been intensified by, for they partially coincide with, differences of religion, and the bitterness of theological animosity has been more intense and has lived on longer in Switzerland than in any other European country. It sounds paradoxical to call the struggle with the Sonderbund the last of the wars of religion.[5] The paradox, however, contains an element of truth. The Sonderbund marked the final stage of the irrepressible and secular conflict between Protestant and Catholic. Nor are the Swiss free from that disease of modern States, the memory of traditional feuds. The forest cantons can recall the time when, as leaders of the Catholics, they maintained a kind of supremacy, for it was not till the beginning of the eighteenth century that the two most powerful Protestant cantons gained the upper hand. The recollection, moreover, of contests stimulated by theological hatred does not form anything like the whole of the bitter reminiscences which the Swiss people inherit from the past. The seventeenth and eighteenth centuries were in Switzerland ages of social and political inequality and occasionally of gross and cruel oppression. The *ancien régime* should be studied by those who want to understand its bad side, as it existed, not in France, but in Bern, or in Zürich, or in Lucerne. In 1787 the whole government of Bern was engrossed by sixty-nine families, and a year or two later French *émigrés* found that from no aristocracy did they receive such cordial sympathy as from the Bernese oligarchs. These facts tell their own tale. They amply explain the meaning and causes of such movements as the peasant war in 1653, the conspiracy of Davel in 1723, or the petition for the most ordinary rights of citizens presented by the Zürich country folk in 1795 and punished by their masters of the city as treason and rebellion.[iii]

---

[5] The Sonderbund War was a conflict which took place in 1847 when seven Catholic cantons (collectively called the *Sonderbund*) formed an alliance against the religious policy of the Federal Diet, in which a majority was held by a radical-liberal party based in the Protestant cantons that had proposed a new centralizing constitution. The Sonderbund was quickly defeated by the Federal Army, and in the aftermath the Constitution of 1848 was passed. This constitution underwent a major revision in 1874, including the introduction of the federal referendum. It is on this latter constitution that Dicey is (almost always) commenting.

[iii] As to the condition of Switzerland during the seventeenth and eighteenth centuries see especially Vulliemin, 'Histoire de la Confédération Suisse,' ii. pp. 177–284. [Louis Vulliemin, *Histoire de la Confédération Suisse*, 2 vols. (Lausanne, 1875–6). Dicey is referring here to three paradigmatic popular uprisings against urban-oligarchic control.]

The French Revolution, while it gave a fatal blow to aristocratic privilege, increased the sources, of Swiss discord; for the foundation of the Helvetic Republic, being an attempt to introduce by foreign aid a political unity inconsistent with the spirit of Swiss nationality, delayed the natural progress of the country towards union. And if the Act of Mediation—that wisest of Napoleon's attempts at constitution-making— gave Switzerland the best constitution which the country had as yet enjoyed, it made the Swiss dependent on France, and by thus outraging national dignity paved the way for the restoration by the Allied Powers of reactionary and oligarchical governments.[6] Hence there is not a part of Switzerland where large portions of the population cannot, if they choose, recall past wrongs. The country remembers the tyranny of the towns; the citizens of Vaud can recall the despotism of Bern; the Italian Swiss may nourish traditions of the time when they suffered from the rapacity of governors sent them by cantons to whose authority they were subject; and if the country folks have historical grievances against the cities, the inhabitants of the cities may remember that civic authority was not so long ago the privilege of an oligarchy. Social exclusiveness still recalls the age of political domination, and, in Bern at least, old families which have ceased in the field of politics to enjoy privilege or to exercise authority hold themselves aloof from statesmen who cannot claim old descent, and affect as much disdain for the officials of the Confederacy as the Faubourg St. Germain for the President and Ministers of the French Republic.[7]

Nor are the difficulties of popular government smoothed away by the prevalence among Swiss citizens of any traditional reverence for law. Many of the institutions of the country still betray to the eyes of an intelligent critic that in Switzerland, as in most small republics, the principle of the division of powers, which is the essential basis for the supremacy of law, has never been fully recognised; both the cantonal constitutions and the federal constitution display a tendency to confound

---

[6] In 1798, under the Directory, the Revolutionary armies invaded Switzerland and established the centralizing and "modernizing" Helvetic Republic. In 1803 Napoleon replaced this with a new constitution known as the Act of Mediation that lasted until his fall in 1814, when the Restoration period saw a reversal of the Revolutionary changes and a return to much of the previous confederal feudal arrangements. Again following French developments, this regime fell in 1830.

[7] The Faubourg St. Germain (part of the current seventh arrondissement) was and remains one of the wealthiest and most exclusive districts in Paris. In the eighteenth century it had become the central area for the *hôtels particuliers* of the upper echelons of the French nobility and it was a bastion of anti-republican sentiment in the nineteenth century.

executive or legislative with judicial functions. In the writings, further, of two of the most eminent among the men of letters who have turned their attention to Swiss politics may be found evidence of a certain lawlessness in the character of the Swiss. Malet du Pan gained from his acquaintance with the revolutionary movements which disturbed Geneva the experience by which to anticipate the course of revolution in France, and Tocqueville noted some fifty years ago the dangers to Swiss democracy which might arise from Swiss lawlessness.[iv]

Behind every other obstacle to the maintenance of legal order lies the national tendency towards the exaggeration of local sentiment. Every federal government involves a division of sovereignty between the confederacy and the States; but in Switzerland each of the cantons has been, and still in feeling is, something like a separate nation. Cantonal unity is itself too great a restraint on the spirit of subdivision to suit the Swiss character. Cantons have broken into half-cantons. Appenzell divides into Inner Appenzell and Outer Appenzell; Unterwald consists of Upper Unterwald and Lower Unterwald. Basle country breaks away from Basle town. Local divisions within each canton have each their distinctive character. It is no great exaggeration to assert that each canton is a confederacy of communes. Federalism, which in the United States is the result of a historical accident, is in Switzerland the necessary consequence of historical developement. America, it has been said, is a nation which under stress of circumstances has adopted the form of a federal State. Switzerland is a federation which under stress of circumstances has developed into a nation.

Swiss democracy has, then, met, and triumphed over, all the obstacles to national unity arising from differences of race, from religious discord, from historical animosities, and from the difficulty inherent in federalism of reconciling national authority with State rights. In 1847 the Sonderbund brought upon Switzerland the perils which fourteen years later Secession brought upon the American Union. Continental statesmen believed that the time had come when foreign intervention might complete the ruin worked by civil discord. Bold would have been the prophet who, on November 4, 1847, when the Diet decreed the

---

[iv] See A. de Tocqueville, 'Œuvres Complètes,' viii. pp. 455–7. [Tocqueville, "Voyage en Suisse," in *Œuvres complètes, publiées par Madame de Tocqueville,* 9 vols. (Paris, 1861–6), vol. 8. Tocqueville did indeed depict a Switzerland so rocked by revolutionary turmoil and so illiberal that it did not merit the description "republican."]

dissolution of the Sonderbund, had predicted that the unity of Switzerland would outlast the authority of the Orleanist monarchy; but 1848, which exiled Louis Philippe and gave France a transitory republic, founded in Switzerland a national government as stable as any in Europe: the Swiss constitution is the one fabric which does honour to the constitution-makers of the year of revolutions.[8]

For profitable criticism of the Swiss constitution it is of primary importance to realise the singularity of the complete success achieved by democracy in Switzerland. It is worth while, therefore, to regard the matter from a general point of view.

Popular government—we use the term with the convenient elasticity given to it by Maine—is apt to be defective in one at least, and it may be in both, of two qualities, namely, ability and stability. On this matter we may consult both American and French experience.

America abounds in talent, in energy, and in resource. The citizens of the Union are a nation of inventors. They are the patentees of the modern world; they promise to be its leaders in the path of scientific discovery; they enjoy institutions of which some are an invaluable inheritance brought by their forefathers from England, and others were framed a century ago by the most skilful of political architects. But the most partial of critics would hesitate to assert that the citizens of America in the management either of national policy or of State business exhibit anything like pre-eminent ability. Whoever reads Mr. Bryce's 'American 'Commonwealth'—the most friendly account of the United States which has ever been written—will be forced to the conclusion that, but for the talent of the people and the fortunate circumstances of the country, the American system of government would be known to all the world as a portentous failure. No one can conceive that the nobodies or mediocrities who have been the usual occupants of the White House represent in any fair degree the political talent of the country. This conclusion is made the more certain when the critic notes that in certain fields of public life the cleverness and the inventiveness of Americans make themselves manifest. The 'machine' is not the creation of a stupid people, but the party mechanism which bears witness to the smartness

---

[8] On the 1848 Swiss constitution see note 5 above. In that year in France, the July Monarchy, the bourgeois constitutional monarchy of King Louis Philippe, fell and the Second Republic was founded, which lasted for four years until the *coup d'état* of Louis-Napoleon Bonaparte established the Second Empire.

of American citizens also gives testimony to the defectiveness of American institutions. The machine promotes party objects and private interests at the expense of the nation; it deprives the state of the advantages derivable from the dedication to the public service of high character and high ability.

France was for long the centre of intellectual movement throughout Europe. A century of revolutions has, it is true, been as unfavourable to the developement of genius as to the maintenance of morality. But it were childishness to fancy that French intelligence is dead, or to deny that France possesses an unexhausted fund of capacity. National calamity, indeed, has in many directions stimulated the spirit of serious and scientific study, and France may, it is likely enough, resume the intellectual leadership of the civilised world. The capacity and character, however, of French public men sink year by year. The permanent administration, indeed, of the country supplies a body of administrators whose talent masks the pettiness, the corruption, or the stupidity of presidents, ministers, and deputies. But the administrative system is the inheritance, not the creation, of French democracy. The politicians whom universal suffrage brings to the front at Paris are as little likely to create or to improve any great institution as ever were any party of respectable nonentities guided by reckless adventurers. The bare chance of Boulanger's triumph convicts his opponents of incapacity. When, sixty years ago, the folly of Charles X. was hurrying the Bourbons to their downfall, France teemed with statesmen and orators.[9] Compare 1830 with 1890, and you have the proof that in France popular government has not created political ability.

From the experience of the Restoration and of the reign of Louis Philippe a thinker may infer that popular government, under the peculiar form of constitutional monarchy, draws the ability of the country into the service of the State. Whether this conclusion be sound admits of doubt. In any case the alleged advantage is purchased at a great price. The party system, whereof the strangeness is concealed from modern Englishmen only by the force of habit, leads, it has been well said, to this

---

[9] Charles X was king when the Bourbon Restoration fell in 1830; he was succeeded by Louis Philippe and the July Monarchy. General George Boulanger had been a leading military and political figure of the 1880s. The political movement of *Boulangisme* that coalesced behind his cult of personality has been said to have combined Catholic, royalist, nationalist, aggressive militarist, and (more controversially) leftist and communard elements. It was feared that Boulanger would lead a coup and destroy the Third Republic.

result: the sixteen cleverest men in Parliament are set to govern the country, whilst the sixteen next cleverest men are employed in hindering the work of government; the talents which should be enlisted in the service of the nation neutralise each other and are rendered almost useless. Under the modern system, moreover, of Parliamentary warfare the weapons of attack are stronger than the means of defence. Politics are turned into a game. The excitement attracts men of talent, but the game is played at the expense of the country: the cost is the perpetuation of political weakness and instability.

The stability of a government includes two things—first, security against revolutionary changes in the constitution, and, secondly, consistency in the policy of the state and in the conduct of the administration. A government is not really stable which does not enjoy at once constitutional stability and administrative stability.

In America the foundations of the commonwealth are as firmly fixed as in any country in the world, and the constitution gives to the non-parliamentary executive an independence not possessed by the ministries of France or of England. But the short tenure of office which in practice is allotted to the President and his ministers, the changes of policy which may result from a thousand votes being cast at New York in favour of, say, a republican instead of a democratic president, the impossibility of forming a permanent civil service, are all circumstances incompatible with the stable and consistent course of administration. The United States have hitherto stood in such a fortunate position that their only wise foreign policy was to have no foreign policy at all. But candid observers may well doubt whether the American administrative system, or want of system, could exist for a year within a European state without involving the country in desperate dangers.

In France popular government has attained neither kind of stability. Within little more than forty years the country has tried a constitutional monarchy, a presidential republic, a democratic empire, and a parliamentary republic. Each change has been the work of violence; each revolution has been carried out against the wish of the vast majority of a people whose one desire is to avoid disturbance and suffering. Revolutionary eras, it may be said, do not fairly represent the habitual condition of France. The observation is not without truth. Let us look, then, at the pacific period covered by the reign of Louis Philippe. The constitution was, indeed, though with difficulty, protected from violent overthrow, but the party system undermined the stability of the

26

executive. Few of our readers, we suspect, realise the constancy of ministerial changes between 1830 and 1848. The ministry of August 4, 1830, the ministry of November 3, 1830, the ministry of March 2, 1832, the ministry of October 11, 1832, the Ministry of Three Days, the cabinets of Mortier, of Broglie, of Thiers, of Molé, of Soult, are forgotten. Englishmen, if they think about the subject at all, remember only Guizot's tenure of power from 1840 to 1848. They forget that the cabinets of Louis Philippe held office for an average period of not two years apiece; they forget that the catastrophe of February 24 was the result, not less of popular impatience at Guizot's long exercise of authority, than of the fatal tendency of the fully developed party system to shake the foundations of the constitution.[10]

Turn now to Switzerland. The Swiss executive, of which we shall say more later, is an elective council or ministry of seven persons. No man can doubt its ability. It transacts a mass of business such as falls to few cabinets. It guides the policy of a State eternally menaced by foreign complications; it preserves harmony throughout a confederacy made up of twenty-two cantons, each jealous of one another and sympathising only in common jealousy of the Federal power. In these tasks the Swiss Council succeeds. Peace and prosperity prevail throughout Switzerland. This is strong proof that the Confederacy is served by ministers of marked ability and of sterling character.[v]

It is not to be expected that the Federal Assembly should, as regards talent, equal the small cabinet made up of the Assembly's ablest members; a country which numbers not much more than half the population of the State of New York cannot, from the nature of things, produce a Parliament of statesmen. But the Assembly is filled with men of sense, of respectability, and of honesty, and compares favourably with the legislatures of larger countries. Let the Swiss Parliament be placed side by side with the Congress of the United States, where five per cent. of the members take bribes in hard cash, and fifteen to twenty per cent. are

[10] The instability of the executive was a major problem of the July Monarchy and was frequently remarked upon by British commentators at the time. François Guizot's tenure was best known for his adamant resistance to extension of the suffrage beyond the limited ranks of the wealthy who then possessed it; a campaign to broaden the franchise ultimately led to the toppling of the regime. Guizot was also among the most important historians and philosophers of the time, exerting a strong influence on heroes of Dicey like Mill and Bagehot.

[v] See Adams, pp. 64, 65.

open to any form of corruption less palpable than the receipt of money;[vi]
or with the senators and representatives of New York, who at Albany pass
'such a witches' Sabbath of jobbing, bribing, thieving, and prostitution of
legislative power to private interest as the world has seldom seen.' If it be
said that we must seek for contrasts from the countries of Europe, let the
Swiss Assembly of States and the National Council be compared with
French legislatures. The charges, indeed, of factiousness and corruption
brought against French representative assemblies may be in many cases
slanders. They are, however, by no means new. No picture of the
Republican National Assembly can be darker than the picture drawn in
1841 of the Orleanist Chamber of Deputies.

> 'Elle [la chambre] possède de fait le pouvoir suprême, inhérent à
> celui de voter l'impôt. Mais ce pouvoir, au lieu de tourner au bien de
> tous, n'est pour elle qu'un objet de trafic, parce qu'elle est le centre
> où aboutissent toutes les corruptions. A quelques rares exceptions
> près, quel est le député qui songe à autre chose qu'à faire ou à refaire
> sa fortune, à revendre les électeurs qui lui ont vendu eux-mêmes le
> pays? Qu'est-ce que la chambre? un grand bazar, où chacun livre sa
> conscience, ou ce qu'il donne pour telle, en échange d'une place,
> d'un emploi, d'un avancement pour soi et les siens, de quelqu'une,
> enfin, de ces faveurs qui toutes se résolvent en argent!'[vii]

These are the words of La Mennais. They may savour of rhetoric and
passion. The point worth notice is that in 1841 thousands of Frenchmen

---

[vi] See Bryce, 'American Commonwealth,' ii. p. 524. [James Bryce, *The American
Commonwealth*, 2 vols. (London, 1888). This volume was heralded as the greatest
treatment of American politics since Tocqueville's *Democracy in America*. Bryce, a
Liberal politician who would occupy several leading administrative posts, was a close
friend of Dicey and a colleague in the Oxford Law faculty. They split on the subject of
Home Rule, although this did not disrupt their friendship.]

[vii] Grégoire, 'Histoire de France,' ii. pp. 220, 221. ["It [the chamber] possesses *de facto* the
supreme power, which is inherent in voting the taxes. But this power, instead of being
made to serve to the good of all, is for the chamber merely an object to be bartered; it is
the center toward which all other corruptions tend. There are a few rare exceptions, but
who is the deputy who dreams of anything other than making or remaking his fortune by
reselling the electors who themselves sold the country to him? What is the chamber? A
great bazar, where each gives away his conscience, or what he takes for his conscience, in
exchange for a post, an employment, an advancement for him or his kin, for some one of
those favors which ultimately turn into cash." Louis Grégoire, *Histoire de France: période
contemporaine, règne de Louis-Philippe, République de 1848, Empire, République jusqu'à la
constitution de 1875...*, 4 vols. (Paris, 1879–83), vol. 2. Gregoire was here quoting from an
anti-government pamphlet by Félicité de Lamennais, a priest who shaped liberal and
socialist currents within Catholicism.]

believed them to be the language of truth, and that in 1890 thousands of Frenchmen bring against the National Assembly of the Republic all the accusations hurled by La Mennais against the Parliament of Louis Philippe. There is no reason to think that a single sensible inhabitant of Switzerland believes the members of the Federal Assembly to be chargeable with the vices imputed, whether justly or not, to American or French legislatures.

The Swiss Parliament, moreover, gives the strongest proof of its own wisdom which can be demanded from any legislative body. It maintains in office a practically permanent executive, which in point of stability stands in the most salient contrast not only with the ephemeral ministries of France, but also with the short-lived cabinets of England. No American President, it should be added, has ever held office for as long a period as have many members of the Swiss Council. Of the stability of the Swiss constitution it is almost needless to speak. It is as firmly established a government as any on the Continent. It is capable of change, and in fact underwent elaborate revision—mainly with a view to increase the authority of the Federal power—in 1874.[11] But revision requires the deliberate sanction of the Swiss people, and the constitution of the Confederacy, which exactly meets the wants and the habits of the Swiss, is as well guarded from sudden attack, carried out either by violence or by hasty legislation, as is any constitution in the world, unless it be the constitution of the United States. Popular government, in short, does in Switzerland display both ability and stability.

Why has the striking success of Swiss democracy failed to attract the attention of thinkers? The question is worth an answer. The failure is due to causes which, though they lie on the surface, deserve attention.

Prosperity, in the case of nations as of men, is uninteresting, and the land of tourists, of guides, and of innkeepers—the 'playground of Europe'—is the most prosperous of countries. It is because France has not prospered that everyone reads modern French history; if the States-General had firmly established a settled plan of liberty, the domestic annals of France, since 1789, might have been as unexciting as the home affairs of England, during the century which followed the Revolution of 1688. Nor even during the period of conflict were the Swiss leaders the

---

[11] See note 5 above. Beyond expanding the purview of the central government and introducing the referendum at the federal level, it is worth noting that this revision was itself ratified by a referendum.

men to enlist widespread sympathy. They knew how to found a constitution which might outlast the hasty creations of 1848, but they were poor revolutionary dramatists. They could not create the surprises which French statesmanship has never failed to produce. They could not provide that series of tragic or pathetic scenes which marked each act of the Italian revolutionary drama. The triumphant suppression of the Sonderbund was a more remarkable feat of arms than the unsuccessful defence of Rome. But the name of Dufour is unknown outside Switzerland; Garibaldi is the saint of European democracy.[12] Swiss history is barren of great men and confutes the creed of hero-worship. The small commonwealths which have coalesced into a nation were, unlike all other small republics, neither adorned by heroes nor oppressed by tyrants. The city of Calvin stands alone, but the men whose names are the glory of Geneva—and Geneva did not till quite recent days belong to the Confederacy—were either, like Calvin himself, foreigners, or else were, like Rousseau, Necker, Clavière, or Malet du Pan, associated by their careers with more important lands than Switzerland. Bigness passes with the world for greatness. It is, after all, the smallness of Switzerland which has diverted the attention of the public from Swiss institutions.

Publicists of intelligence perceive that the interest of a political organism is independent of its size, and that England, or the United States, may learn much from the experience of a country smaller than more than one American State. But the complexity of the Swiss constitution has made the study thereof difficult, whilst the fact that the constitution of Switzerland is neither, like the French Republic, a modern creation, nor, like the United Kingdom, the result of long and uninterrupted historical developement, perplexes students, who sorely need that guidance through the annals of Switzerland which Mr. Freeman has so long promised, and which can be provided by Mr. Freeman alone.[13] A cursory examination, moreover, of Swiss federalism suggests the idea that the Confederation is a mere copy of the American Union. In Switzerland, as in America, you have a federation in which the authority

---

[12] Guillaume Henri Dufour led the Federal Army to victory in the Sonderbund War and was later president of the first Geneva Convention. Giuseppe Garibaldi was one of the great figures of the struggle for Italian unification and a leading left-wing politician during the early decades of the Kingdom of Italy.

[13] Edward Augustus Freeman was Dicey's colleague at Oxford, where he was Professor of Modern History. Freeman was a prominent champion and scholar of federalism and was one of the rare Victorians to follow Swiss affairs closely.

of the central government is artfully balanced against the sovereignty of the several federated States. In both countries you have a President of the Republic, in both you find a senate representing the States and a lower chamber representing the people. In both a federal court exercises, if not identical, yet analogous functions. In each country democracy has reached its final developement. The smaller republic copies the features of the great American commonwealth. Why, it may be asked, study a miniature copy when you can with more profit examine the traits of the full-sized original? The answer is that Swiss constitutionalists, though profiting by the experience of the United States, were no servile imitators. Their work is as noticeable on account of its essential unlikeness as on account of its superficial similarity to the constitution of the United States. The resemblance is in many instances merely nominal. The President of the Confederation, for example, is merely the annually appointed chairman of a board, and bears as little resemblance to an American president as to an English premier. Democracy in Switzerland has reached a stage beyond that which it has attained in America. Add to this that it is where Swiss statesmen have followed Transatlantic precedents that their success is most doubtful. The Swiss Senate is as distinctly the least as the American Senate is the most successful among the institutions of the two republics. It is when Swiss statesmanship has displayed most originality that it has been most successful and is most full of instruction.

To any inquirer even moderately versed in the comparative study of constitutions a thoughtful perusal of Sir Francis Adams's work, combined with a knowledge of such authorities as Orelli's admirable 'Staatsrecht der Schweizerischen Eidgenossenschaft,' or Dubs's popular exposition of the public law of the Swiss Confederation,[14] will show that the most original among the Federal institutions of Switzerland are the Council of State and the Referendum. Our aim in the remainder of this article is to fix our readers' almost exclusive attention upon the nature and working of these institutions. They are closely connected together; they give to Swiss democratic federalism its peculiar colour.

---

[14] The first two are cited at the opening of the article; the latter was a textbook of Swiss Constitutionalism by the politician-humanitarian Jakob Dubs: *Le droit public de la Confédération suisse; exposé pour le people*, 2 vols. (Neuchâtel, 1878); *Das oeffentliche recht der Schweizerischen eidgenossenschaft: Dargestellt für das volk*, 2 vols. (Zurich, 1878).

Many other subjects suggested by Sir Francis Adams's pages are, it is true, of equal if not of greater importance. The cantonal governments and the communes deserve separate investigation. The communal life, indeed, of Switzerland and the character of the population, especially of the German portion thereof, are essential conditions for the success of the Swiss experiment in democratic government. But they are not the means by which this success is achieved. Switzerland has always possessed communes and cantons. The German-Swiss have from time immemorial been accustomed to self-government; but Switzerland, in spite of these advantages, has been distracted by civil and religious discord. Her present peace and unity are due, as far as national prosperity is ever in reality caused by forms of government, to the Swiss constitution, which has achieved all that the best-framed of polities can achieve—namely, the giving free scope to the energy and ability of the nation. Of Swiss constitutionalism the Council and the Referendum are the corner stones.

1. *The Council.*—The annually elected chairman of the Federal Council is officially styled President of the Confederation; but there exists in reality no official of the Swiss Republic occupying a position like that held by President Carnot or President Harrison.[15] The Council consists of seven members, each of whom presides over a special department of the administration—e.g. foreign affairs or finance. The councillors may for convenience be called ministers, and the Council a cabinet. But there exists in Switzerland no council or committee resembling the Ministry or Cabinet either of France or of England.

Four noticeable characteristics distinguish the Swiss Council from the executives of other popularly governed countries, and, when examined, prove that Switzerland has invented a scheme of administration which is marked by singular originality and differs as much from the Presidential system of the United States as from the Cabinet system of the United Kingdom.[16]

---

[15] In 1890 Sadi Carnot was President of France and Benjamin Harrison was President of the United States.

[16] While it may sound odd to twenty-first-century readers to hear the Swiss model set up as an equal and alternative to American presidentialism or British parliamentarism, Dicey's point here had purchase for many years. In his friend James Bryce's *Modern Democracies* of 1921, for instance, one can find this view that the American, British, and Swiss were the three archetypes of modern democratic constitutionalism.

First, as already intimated, no member of the Council occupies the position either of an American President or of an English Prime Minister. The President of the Confederation, who is elected by the Federal Assembly from among the members of the Council for one year only, and cannot be re-elected for more than one year in succession, receives a slightly larger salary and occupies a higher rank than any of his colleagues. He is, however, in reality nothing but the chairman of the Council, and does not, except from the influence of personal character, exercise as much authority over the councillors as does the chairman of a company over his board of directors.

Secondly, the Council is elected by the Federal Assembly at the Assembly's first meeting for a fixed term of three years. As each Federal Assembly, or, as the Americans would say, each Congress, is elected for a period of three years in the month of October, and the Council is elected at the first session of the Assembly in the following November, it follows that the Council continues in office from the moment of its election until the first meeting of the Federal Assembly. For the election of the Council, of the so-called President of the Confederacy for the year, and of some other officers, the Chambers of the Federal Assembly, i.e. the Council of the States (or Senate) and the National Council (or Chamber of Deputies or Representatives), sit and vote together as one body. The members of the Council are in general, though not invariably, elected from among the members of the Federal Assembly, or from among the outgoing councillors. Membership of the Council is inconsistent with the holding of a seat in the Assembly. But the councillors have a right to speak in either Chamber and to take part in its debates. They have, of course, not the right to vote on divisions.

The Council is elected, as already stated, for a term of three years. Critics, therefore, impressed with a traditional belief in democratic fickleness, or observers of the mutability which weakens the Ministries of France, or even of England, would naturally assume that the Swiss councillors, in fact, held office for no longer than three years at a time. The assumption, plausible though it be, is baseless. The members of the Council are not only re-eligible, but are usually re-elected.

'There have been hitherto only two instances of a member willing to serve not being re-elected, but from time to time some naturally resign, one for a more lucrative post, another to become head of a diplomatic mission, another from a desire to retire into private life.'[17]

A councillor in any case is, unlike an English, or a French Minister, absolutely certain of holding office for at least three years, for[:]

Thirdly, the Council, though elected by the Assembly, cannot, according to either the theory, or the practice, of the constitution, be dismissed from office by the Assembly. Nor, on the other hand, can the Council dissolve the Assembly.

Fourthly, the Council 'is not a purely party government: it is rather an executive committee for the management of business than a real executive power, such as exists in other countries.'[18] This fourth characteristic, which we have purposely expressed in the language of Sir Francis Adams, requires some further explanation. In the words 'a committee for the management of business' lies the explanation of all the main peculiarities in the nature and in the position of the Council. It is a board of experienced men appointed by the Assembly to carry on the business of the nation; and it is appointed, speaking generally, on business principles. What Englishmen fail to perceive when they criticise their own institutions, though they see it plainly when censuring the institutions of America, is the fundamental opposition between the party system and the business system of management. On the party system men are placed in power because they are party leaders, i.e. because they can manage men, not because they can manage business. The party system tends, at any rate where the scheme of cabinet government exists, to enforce the collective responsibility of the cabinet. The party system also generates an Opposition, 'whose business it is to oppose,' or, in other words, to hinder the efficient transaction of public affairs. The party system, lastly, absolutely requires a change of executive when the policy or the proposals of the executive meet with the disapproval of the persons, whether members of Parliament or electors, by whom the executive is appointed. The business method of management is utterly different. Where ministers are appointed, whether by an absolute monarch or by an Assembly, mainly as agents who may carry on the work of the country, they are, or may be, appointed for capacity in business—for skill, that is to say, in administration. With ideas of business the notion of the collective responsibility of the executive is inconsistent. Departmental takes the

---

[17] Adams and Cunningham, *Swiss Confederation*, 59.   [18] Ibid. 65.

place of general responsibility. Hence a ministry of affairs may be made of experts who, on many points, are not in full agreement with each other; for the proper management of business does not require that a minister who has made—say, to an Assembly—a proposal which the Assembly rejects should thereupon resign office. Still less does it require that because, say, the Minister of Education produces a Bill which the Assembly cannot approve, the whole ministry should retire from power. If a manager proposes to his employer a scheme which the master disapproves, the head of the firm rejects the proposal, but he does not in general dismiss the manager. Still less does any sane merchant discharge all his clerks because he rejects plans proposed to him by the head clerk. Now, the rules which fix the position and action of the Council are, on the whole, based on the requirements of the business system rather than of the party system of government. The Council are not the leaders so much as the experienced agents of the Swiss people. The councillors are selected for capacity. Hence the continuance in office of men recommended, at any rate, by the possession of experience. Hence the absence of any rule that the councillors need absolutely agree, or pretend to agree, as to every proposal made by the Council. As in every board for the management of affairs, the minority practically gives way to the majority. But it may well happen that members of the Council oppose one another in debate.

> 'The most remarkable sight is that which occurs where a debate arises in either Chamber upon a question where the difference of opinion of members of the Federal Council is very marked, and it has happened that two of the body have risen in succession to support dissimilar views. The debate once over, no particular fric-tion results between the two colleagues; both victor and vanquished may spend the evening at the same café, continue their discussion amicably or not at all, and they will sit serenely together on the morrow in Cabinet Council as if nothing particular had happened.'[19]

To the same cause it is due that the Council never is permanently at variance with the Assembly, and never retires on account of a Parliamentary defeat.

> '...Collisions between the Federal Council and the Federal Assembly do not exist. If any measure proposed by the former is

---

[19] Ibid. 58.

rejected by both Chambers, or by one, and thus does not become valid, the Federal Council, as seen in the preceding chapter, accepts the rejection; it asks for no vote of confidence, nor does anything ensue in the shape of what we should call a ministerial crisis. Similarly, there is no question of a dissolution of the Chambers when the people reject measures passed by them. The Federal authorities, whether legislative or executive, being chosen for a fixed term, remain at their posts during that term.' (P. 60.)

When a Minister failed, in 1882, to carry a measure relating to education, there was no question of his giving in his resignation; and a Swiss paper, 'opposed to him in politics, remarked that it was lucky the parliamentary system did not exist in Switzerland, as otherwise there would have been an immediate resignation of a capable, honest, and devoted administrator.'[20]

A moment's examination of what is meant by the allegation, that 'the parliamentary system does not exist in Switzerland,' will enable us to see more truly than did perhaps the Swiss critic the real points of resemblance and difference between the Swiss scheme of government by council and the system either of presidential or of cabinet government. In any country where there exists an elective legislature or parliament the relation between the executive and the legislature may be of two totally different characters. The executive may be a non-parliamentary government—that is, a person or body of persons standing totally outside the legislature, and owing to the legislature neither its creation nor its continuance in power. The best known type of such a non-parliamentary executive is the American President, and another example of it may be found in the Government of the German Empire. Wherever such an executive exists several other phenomena coexist with it. The legislature legislates, but it does not govern. There exists some authority in the State which supports the executive, and exercises power at least equal to that of the legislature, and probably greater. The American President represents the true sovereign of America—namely, the American people —at least as truly as do the Houses of Congress.[21] The consequence is

---

[20] Ibid. 61.

[21] This judgment about the relative representativeness of the President and Congress was controversial then as it is now. Here there is once again overlap with James Bryce, who had rendered a similar judgment in *The American Commonwealth*.

that an extra-parliamentary executive possesses a kind of strength and independence not to be found in governments depending for their existence on the will of a legislature. But such an executive is likely, or certain, to come into collision with the legislative body; the history of the United States or of the French Republic of 1848 sufficiently proves the truth of this statement.

The executive, on the other hand, may be a parliamentary government, i.e. a person or body of persons belonging to the legislature, and created as well as continued in power by the will of Parliament. The best developed type of such a parliamentary executive is, of course, the English Cabinet. If another example be wanted, it may be found in the so-called Presidential Government of the existing French Republic. This illustration is instructive. The founders of the constitution meant that the President should be independent of the legislature. The fall of President Grévy, which involved a constitutional revolution, shows that the founders of the Republic have failed in attaining their object.[22] The President, who was meant to wield independent authority, is the servant of the Assembly; for by the Assembly he is not only appointed, but may be displaced. The Government of France has become a parliamentary executive, and in France, as in every country where such an executive exists, two further results ensue.[23] The legislature governs as well as legislates; there exists no acknowledged authority in the State with power equal to that of the legislative body. Monsieur Carnot and Lord Salisbury alike govern by the grace of Parliament, and represent a parliamentary majority.[24] Such a parliamentary executive avoids conflicts with the legislature, but it can boast of no real independence, for its actions waver in accordance with the will or the whims of the party which predominates in the National Assembly or Parliament.

The authors of the Swiss constitution attempted to create an executive which should be in harmony with the legislature, but not be dependent upon it—that is, a government which should to a certain extent combine

[22] Jules Grévy was President of France from 1879 to 1887, and is often credited for putting the Third Republic on a stable footing after the preceding monarchist government. He was forced to resign due to a corruption scandal.

[23] For more on the distinction between parliamentary and non-parliamentary executives, see appendix III to the eighth edition of the *Law of the Constitution*.

[24] Carnot was then President of France. Robert Cecil, Marquess of Salisbury, was in the middle of his second stint as Prime Minister at the time of writing, heading a coalition of Conservatives and Liberal Unionists. Dicey supported his government.

the characteristics of the presidential system with the characteristics of the cabinet system. The statement that parliamentary government does not exist in Switzerland means that this endeavour has succeeded, that the executive acts in general harmony with parliament, but possesses a real independence, and that the legislature, while it legislates, does not govern. The statement is to a great extent true.

The Swiss Council, as compared with the presidential government of America, may be called a parliamentary executive, for it is elected by the Federal Assembly, and looks to the Assembly for re-election. The Council as compared with an English Cabinet may be called a non-parliamentary executive, for it cannot be dismissed by the Assembly, nor does rejection of the Council's proposals by the Assembly make it impossible to carry on the work of administration. In another most important respect the Council differs both from an American President and from an English Cabinet. The Council to a great extent represents the nation; a president or a cabinet each must represent not the nation but a party. For the completion of this comparison or contrast it must in fairness be added that while the American and the English systems each permit the rise of some leader whose authority with the country makes him a temporary dictator, the Swiss system keeps the executive government permanently in commission. Under the constitution of the Confederation no place is left for authoritative leadership. Switzerland does not provide a sphere for the powers of men such as were Walpole, or Chatham, or Washington, or Lincoln.[25] Switzerland does not foster the production of either Heaven-sent Ministers or Saviours of Society.

To an English inquirer the peculiarities of the Swiss Council suggest at once two questions. How, in the first place, does the system work? The answer is simple. The system works admirably. Of this we may adduce two proofs.

The first is that the Confederacy prospers, and that its prosperity depends upon the successful performance by the Council of multifarious and arduous duties. The existence, indeed, of cantonal governments relieves the central power from duties which overburden an English

---

[25] Robert Walpole was *de facto* the first Prime Minister of England (roughly 1721–42), consolidating the Whig supremacy and parliamentary-constitutional monarchy after the Glorious Revolution. The First Earl of Chatham, William Pitt the elder, was the Whig leader during the Seven Years' War. George Washington was the first and Abraham Lincoln the sixteenth president of the United States. Dicey was a great admirer of Lincoln and had been a fervent advocate of the Union during the Civil War.

Cabinet. But State rights and State jealousies impose upon the Council tasks unknown to a French or to an English Ministry. In any case its labours are heavy. The Council, unprovided with any standing army, is responsible for the general maintenance of order. The Council conducts the whole Federal administration. The Council proposes legislation to the Federal Assembly, and apparently drafts every 'Bill,' to use an English expression, which is submitted to the legislature. If, for example, the Assembly, on the proposal of a private member, passes a resolution in favour of some legislative innovation, it is for the Council to reduce the proposed change to the form of a law. The Council takes in hand all schemes of constitutional revision. The Council conducts the whole foreign policy of the State; if Germany or France complain because refugees are not expelled, it is for the Council at the same time to maintain the dignity of the Confederacy and to satisfy the exigencies of a powerful neighbour. The Council is under the constitution often forced to determine questions which are rather judicial than political, and, in a way which foreigners can hardly understand, exercises in some matters, as, for instance, in the case of the complaints brought both by and against the Salvation Army, a jurisdiction concurrent with that of the Federal Court. The decrees of the Court itself are enforceable not by the officers of the tribunal but by the Council, and the Council must enforce them through the agency of the often jealous and refractory cantonal authorities. It is, indeed, in dealing with the cantons that the skill and the difficulties of the Council are chiefly apparent. The Council must see that no provision of a cantonal constitution which violates the constitution of the Confederacy is sanctioned. The Council must insist that the cantons observe the Federal laws. But the Council must not excite unnecessary conflicts between the cantons and the Federal power. That Switzerland is prosperous and contented, and that the same councillors are re-elected from one triennial period to another, shows, then, that the Council performs complicated tasks with extraordinary success.

The second proof of the same fact is to be found in the language of Sir Francis Adams.

'The members of the Federal Council, we will venture to affirm, yield to no other government in Europe in devotion to their country, in incessant hard work for a poor salary, and in thorough honesty and incorruptibility. A diplomatist who knew them well and appreciated their good qualities aptly remarked that they reminded him of a characteristic industry of their own country—of watchmaking—for, having to deal with very minute and intricate affairs, their attention is unremittingly engaged by the most delicate mechanism of government, by the wheels within wheels of Federal and cantonal attributes, by the most careful balancing of relations between contending sects and Churches, and by endeavours to preserve the proper counterpoise between two (French and German), not to say three (the third being Italian), nationalities. Their task is thus essentially one of constant vigilance and careful supervision.' (P. 64.)

This is the evidence of an unbiassed witness who testifies to facts of which he has accurate knowledge.

How, in the second place, is it possible that in Switzerland men of character and capacity should be able, without loss of self-respect, to retain office, though the measures they propose to the legislature have been rejected by the Assembly, or, as may be the case, by the people? This is an inquiry which perplexes an Englishman. In England, as he knows, the Ministry is virtually elected by Parliament, and no Cabinet could retain office for a week if a Parliament which it could not dissolve rejected the Government's chief Bills. The Swiss Council or Cabinet is, he learns, elected by the Federal Assembly, or, in other words, by the Swiss Parliament; the Council has, further, no power of dissolving the Assembly. How, then, be asks, is it possible for the Council to maintain office when the measures it proposes are rejected? The answer can be gained only by studying the best known and the least understood of Swiss institutions. The position of the Council depends on the legislative authority of the Swiss people.

2. *The Referendum.*—This term—utterly foreign to English constitutionalism—means 'the reference to all vote-possessing citizens, either of the Confederation or of a canton, of laws and resolutions framed by their representatives,'[viii] and denotes a constitutional arrangement which governs the whole working of Swiss democracy. Under the Federal constitution the referendum plays a twofold part. It forms, in the first place, an essential portion of the machinery for the revision of the constitution. Such revision always takes place by means of a law regularly

---

[viii] Adams, pp. 76–87; Orelli, 'Das Staatsrecht der Schweizerisclien Eidgenossenschaft,' pp. 83–8 and 79, 80.

passed by the two Houses of the Assembly. If the two Houses agree on their scheme of revision, or, as Englishmen would say, on a 'Reform Bill,' then the Bill is made the subject of a referendum, and is submitted to the Swiss people for their rejection or approval. If the Bill is accepted by the majority both of the citizens voting and of the cantons, it becomes law; if not, it falls to the ground. But the course of procedure may be a little more complicated. If the two Houses disagree, or if fifty thousand citizens demand a revision of the constitution, then the question whether there shall be a revision or not is put to the people. If the majority of the voters answer in the negative the matter is ended; if the majority answer in the affirmative, then there is a new election of both Houses for the taking in hand of a revision of the constitution, or, as we should say, the passing of a Reform Bill.[ix] The measure itself is, thereupon, prepared by the Council, and submitted by it to the Houses. When the Bill has passed the Houses it is laid before the people, and becomes law or not according as it is or is not accepted by a majority both of the citizens voting and of the cantons. The referendum, when employed to effect a constitutional reform, is what the Swiss call an 'obligatory' referendum; in other words, the express assent of the Swiss people is necessary for the passing of any law modifying any of the articles of the constitution, and English readers must be reminded that these 121 articles contain a multitude of general principles which are not in their own nature constitutional, as, for example, the article which absolutely prohibits the establishment of gambling houses.[x]

The referendum, in the second place, may be necessary for the validity of any law whatever passed by the Assembly; for since 1874 any such law must, on demand being duly made within the proper time by thirty thousand voters, be submitted for ratification or rejection to the Swiss people, and unless ratified by a majority of persons voting does not come into force. The referendum is in this case what the Swiss call 'facultative' or 'optional,' i.e. it must be employed if required by the proper number of citizens, but not otherwise. It is rarely demanded. From 1874 to 1884, of ninety-nine laws which had passed the Assembly

---

[ix] Constitution Fédérale, art. 120. [*Constitution fédérale de la Confédération Suisse du 29 mai 1874* (Berne, 1874).]
[x] Constitution Fédérale, art. 35.

seventeen only were the subject of a referendum. Of these seventeen thirteen were vetoed by the people.

The word 'vetoed' is suggestive; it recalls the striking analogy between the referendum of democratic Switzerland and the miscalled veto of an English king. When Elizabeth, or James I., or William III.,[26] refused assent to a Bill which had passed the Houses of Parliament, the sovereign acted in just the same manner in which the citizens of Switzerland now act when they refuse their sanction to a Reform Bill, or it may be to an ordinary Bill, which has been passed by the National Assembly. For the analogy between the royal veto and the popular referendum is much more than formal. When the English king was the most influential member of the sovereign legislature, he naturally, in common with each House of Parliament, approved or rejected Bills submitted to him for his consideration, and, if he were a ruler of high character, exercised his right in accordance with his opinion as to the feeling and the interest of the nation. Under the Swiss democracy the electors are the sovereign power: they, as did the kings of England, think that laws ought to be prepared and approved by a parliament; but they, like an English monarch[xi] of the sixteenth or seventeenth century, claim to be part of the legislature, and to reject any proposed measure, at any rate when it affects the foundations of the State. Where democracy is king the referendum is the royal veto. This is an analogy which should never be absent from the minds of Englishmen, for there is more than one circumstance which makes it difficult for them to estimate fairly the character and effects of the most noteworthy among Swiss institutions.

---

[26] Elizabeth I, the last of the Tudor monarchs, was Queen of England and Ireland from 1558 to 1603. James I was her successor, the first Stuart monarch, serving until 1625; as James VI he had been King of Scotland since 1567. William III was King of England, Scotland, and Ireland from 1689 to 1702, having been granted the Crown after his invasion from Holland in the Glorious Revolution. The last exercise of the royal veto was by William's successor, Queen Anne, in 1708.

[xi] Elizabeth in the Parliament of 1597 assented to forty-three Bills, public and private, and rejected forty-eight, that had passed both Houses (1 'Parliamentary History,' p. 905; and see Hearn, 'Government of England,' 2nd ed. p. 60). [*The Parliamentary History of England from the Earliest Period to the Year 1803*, ed. William Cobbett 36 vols. (London, 1802–20); William Edward Hearn, *The Government of England: Its Structure and Its Development*, second edition (London, 1887). Hearn was an Irish emigrant to Australia who established the University of Melbourne Law School. Originally published two decades prior, *The Government of England* was a touchstone for mid-Victorian political and constitutional debates and was lauded by Dicey.]

The referendum is discredited in English eyes by its apparent likeness to a French *plebiscite*.[27] The character of the sham appeal to a popular vote by which revolutionary and imperial tyranny has fraudulently obtained the moral consecration of the *vox populi* can even now hardly be better described than in the language of Thiers:—

> 'J'admets la différence qu'il y a entre un article de la Charte et un article de loi; mais cela ne fait pas que je croie au pouvoir constitu-ant. Le pouvoir constituant a existé, je le sais; il a existé à plusieurs époques de notre histoire; mais, permettez-moi de vous le dire, s'il était le vrai souverain il aurait joué par lui-même un triste rôle. En effet il a été, dans les assemblées primaires, à la suite des factions; sous le Consulat et sous l'Empire, il a été au service d'un grand homme; il avait alors la forme d'un sénat conservateur qui, à un signal donné par cet homme, faisait toutes les constitutions qu'on lui demandait. Sous la Restauration, il a pris une autre forme; il s'est caché sous l'article xiv de la Charte; c'était le pouvoir d'octroyer la Charte et de la modifier. ... Je ne respecte donc pas le pouvoir constituant.'[xii]

Forty-nine years have passed since these words were spoken; the experi-ence of nearly half a century has illustrated and confirmed their truth.

---

[27] To ratify important aspects of their Imperial rule, both Napoleon and his nephew Louis-Napoleon held votes under universal suffrage, which they called *plébiscites* after the Ancient Roman institution of direct legislation by the plebs.

[xii] Grégoire, 'Histoire de France,' ii. p. 298. ['I admit that there is a difference between an article of the Charter and a (regular) article of law; but it does not follow that I believe in constituent power. Constituent power has existed, I am aware; it has existed at several moments in our history. But let me tell you, if it were the true sovereign it would by itself have played a sad role. Indeed it was present in the primary assemblies at the behest of the factions; under the Consulate and the Empire it was at the service of a great man. Then it took the shape of a conservative senate which, at the signal of this great man, created all the constitutions that were asked of it. During the Restoration, it took another form; it was hidden under article 14 of the Charter; it was the power of granting and modifying the Charter. (*Thiers continued:* Take a look at the diverse roles that constituent power has played over the last fifty years. Don't say that it is the glory of our history, because the victories of Zürich, Marengo, and Austerlitz have nothing in common with these miserable constitutional comedies.) ...Thus I have no respect for constituent power.' Adolphe Thiers was a leading intellectual and political figure of the center-left across the middle two quarters of the nineteenth century. The Charter of 1814 was the written constitution of the Bourbon Restoration, which succeeded when Louis XVIII took the throne after Napoleon's fall. The Consulate (1799–1804) and the First Empire (1804–14) were periods of Napoleon's personal rule.]

If the referendum were a *plébiscite* it would merit nothing but unqualified condemnation. But the Swiss reference to the people is no *plébiscite*; it has nothing of a revolutionary character; it is as regular and normal a proceeding as the sending of a Bill from the Commons to the Lords. The people to whose judgement a reform or a law is submitted have had the fullest opportunity of following the discussions to which it has given rise. They know, or can know, all that has been urged by its advocates and by its opponents. A proposed constitutional change must have excited general attention; a special enactment provides for the bringing of every law on which a referendum may be required to the knowledge of the cantons and the communes.[xiii] The Government cannot either intimidate or corrupt the citizens; the popular vote is taken with perfect freedom. That the voters act without constraint is proved by the main charge which critics or reformers bring against the referendum, which is that the Swiss people reject improvements or innovations approved by the Federal Assembly.

To the few Englishmen, again, who have glanced at the writings of Swiss democrats the idea naturally occurs that the referendum is merely the practical outcome of most dubious political theories. Deductions supposed to be drawn from the dogma of the sovereignty of the people excite in the mind of an English thinker a prejudice against the arrangements which they are intended to recommend. Herzog or Curti may influence their Swiss disciples, but their pamphlets suggest to English critics that the referendum is defensible only by arguments which display all the unsoundness, but none of the ingenuity, of Rousseau's fallacies.

Whoever would free himself from prejudice must remember that the institution under criticism is the natural growth of Swiss constitutionalism. In the face of vigorous opposition it has, during the last fifty years, spread from canton to canton. Since 1848 it has been part of the Federal constitution, and under the revision of 1874 it has received further developement. The referendum, it should be noted, though introduced by democrats, is supported by Conservatives. It 'has struck root and expanded wherever it has been introduced, and no serious politician of any party would now think of attempting its abolition. The

---

[xiii] See B. Moses, 'Federal Government in Switzerland,' pp. 117–20. [Bernard Moses, *The Federal Government of Switzerland: An Essay on the Constitution* (Oakland, 1889). Moses was a political scientist at the University of California and a diplomat.]

Conservatives, who violently opposed its introduction, became its earnest supporters when they found that it undoubtedly acted as a drag upon hasty and radical law-making.'[xiv]

Criticism is neither censure nor apology.

> 'Steady, independent minds, when they have an object of so serious a concern to mankind as government under their contemplation, will disdain to assume the part of satirists and disclaimers. They will judge of human institutions as they do of human characters. They will sort out the good from the evil, which is mixed in mortal institutions as it is in mortal men.'[xv]

To a critic who follows these precepts of Burke's it will easily become apparent that the latest of democratic inventions is an institution marked by patent defects which are balanced, at any rate in the case of Switzerland, by equally real, though less obvious, merits.

The referendum is open to two grave objections. The first objection is that the reference of parliamentary legislation to a popular vote is, on the face of the matter, a reference from the judgement of the instructed to the opinion of the uninstructed—from knowledge to ignorance. A legislature must be worse constituted than is the Federal Assembly if it does not contain members whose education and intellectual capacity are far higher than the education and the intelligence of the ordinary elector. It is *a priori* improbable that the judgement of the Swiss people should be sounder than the judgement of the Swiss people's chosen representatives. If a popular vote be needed to correct the errors of a parliament, the natural inference is, not that the electors are specially wise, but that the parliament is specially foolish. If in Switzerland the referendum be a public benefit, this fact will suggest to most Englishmen that the Swiss Federal Assembly is badly chosen. The *a priori* conclusion that the people are not so wise as their Parliamentary representatives is, it may be suggested, confirmed by the historical experience of England. Parliament supported 'revolution principles' when a popular vote would have restored the Stuarts. The Septennial Act saved England from a reaction. The reform of the calendar, the gradual spread of religious

---

[xiv] Adams, pp. 77, 78. Something like the referendum exists in some of the States of America, and the principle on which it depends has crept into some portions of British legislation.

[xv] Reflections on the Revolution in France. [Edmund Burke, *Reflections on the Revolution in France, in Revolutionary Writings*, ed. Iain Hampsher-Monk (Cambridge, 2014), 131.]

toleration, Catholic emancipation, are events each of which marks a step in the path of progress taken by the wisdom of Parliament in opposition to the prejudices of the English people. Even to-day the referendum might in England be fatal to the maintenance of wise sanitary legislation.[28]

The point of this objection to every method of appeal from parliament to the populace cannot be got rid of. It may, however, to a certain extent be blunted by the consideration that to attack the referendum is to attack democratic government. The line of argument which tells against the referendum proves that where the people are, as a mass, far less highly educated than the class to whose leadership they in fact submit there is little wisdom in handing over sovereignty to the people. But it does not —conclusively at least—show that where a democracy exists and the representative assembly does, in truth, obey the behests of the electors, direct reference of legislative proposals to the decision of the electorate is of necessity an evil. No British Parliament could at the present day enact statutes, however wise, which ran counter to the wish of a decided majority among the British people; but Parliament may easily mistake the vociferation of a faction for the voice of the country, and hesitate at the adoption of measures which, if adopted, would command the unhesitating support of the nation.

The second objection is that the referendum undermines the influence of the legislature. The partial truth of this assertion admits of no denial. An assembly, the decisions whereof are liable to reversal, cannot possess the authority of a sovereign parliament, and debates which are indecisive lose their importance. Where, as in Switzerland, a parliamentary vote may be overriden by a popular veto, parliamentary debates cannot be carried on with the same energy or vivacity as in France or in England. It is vain to suppose that you can possess at the same time inconsistent advantages. England has at times gained much from the sovereignty of Parliament. Switzerland may derive considerable benefit from the direct participation of the Swiss people in Federal legislation. But it is impossible to combine all the advantages of parliamentary government, as it exists in England, with all the advantages of fully developed popular government as it exists in Switzerland. If the authority of Parliament

---

[28] These examples, some of which were tropes of the period, are lifted directly from Henry Maine's *Popular Government*. See his later invocations of this passage in Chapters 3, 7, and 9 of this collection.

must be maintained at the highest possible point, then Parliament must be supreme, and the decrees of Parliament must be final. If, on the other hand, it be desirable that the people should act as legislators, then the authority of Parliament, and with it the importance of parliamentary debates, must suffer diminution. This becomes clear as day if we recur to the analogy between the referendum and the veto. To revive the obsolete prerogative of the Crown would be of necessity to diminish the weight of Parliament. When Elizabeth rejected more than half the Bills which had been passed by the Houses statesmen thought more of convincing or conciliating the Queen than of securing the approval of a parliamentary majority. Discussion in the closet was more important than debate in the House of Commons. Whether the veto be pronounced by the Crown or by the people the effect must in one respect be the same. Parliamentary statesmanship is discouraged, and statesmen court, not the representative assembly, but the sovereign king or the sovereign democracy.

All this is true. Still it is, we must remember, not quite the whole truth. Just as the management of Parliament was of importance even when the veto was a reality, so in Switzerland the legislature plays a leading part, even though parliamentary authority is diminished by the existence of the referendum. Debates at Bern do more than convince the representatives of the people; they also affect the judgement of the citizens. Knowledge that a law passed by the legislature will be submitted to a popular vote may sometimes give additional reality to legislative debate. The most successful of English advocates has contrasted the reality of a counsel's address to a jury with the unreality of an orator's speeches in Parliament. He meant to persuade, and did persuade or mislead, juries; he never dreamt that his ingenuity would turn the vote of a single M.P. Hence arguments which will never affect the conduct of sworn partisans may conceivably tell on the votes of citizens not bound over to party allegiance. A sham debate before the Federal Assembly may be a real appeal to the sense of the Swiss people. Nor in England itself does parliamentary discussion possess its ancient importance. We have introduced into our constitution the spirit, though not as yet the form, of the referendum.

The celebrated Swiss institution is, however, indisputably opposed to that highest form of representative government under which the nation *bona fide* entrusts the management of affairs to the best educated and most intelligent of the citizens. Whether this form now exists, either in England or elsewhere, is open to question. But, be this as it may, the error of English criticism on the Swiss constitution lies not in an over-estimate of the faults, but in an under-estimate of the merits which, under the circumstances of Switzerland, may be justly attributed to the most original creation of the Swiss democracy.

These virtues are twofold. The referendum, in the first place, is both a democratic and a conservative institution. This constitutes its great recommendation in the eyes of thinkers who recognise the necessity of loyally accepting the principles of democracy, and, at the same time, wish to give to a democratic polity that stability which has been the special merit of the best monarchical or aristocratic polities. An appeal to the people is, on the very face of it, a democratic arrangement.

Every argument and every sentiment which tells in favour of a wide extension of the suffrage also favours the reference of fundamental changes in the constitution to a popular vote. Much may be justly urged against the moral or intellectual decisiveness of the *vox populi*; but in the field of political speculation the main thing to be considered is not so much the speculative worth, as the actual authority, of the person, or class, to whom political power is to be committed. When faith in the Divine right of kings gave to the commands of a monarch a weight not attached to a parliamentary vote, statesmen and patriots, while attempting to restrain the abuses of the prerogative, wisely acquiesced in the authority of the Crown, and strove to employ the dignity of the king for the benefit of the state. In modern Europe the voice of the people, as a matter of fact, commands reverence. Enlightened statesman-ship, therefore, consists in using this faith in the supremacy of the majority for the promotion of good government. One way in which this faith may be thus employed is to make it lend moral strength to law, and be a check upon sudden changes either of policy or of legislation. The referendum, as it exists in Switzerland, produces precisely these desired results. The fundamental laws of the land are sanctioned by popular consent; they cannot be lightly changed, yet their unchangeableness can produce no popular complaint. The charges against the referendum are, in this point of view, its best apology. The referendum, it is said, obstructs reforms. So be it. The referendum, then, must also hinder sudden innovation. The arguments, in short, no less for than against the maintenance of a strong second chamber, apply with double force as well for as against the constituting the people a sort of third chamber, and securing to the citizens that share in legislation which in England used to belong to the Crown. A popular veto possesses a strength which cannot belong to a second chamber. If the English Peers or the French Senate reject an alleged reform, the rejection itself excites anger, and becomes an argument in support of the very measure which it was meant to prevent or delay. If the French Senate oppose a scheme of revision, the scheme is extended so as to include the abolition of the Senate. If the Swiss people refuse to revise the constitution no irritation ensues, and no one dreams of arguing that the Swiss people ought to lose the popular veto.

The referendum, whenever fairly applied, has turned out a conservative force. This is in itself a gain, nor can the rejection of even salutary measures be in all cases counted an evil. The advisability, or rather the practicability, of a given line of policy depends in many, though not in all, cases on the sentiment with which it will be received by the mass of the citizens. It were possible to find Acts of Parliament which, had they been submitted to the popular vote, either would never have passed or would never have been repealed. Inconsiderate reform is the parent of disgraceful reaction. The existence of the referendum brings into view a consideration which escapes partisans. There are many matters which become party questions, but are not popular questions. A historian may doubt whether between 1850 and 1866 there existed in England any genuine demand for parliamentary reform. A direct appeal to the electors might have shown that no change was ardently desired. At the present moment both the advocates of denominational education and the advocates of secular education might discover, were it possible to ascertain the genuine feeling of Englishmen, that thousands of parents are profoundly indifferent to the controversies by which they are conventionally supposed to be warmly excited.[29] An appeal to the people may, in short, be the death blow to factitious agitation carried on in the name, but without the sanction, of the democracy.

Here we come across the second merit of the referendum. It checks the growth of the party system. The fact that the articles of the constitution cannot be changed without the assent of the Swiss people extinguishes much of the petty management, the intrigue, and the compromise which in England marks the passing of every important

---

[29] Fights over the acceptability of public funding for denominational schools were among the most bitter conflicts of the late nineteenth century, following nonconformist Liberals' discontent with the 1870 Elementary Education Act's acceptance of subsidies for Church of England schools.

Act of Parliament. Whoever studies the history either of the great Reform Act of 1832, or of the subsequent legislation by which it has been amended, will be forced to admit that some of the most vital provisions of the existing English constitution owe their introduction neither to the foresight of statesmen nor to the wishes of the people, but to the skill or the art of parliamentary leaders, whose immediate object was to secure a momentary party success. The referendum, however, does much more than diminish the importance of parliamentary adroitness. It strikes at the root of modern parliamentary government, because it makes it possible for statesmen to retain office without discredit, though unable to carry particular measures of which they advocate the adoption. The idea which pervades the system of government by Parliament as it exists in England, or in France, is that the support of a parliamentary majority is the necessary condition for the continued existence of a cabinet. Ministers who hold office when this condition is not fulfilled occupy a position absolutely unbearable to men of common self-respect. They are responsible for the government of the country, whilst compelled to obey the behests of an Opposition whose very object it is to make it impossible for the Ministry to govern the country with credit. In Switzerland, on the other hand, the theory and the practice of the constitution make the Swiss people the real sovereign. Hence the Council or Ministry may with credit serve the people, even though some of the Council's proposals are negatived by a popular veto. Thus, to recur to an example given by Sir Francis Adams, the Council in 1882 proposed what we should call an Education Act, which, though passed by the Assembly, was rejected by the people. Neither the Council nor the member primarily responsible for the proposal felt bound to resign, or suffered moral injury by retaining office. The sovereign of the country—the Swiss people—had declined to approve a proposal made by competent public servants whom the sovereign had no wish to dismiss. The Council stood towards the people in the very relation in which the servants of Queen Elizabeth stood towards the Crown. No one supposed that difference of opinion between the Queen and a Secretary of State made the Secretary's retirement either a matter of decency or a matter of duty. She might well reject his advice while wishing to retain him in her service.

That laws of primary importance are referred to the decisive arbitrament of a popular vote, enables the Swiss Council to retain office with dignity even after it has become clear that a whole line of policy advocated by the Council will not be accepted by the country. Under the parliamentary system, indeed, a time arrives when a statesman who has long struggled in favour of a particular policy must acknowledge that his views have been decisively rejected by the nation, and that he ought not any longer to sacrifice all chance of serving his country for the sake of a policy which the country has refused to adopt. No sane critic blames Sir Robert Peel for having after 1832 acquiesced in the Reform Act, and there are few critics who would now censure Lord Derby for having after 1852 accepted Free Trade.[30] But the acquiescence of a parliamentary statesman in a policy he has opposed generally lays him open to some charge of inconsistency, and he himself, no less than others, may reasonably hesitate to decide what is the moment at which the time has arrived for honourable acquiescence in defeat without disgraceful surrender of principle. The referendum, or even the possibility of the referendum, greatly clears the path of men anxious to serve the country, and anxious also not to compromise their principles; for the appeal to the people enables statesmen honestly to assert that certain questions are for the time removed out of the field of practical politics. A proposition, for example, is made to increase the power of the Federal Government. The proposal on reference to the popular vote is decisively rejected. There is nothing either immoral or undignified in the position of a minister who acquiesces in the people's decision. He does not retain office by pretending to think the people right; he maintains that the people's decision is a mistake, but he retains office because the sovereign wishes him to retain it, because he can faithfully discharge his duties, and because the question of increasing the Federal power has received its decision.

This at any rate is the view of their duties taken by Swiss Ministers. Hence, as already intimated, the admirable stability of the Federal Executive is more or less directly due to the existence of the referendum. This stability is no doubt gained at a considerable cost, for it involves some diminution in the authority of the Federal Assembly. What to the Swiss people be the balance of loss and gain is a question deserving the attentive consideration of thinkers occupied in the study of modern

---

[30] Robert Peel was a leading Tory statesman who, after having opposed the Reform Act, urged his party to make peace with its passage. After the repeal of the Corn Laws in 1846 (the triumph of free trade to which Dicey is referring) the bulk of the Conservative party supported reinstitution of agricultural protections, although the Conservative premier Edward Smith-Stanley, 14th Earl of Derby, accepted repeal.

democracy. Whatever be on this matter the ultimate verdict of impartial criticism, one thing is clear. The Swiss Confederation presents a peculiar type of democratic government, as different from the parliamentary democracy of France and of England as from the presidential democracy of the United States. In Switzerland, as in every country where popular government exists, a representative legislature, or parliament, forms a most important part of the constitution. But this parliament is not, like the parliament of England or of France, the master of the executive. It is not, like the Congress of the United States, an authority so unconnected with the administration as to be quite as often the rival or opponent as the ally or supporter of the President. At a time when the novel term 'parliamentarism' is coming into vogue, thinkers, who are well aware that Swiss federalism can, from the nature of things, never present a model for the reform of English institutions, may yet study with interest and instruction the constitution of the Swiss democracy.[31] For in Switzerland, and in Switzerland alone, representative government has hitherto escaped both from the evils of the party mechanism which corrupts the politics of the American Republic, and from the equal evils of that transformation of parliamentary government into government by Parliament which threatens, in England no less than in France, to undermine the stability and destroy the authority of the National Executive.

---

[31] For the historian of concepts, who usually now uses *parliamentary government* and *parliamentarianism/parliamentarism* interchangeably, it is worth noting that Dicey did not treat the two as equivalent. He consistently (see also Chapter 6) viewed the latter as a recent coinage indicative of growing disaffection with the pathologies exhibited by legislative assemblies. As he had written a couple of years prior to this: "In every country there are thinkers and politicians to whom Parliamentarianism means the rule of an Assembly torn by factions, whose strife is fatal to the existence of good administration, and sacrifices (as is alleged) to the interest of party the welfare, it may be the existence, of the country."

3

Ought the Referendum to Be Introduced into England? (1890)

"It is a question for us Englishmen to consider whether it would be possible and advantageous to introduce the Referendum at home. For instance, it might well be that such a vexatious question as Home Rule for Ireland could once for all be settled one way or the other, by a vote of the whole electoral body in the United Kingdom. We merely throw this out as a suggestion, but of course the conditions of Great Britain are very different from those of Switzerland, where the nation is so eminently democratic, and where the Referendum has been habitually employed for a variety of local matters."[i]

These are the words of the only Englishman who has treated of modern Swiss politics both with adequate knowledge and with perfect impartiality. They will not in the long run fall unheeded on the public ear. The British Constitution, while preserving its monarchical form, has for all intents and purposes become a Parliamentary democracy. When this fact with all its bearings is once clearly perceived by Englishmen, theorists and politicians will assuredly ask themselves what may be the effect, for good or bad, of transplanting to England the newest and the most popular among the institutions of the single European State where the experiment of democratic government has, though tested by every possible difficulty, turned out a striking, and, to all appearance, a permanent, success.

My aim in this article is (following out the line of thought suggested by Sir Francis Adams), to examine three questions: first, what is the

---

[i] Adams, "Swiss Confederation," p. 87.

nature of the Swiss Referendum? secondly, whether it be possible to introduce the principle of the Referendum into the world of English politics; and, thirdly, whether such introduction would be beneficial to the nation?[ii]

I.

The Referendum may be roughly defined as the reference to all vote-possessing citizens of the Confederation for their acceptance or rejection, of laws passed by their representatives in the Federal Assembly.[iii]

Under the Swiss Constitution as amended or re-enacted in 1874, all legislation of the Federal Parliament is or may be subject to the Referendum,[iv] but an important distinction is drawn between laws which do, and laws which do not, effect changes in the Constitution.

In Switzerland, as in England, the Constitution can always be revised or altered by the National Parliament. But in Switzerland no law which revises the Constitution, either wholly or in part, can come into force until it has been regularly submitted by means of the Referendum to the vote of the people, and has been approved both by a majority of the citizens who on the particular occasion give their votes, and also by a majority of the Cantons. With the elaborate provisions which secure that under certain circumstances a vote of the people shall be taken, not only on the question whether a particular amendment or revision of the Constitution approved by the Federal Assembly shall or shall not come

---

[ii] The Referendum is throughout this article described only in its broadest outline, for Englishmen are much more concerned with the principle of the Swiss institution than with the particular constitutional mechanism by which effect is given to the principle in Switzerland. Whoever desires further information should consult, among other authorities, Adams' "Swiss Confederation," cap. vi.; Orelli's "Das Staaterecht der Schweizerischen Eidgenossenschaft," pp. 79, 80, 83–88; Constitution Fédérale, arts. 89, 90, and 121; and also a notice of Adams' work in the *Edinburgh Review* for January 1890. [The *Edinburgh Review* article is Chapter 1 of this collection; the other works listed are examined there.] The Referendum, it should also be noted, is in this article treated all but exclusively as a part of the Swiss Federal or National Constitution. It exists, however, and flourishes as a local institution in all but one or two Cantons. A competent English observer who should report minutely upon the working of the Referendum as a cantonal institution, and especially at Zurich, would render a service of inestimable value to all students of political science.

[iii] See Adams, p. 76.

[iv] See Constitution Fédérale, arts. 89, 118–121. Swiss authorities do not apparently apply the term "Referendum" to the popular sanction required for the validity of any revision of the Constitution under Const. Fed., art. 121. It is, however, clear that the popular assent which is required for all constitutional amendments partakes of the nature of a Referendum.

into force, but also on the preliminary question whether any revision or reform of the Constitution shall take place at all, we need for our present purpose hardly trouble ourselves. What Englishmen should note is that when any law, or as we should say Bill, amending the Constitution has passed the two Houses of the Federal Assembly, it cannot take effect until it has been made the subject of a Referendum and has received the assent of a majority both of the voters and of the Cantons. For the validity, in short, of a constitutional change a reference to the people is an absolute necessity. The Referendum is here, in the language of Swiss constitutionalists, an "obligatory" or "necessary" Referendum.

Critics ought further to note that the necessity for the Referendum extends to many laws which under our English system would not be called Reform Bills, or be considered to effect any amendment of the Constitution. The reason of this is that the Swiss Constitution contains a large number of articles which have no reference to the distribution or exercise of Sovereign power, but which embody general maxims of policy, or (it may be) special provisions as to matters of detail, to which the Swiss attach great importance, and which therefore they do not wish to be easily alterable. All the enactments, however, contained in the Constitution, form, whatever be their essential character, part thereof. No one of them can therefore be legally abolished or modified without the employment of the Referendum. Thus a law which limited the liberty of conscience secured by Article 49 of the Federal Constitution, or which interfered with the liberty of the press guaranteed by Article 55, or which in contravention of Article 55 enacted that treason or any political offence should be punished by death, would not, according to English ways of thinking, bring about a constitutional change; but it would undoubtedly modify a part of the Federal Constitution, and could not therefore be enacted without the use of the Referendum.

Laws which do not affect the articles of the Constitution come (or may come) into force on being passed by the Federal Parliament without the necessity for being submitted to a popular vote.

But in the case even of ordinary legislation 30,000 voters, or eight Cantons, may, within a definite period, fixed by statute, after the passing of any law, demand that it shall be submitted to the Swiss people for approval or rejection. When once this demand has been duly made the particular law, say an Education Act, to which it applies, must of necessity be made the subject of a Referendum. Whether it comes into force or not depends on the result of the popular vote. There is, be it observed, no need in this instance for obtaining the assent of the majority of the Cantons. This Referendum, which may or may not be required according as it is or is not demanded, is called, in the language of Swiss jurists, a "facultative" or "optional" Referendum.[v]

The matter then stands shortly thus: No change can be introduced into the Constitution which is not sanctioned by the vote of the Swiss people. The Federal Assembly, indeed, may of its own authority pass laws which take effect without any popular vote, provided these laws do not affect the Constitution; but it is practically certain that no enactment important enough to excite effective opposition can ever become law until it has received the deliberately expressed sanction of the Swiss people.

Foreigners often miss the true characteristics of the Referendum in Switzerland, because they confuse it with essentially different forms of appeal to the people which are known to other countries.

The Referendum looks at first sight like a French *plébiscite*,[vi] but no two institutions can be marked by more essential differences.

A *plébiscite* is a mass vote of the French people by which a Revolutionary or Imperial Executive obtains for its policy, or its crimes, the apparent sanction or condonation of France. Frenchmen are asked at the moment, and in the form most convenient to the statesmen or conspirators who rule in Paris, to say "Aye" or "No" whether they will, or will not, accept a given Constitution or a given policy. The crowd of voters are expected to reply in accordance with the wishes or the orders of the Executive, and the expectation always has met, and an observer may confidently predict always will meet, with fulfilment. The *plébiscite* is a revolutionary, or at least abnormal, proceeding. It is not preceded by debate. The form and nature of the question to be submitted to the nation is chosen and settled by the men in power. Rarely indeed, when a *plébiscite* has been taken, has the voting itself been either free or fair. Taine has a strange tale to tell of the methods by which a Terrorist faction, when all but crushed by general odium, extorted from the country by means of the *plébiscite* a sham assent to the prolongation of

---

[v] It would appear further that, as a matter of practice even where no demand is made for an appeal to the people, the Federal Council or Ministry may, if it thinks fit, make any ordinary law the subject of a Referendum.

[vi] See Maine, "Popular Government," pp. 38–41.

revolutionary despotism.[vii] The credulity of partisanship can nowadays hardly induce even Imperialists to imagine that the *plébiscites* which sanctioned the establishment of the Empire, which declared Louis Napoleon President for life, which first re-established Imperialism, and then approved more or less Liberal reforms, fatal at bottom to the Imperial system, were the free, deliberate, carefully considered votes of the French nation given after the people had heard all that could be said for and against the proposed innovation. Grant that in more than one of these cases the verdict of the *plébiscite* corresponded with the wish of the nation. *The plébiscite* itself still remains without value, for, at the moment when the nation was asked to express the national will, France was placed in such a position that it would have been scarcely possible for any sane man to form any other wish than that assent to the Government's proposals might remove all excuse for prolonging a period of lawlessness or despotism. It is reasonable enough to believe that France desired the rule of the First Napoleon. But this belief depends on the result not of Napoleonic *plébiscites*, but of a fair estimate of the condition of affairs and of the state of public opinion. We may believe, in short, that the *plébiscite* which sanctioned the foundation of the Empire expressed the will of the nation, because there are rational grounds for believing that France might desire Imperial government. But no one bases his belief in the desire for the Empire on the result of the *plébiscite* which nominally sanctioned its establishment. Deliberation and discussion are the requisite conditions for rational decision. Where effective opposition is an impossibility, nominal assent is an unmeaning compliment.

The essential characteristics, however, the lack of which deprives a French *plébiscite* of all moral significance, are the undoubted properties of the Swiss Referendum. When a law revising the Constitution is placed before the people of Switzerland, every citizen throughout the land has enjoyed the opportunity of learning the merits and the demerits of the proposed alteration. The subject has been "threshed out," as the expression goes, in Parliament; the scheme, whatever its worth, has received

---

[vii] See Taine, "La Révolution," tome iii.; "Le Gouvernement Révolutionnaire," pp. 551 and following. [Hippolyte Taine was one of the most influential historians and critics of nineteenth-century France. His study of the Revolution, which was relentlessly critical of the Jacobins and deeply influential for Third-Republican liberalism, consisted of volumes 3–8 of his eventual eleven-volume series, *Les Origines de la France contemporaine* (Paris, 1875–93).]

the deliberately given approval of the elected Legislature; it comes before the people with as much authority in its favour as a Bill which in England has passed through both Houses. The voters have been given the opportunity before pronouncing their decision of learning all that can be said for, and (what is still more important) all that can be said against, a definite measure, by every man who, either from a public platform, or in the columns of the press, or in private conversation, advocates or deprecates its adoption. The position of the Swiss people when summoned to vote upon a constitutional amendment is pretty much what would have been the position of the British electorate if, in 1886, the Home Rule Bill had, after ample discussion and amendment, passed through both Houses of Parliament, and thereupon the Queen, feeling the extreme importance of the occasion, had called upon the voters of the United Kingdom to give an answer by a mass vote "Aye" or "No" to the question whether she should or should not give her assent to the Government of Ireland Bill, 1886. Swiss citizens, be it added, vote on the occasion of a Referendum at least as freely as do English electors at a general election. Neither the Council nor the Federal Assembly can constrain or influence their votes; as a matter of fact, the voters constantly reject measures referred to them for approval. The gravest charge brought against the Referendum by its critics, and brought with much show of reason, is that it obstructs improvement. Whatever be the force of this criticism, the mere fact that it can be made with plausibility affords conclusive proof that the Referendum is a real appeal to the true judgment of the nation, and that the appeal is free from the coercion, the unreality, and the fraud which taint or vitiate a *plébiscite*. The Referendum, in short, is a regular, normal, peaceful proceeding, as unconnected with revolutionary violence or despotic coercion, and as easily carried out, as the sending up of a Bill from the House of Commons to the House of Lords. It causes less disturbance, and probably less excitement, throughout the country than is occasioned in the United Kingdom by a general election.

To an Englishman the idea naturally occurs that a general election is in its nature, though not in its form, a Referendum.

The idea is plausible, and falls in with our ordinary way of speaking. We are accustomed to say that the passing of an important Bill is finally determined by an appeal to the electors; that, for example, the great Reform Bill was carried by the general election of 1831; that the Irish Church was disestablished by the verdict of the electors in 1868; or that in 1886 the Home Rule Bill was rejected by the British people.[1] This mode of speaking contains in itself an element of truth. A general election is an appeal to the people, and may under peculiar circumstances be made to serve, though in an awkward and imperfect manner, the purpose of a Referendum. But we must not be deceived by words. A general election is an appeal to the people; so also is the exercise of the Referendum; but the two appeals differ fundamentally from each other, and their points of difference are for our present purpose of vital consequence.

An election, after all, has for its primary and immediate object the appointment of representatives. It is a choice of persons or of parties: it is not a judgment on the merits or the demerits of a proposed law. No doubt the choice of members approaches every day more and more nearly to a decision on matters of policy, and at times an election really sanctions or vetoes proposed legislation. The personal element, however, is at every election a matter of moment; a strong candidate may carry a seat by his own individual strength. The main and avowed object, moreover, of electors in voting for *A* rather than *B*, is not to determine whether a particular Bill shall, or shall not, be passed, but whether the members of a particular party shall, or shall not, keep, or acquire, office. Thus, to take an example from the current events of the day, we all know that at the next general election, whenever it occurs, the question submitted to the electors will not be the advisability or impolicy of enacting a known scheme for the establishment of Home Rule in Ireland, but the expediency of keeping the Unionists, or of placing the Gladstonians, in office.[2] The electors will certainly not have before them a definite drafted bill, which they are finally called upon to disallow or approve. Never did an election approach more nearly to a Referendum than that which followed the dissolution of 1831. The country pronounced by a crushing majority in favour of the Bill, the whole Bill, and nothing but the Bill. Yet the Bill which ultimately became law

---

[1] The First Reform Act was passed in 1832 after the Whigs' general election victory, the Irish Church Act 1869 was passed after the Liberals' general election victory, and the Liberals lost their majority in the 1886 general election after the First Home Rule Bill failed.

[2] By Gladstonians Dicey means those Liberals who remained in the Liberal party and stayed faithful to Gladstone after his announcement of Home Rule. The Unionists embraced the alliance to oppose Home Rule formed between Conservatives and former Liberals who now fashioned themselves the Liberal Unionists.

differed in important particulars from the first and second Reform Bills. The crises, moreover, when as in 1831 the vote of the electors is determined almost wholly by their desire for a particular measure, or their aversion to it, are of rare occurrence.[3] An election must be a decision on general policy. It is usually in England an answer to the question, not whether a particular Bill shall become law, but whether a given set of men shall govern the country. It were difficult in any case to keep clear from each other questions of persons, of policy, and of legislation. But our English system of government makes it a certainty that statesmen of all parties will do their best to confuse the issues which at an election are nominally submitted to the verdict of the nation. A Ministry will always, if possible, dissolve at the moment when any adventitious circumstance enhances the popularity of the Cabinet. A success abroad, any circumstance which for the moment discredits a leading opponent, any sudden event which may have raised the reputation of the Government or brought odium upon the Opposition, will be used as a means for inducing the electors to favour the Ministerial policy, and to return representatives who may support the legislation recommended by the Ministry. The Opposition of the day will follow suit. Every accident which tells against the party in office, every error or alleged error of judgment, whether important or trifling, which affects the momentary popularity of the Cabinet—the inconsiderate utterances of a Premier, the inopportune severity, or the undue leniency, of a Home Secretary in the execution of the law, the badness of the seasons, and the depression of trade—are each and all of them matters which respectable politicians turn to account in the effort to deprive the Government of the day of public goodwill, and to divert the attention of the electors from the serious and substantial issue whether the kind of legislation which is opposed by the one, and supported by the other, of the great parties in the State, be or be not likely to benefit the country. It were useless and pedantic to blame or deplore conduct which, however disastrous to the country, results naturally from the faults of human nature when these vices are fostered by a scheme of public life, which links indissolubly together the personal success and influence of politicians with the triumph of particular schemes of legislation. Nor is partisanship always to blame for the confusion of issues which the public

---

[3] The 1831 general election, which returned a huge majority for the Whigs, was fought amidst enormous upheaval over parliamentary reform.

interest imperatively requires to be kept clear of each other. An election determines which of two parties shall enjoy the advantages, and incur the responsibilities, of government. Now it may well happen that men of sense and patriotism wish, on the whole, to keep a particular body of statesmen in power, whilst severely condemning some legislative proposal which these statesmen advocate. These well-meaning citizens are at a general election placed upon the horns of a dilemma from which there is no practical escape. They must either banish from office men whose policy they in many respects approve, or else sanction the passing of a law which they believe to be impolitic. Contrast this state of things with the position of the Swiss people when appealed to by means of the Referendum. The appeal is exactly what it purports to be, a reference to the people's judgment of a distinct, definite, clearly stated law. Every "Bill" laid before the Swiss for their acceptance has, be it again noted—for this is a fact which can hardly be too strongly insisted upon—passed through both Houses of the Federal Parliament. It has been drafted by the Federal Ministry or Council; it has been the object of ample discussion; its fair consideration has been, or certainly may be, secured by all the safeguards known to the Parliamentary system. The Referendum does not hurry on a single law, nor facilitate any legislation which Parliamentary wisdom or caution disapproves. It merely adds an additional safeguard against the hastiness or violence of party. It is not a spur to democratic innovation; it is a check placed on popular impatience.[vii]

It may be worth adding that the most trustworthy Swiss authorities consider an "obligatory" far preferable to an "optional" Referendum; the latter is the result of an agitation which gives a character of partisanship to the resulting Referendum.

The law to be accepted or rejected is laid before the citizens of Switzerland in its precise terms; they are concerned solely with its merits or demerits, their thoughts are not distracted by the necessity for considering any other topic. No one's seat either at the Council board or in the Assembly depends upon the law's passing. The Councillors will

---

[viii] Of course in making this statement, I do not refer to the right given under Constitutional Fédérale, art. 120, to 50,000 Swiss citizens of demanding the preparation of a scheme for revising the Constitution. This right is what Swiss authors call the Initiative, and is certainly not an essential part of the Referendum.

A law which has passed the Houses is sometimes submitted to the people in such a form that the voters may accept it either wholly or in part, but in general I believe laws for the amendment of the Constitution are voted upon as a whole.

continue to discharge their administrative duties whether the measures submitted to the Swiss people are or are not sanctioned by the citizens. The rejection of measures approved by the Federal Parliament does not, it would appear, injure the position of the majority by whom the rejected schemes have been proposed or supported. The Swiss distinguish between men and measures; they send to Parliament the members, say the Radicals, with whose policy they on the whole agree, even though these representatives have carried through Parliament Bills to which the Swiss voters refuse their assent. This fact is well established; it is quite of a piece with the absolutely indisputable fact that the members of the Swiss Council, or Ministry, though they require triennial re-election by the Federal Assembly, hold office by what is practically a permanent tenure. All this appears odd enough to Englishmen. To a stranger from China or Persia, such as philosophers of the eighteenth century introduced into their essays as the observer, critic, or satirist of European customs, the habits of English public life may appear more opposed to the dictates of right reason than the practice of the Swiss democracy. However this may be, the people of Switzerland have recognized to the full their own sovereignty, and act in the main on the principles which guided an English monarch during the ages when, though Parliament was the acknowledged and sovereign Legislature of the land, the king was the most influential member of the sovereign power. A Tudor monarch retained valued servants in his employment, even though he rejected their advice. He acknowledged the legislative authority of Parliament, but he maintained his claim to be part of the Legislature and refused assent to Bills which, though passed by the Houses, seemed to him impolitic. The Swiss people in like manner, being the true Sovereign of Switzerland, retain, in the service of the State, Ministers whose measures the voters nevertheless often refuse to sanction. The Swiss democracy values the legislative ability of the Federal Parliament, but, like an English king of the sixteenth century, constantly withholds assent from Bills passed by the two Houses. The Referendum is a revival of the miscalled "veto," but is a veto lodged in the hands, not of a sovereign monarch, but of a sovereign people. Such a veto produces the same effects, whatever be the power by which it is exercised. It secures the Constitution against any change which the Sovereign does not deliberately approve; it tends to produce permanence in the tenure of office; it undermines the strength of that elaborate party system which in England lies at the basis not of Parliamentary government, but of government by Parliament.

II.

No vital change in either the law or the customs of the Constitution would be so easy of introduction into England as the establishment in principle of the Referendum, or of a popular veto on any amendment or alteration in the Constitution; such, for example, as the disestablishment of the Church, or a considerable diminution in the numbers of the House of Commons.

The methods by which this popular veto might be established are various and of different merit.

First. The House of Lords might adopt a new policy with regard to all Bills which, in the judgment of the Peers, modified the Constitution. They might announce their resolution, on the one hand, to reject every Bill, from whatever party it might proceed, which contained constitutional amendments, until the Bill, after having passed the House of Commons, had been in effect submitted to the electors at a general election, and had received their sanction by the return of a decisive majority in its favour; and, on the other hand, when once such a majority had been obtained, to pass as a matter of constitutional duty any Bill which, being again approved by the House of Commons, substantially corresponded with the measure the Peers had before rejected, with a view to ensuring its submission to the judgment of the nation.

Such a policy, if carried out with vigour and impartiality, would constitute the House of Lords the guardian of the Constitution. It would involve a great nominal sacrifice of authority, but the real loss would be little or nothing, for the Peers would exchange an unrestricted veto, which they cannot exercise, for a suspensive veto which would be real, because its exercise would be supported by popular approval.

This is the easiest mode of establishing the Referendum. It is, however, the least satisfactory. The Act finally passed after a general election, would not be the Bill on which the nation had pronounced a verdict. What is of far more importance, a general election is, for reasons already stated, but an indifferent imitation of a true Referendum.

Secondly. Either House of Parliament might petition the Crown not to assent to the passing of a particular Bill, say for the disestablishment of the Church, or for granting the Parliamentary suffrage to women, unless and until a vote of the electors throughout the United Kingdom had been taken, and the majority of the electorate had voted in favour of the Crown giving its assent.

The Queen might further conceivably *motu proprio*—*i.e.*, in truth, on the advice of the Cabinet for the time being—announce that her Majesty would give or refuse her assent to a given Bill which had passed the two Houses, according to the results of the votes given on the matter by the electors of the United Kingdom.

This use of the royal prerogative has been suggested by Mr. Frank Hill, in a recent number of the *Contemporary*.[4] It would, of course, be new and anomalous; it would therefore be called "unconstitutional" by every man who feared the result of an appeal to the people. But this employment of the veto would be in strict conformity with the principles which have governed the growth of the Constitution. English history, from a constitutional point of view, is little else than a record of the transactions by which the prerogatives of the Crown have been transformed into the privileges of the people. The exercise of the prerogative has no doubt hitherto been in effect transferred from the Crown to the House of Commons. But now that the true political Sovereign of the State is the electorate, the Crown may rightly exercise the royal veto, so as to ensure that changes in the Constitution shall not be in reality opposed to the will of the electors. It were impossible for the Queen to make a more legitimate exertion of her prerogative than to use it as the means for checking the arrogance of party by ensuring the supremacy of the nation.

Thirdly. Parliament might insert in any important Act (such, for example, as any statute for the repeal or modification of the Act of

---

[4] Hill was a journalist who, like Dicey, broke with the Liberal party over Home Rule. In the article in question Hill had written as follows: "Why may not the country at large have the opportunity of imposing its veto upon a measure which represents not its own convictions, but the successful electioneering tactics of busy and unscrupulous organizations, and the cowardice and want of principle of political candidates and leaders? Supposing an Anti-Vaccination Bill or an Eight Hours Bill to become law in the circumstances which have been supposed – and it could scarcely become so in any other – why should not an appeal be made, on the principle of the Swiss *Referendum*, to the general sense of the country? The Sovereign of the country, standing aloof from political parties, would naturally be the person in whom, when there was reason to suppose that the voice of the nation had been falsified in the Parliamentary representation, this right of appealing to the nation at large would be vested. Instead of the merely formal assent, '*La Reine le veut*,' or the obsolete form of veto, '*La Reine s'avisera*,' we should have at the initiative of the Crown the decision, '*Le peuple le veut*,' or '*Le peuple s'avisera*'"; F. Hill, "The Future of the English Monarchy," *Contemporary Review* 57 (1890): 187–205.

Union with Ireland⁵) the provision that the Act should not come into force unless and until, within six months of its passing, a vote of the electors throughout the United Kingdom had been taken, and a majority of the voters had voted in favour of the Act.

Fourthly. A general Act might be passed containing two main provisions: first, that the Act itself should not come into force until sanctioned by such a vote of the electors of the United Kingdom as already mentioned; and secondly, that no future enactment affecting certain subjects—*e.g.*, the position of the Crown, the constitution of either House of Parliament, or any part of either of the Acts of Union—should come into force, or have any effect, until sanctioned by such vote as aforesaid of the electors of the United Kingdom.

It is not my object to draft even in outline an enactment for the introduction of an appeal to the electors with reference to legislation of grave importance. Any Act establishing a Referendum would necessarily lay down the conditions on which the vote of the electors should be taken and the mode of taking it. Such a statute might, it is clear, make the validity of the law which was to be submitted to popular approval depend either upon its obtaining in its favour the vote of the majority of the electorate, or upon its obtaining, as in Switzerland, the approval of the majority of the electors who actually vote. With these and other details no man of sense will at present trouble his mind; what needs to be insisted upon is that, either by the use of the prerogative, or by direct Parliamentary enactment, the Referendum may easily be introduced among the political institutions of the United Kingdom; it may be introduced either in a general form, or experimentally in regard to a particular enactment. There is no lack of mechanism for achieving this object; the resources of the Constitution are infinite.

Some theorist will object that any Act introducing the Referendum will have little validity, since Parliament might by a subsequent, statute undo its own handiwork. This objection, whatever be its speculative

---

⁵ The "Act for the Union of Great Britain and Ireland" was passed in 1800 and came into effect on New Year's Day, 1801. Among other notable features of the Act which set the tone for politics in the nineteenth century were the uniting of the Church of England and Ireland (a union that was only dissolved in 1869 in the aforementioned Irish Church Act 1869) and the provisions for Ireland's parliamentary representation. However, in a move that would cause considerable damage to Anglo-Irish relations, King George III prevented the Act from including permission for Catholics to serve as MPs; Catholics remained forbidden to sit in Parliament, among other restrictions, until the Catholic Emancipation of 1829.

force, is in the particular case of no practical moment. Any careful student of the Swiss Constitution will perceive that the Federal Assembly might, under the articles of the Constitution itself, occasionally dispense with or override the Referendum.[ix] This possibility of rapid legislation may conceivably be of great advantage at a crisis, which places the existence of the nation in peril. But in Switzerland the rights of the people are never in fact overridden. As it is in Switzerland, so would it be in England. Let a popular veto be established, and the popular veto will command respect.

A critic may again suggest that the introduction of the Referendum is practically impossible, because the change it involves is opposed at once to the interests and to the instincts of members of Parliament. That the House of Commons would cordially dislike an innovation which tends to diminish the importance of the House admits not of dispute. In this one instance, however, the feeling of members of Parliament is of small importance; the authority of the House depends on the support of the electors. An appeal to the electorate, by whatever party and by whatever means it is introduced, will never offend the electors. The rejection of a Bill by the Lords excites indignation because it may be represented as a defiance offered by the aristocracy to the will of the people. But were the Crown, or the Lords, to prevent a Bill coming immediately into force solely for the sake of submitting it to the people for popular approval or rejection, a course of proceeding which would elicit Parliamentary rhetoric and reprobation, could provoke no popular censure. The nation would condone or applaud a direct appeal to the nation's own sovereignty.

The possibility of introducing the principle of the Referendum into English legislation admits not of doubt. The far more important question is whether a change of immense moment, which is certainly feasible, is also expedient.

III.

Would the introduction of the Referendum into England be of benefit to the nation?

This is an inquiry which no competent student of comparative politics will answer offhand, or with dogmatic assurance.

[ix] Constitution Fédérale, art. 89.

The assumption were rash that even in Switzerland, where the recognition of the popular veto on legislation is firmly established, the Referendum is entirely successful, and does not produce evils which must be carefully weighed against its alleged beneficial results; and though Conservative Swiss opinion now, on the whole, favours an institution originally invented and introduced by Radicals, there is no doubt that the Referendum is, in the opinion of fair-minded and competent judges among the Swiss, open to criticism and to censure.

It were, again, the rashest of assumptions that arrangements which work well in Switzerland are certain to produce good effects in England. The Swiss Republic is no ideal commonwealth. And the experience of more than a century makes it impossible for honest thinkers to fancy that in the world, either of fact or of imagination, they can discover some perfect constitution which may serve as a model for the correction of the vices to be found in existing polities. No man endowed with a tithe of Montesquieu's learning and sagacity could at the present day treat the institutions of any country after the manner in which the Constitution of England was treated by the author of the "Esprit des Lois."[6] It were invidious to dwell on the shortcomings of that immortal work, for modern critics are far more likely to neglect the vital truths contained, and to a certain extent concealed, under the dogmas of the French jurist than to exaggerate the importance of teaching expressed in formulas which have ceased to be the commonplaces of the day. Yet the mistakes of Montesquieu contain a lasting warning. He studied English institutions with infinite care, yet in some points he profoundly misunderstood the Constitution which was the object of his intellectual adoration and his misunderstandings, just because [of] their ingenuity[,] have misled generation after generation.[7] The errors of Montesquieu are not more instructive than the mistakes made by the greatest among his disciples. The more minutely the details of the French Revolution are studied the stronger becomes the conviction of capable judges that the

[6] Charles de Secondat, Baron de Montesquieu, *The Spirit of the Laws*, ed. Anne M. Cohler, Basia Carolyn Miller, and Harold Samuel Stone (Cambridge, 1989). The principal discussion of the English constitution comes in II.6. Dicey certainly would not have been alone in criticizing Montesquieu's analysis as antiquated after the more clear-sighted examination of Walter Bagehot's *English Constitution* (1867). But the charge here that Montesquieu presented the English system as an ideal for all societies whatever their histories and circumstances is inapt.

[7] I have had to make slight amendments to this sentence for the sake of sense.

genius of Burke was, even when swayed by passion, endowed with something of prophetic insight into the nature and the perils of the most astounding movement or catastrophe which, since the days of the Reformation, has convulsed Europe. But every increase in historical knowledge, just as it enhances our veneration for Burke's insight into the follies and the vices of the Revolution, also increases our sense of the gravity of those misconceptions as to French history and character which, for the purposes of practical guidance, made his prophetic power all but useless.

We have all now learnt that *cælum non animum mutant*,[8] if true of individuals, is profoundly untrue of institutions. English constitutional-ism has been transplanted from its native soil to every civilized land, but in no single instance has the exported plant reproduced the characteris-tics of the original stock. Even if the condition of Switzerland strikingly resembled the state of England, the Referendum might probably change its character and working when transplanted from the Alpine Republic to the insular monarchy. But the two countries differ as widely from each other as can any two lands, each of which is the home of rational freedom. Switzerland is the smallest of independent States; her popula-tion is less than that of London; federalism and localism of an extreme type are as natural to the Swiss as they are foreign to the inhabitants of the United Kingdom. Fortune has not given to us, and no human art can create in any part of the United Kingdom, the cantons and the com-munes which are the backbone of the Swiss political organization. In Switzerland, again, popular education has reached a level as high as perhaps is attainable in any modern European country; the Swiss are, in more points than one, the Scotch of continental Europe.[9] The system of party, moreover, which flourishes with exuberant, or ominous, vigour in all countries inhabited by the English people, is, it would seem, but incompletely developed in the Swiss Republic. This is a point on which a foreigner must speak with the greatest caution. Swiss institutions, there is reason to believe, check the growth of the party system; but the imperfect development, not indeed of party feeling but of party

---

[8] *Cælum non animum mutant qui trans mare currunt* (those who cross the sea change the sky but not their souls) is a Latin proverb from the poet Horace.

[9] The English were latecomers in the provision of education, whereas Scotland had provided widespread elementary education since the mid-seventeenth century.

organization, may well facilitate the working of Swiss institutions. Any thinker who gives fair weight to these obvious reflections will conclude that the success of the Referendum in Switzerland falls far short of proof that a similar institution would work beneficially in England. Swiss experience is evidence that the popular veto may, under certain circumstances, produce good effects. This it does prove; but it proves nothing more. Any one who wishes to weigh the expediency of introducing such a veto into the institutions of England under forms and limitations suitable to the genius of the country, will give less importance to the specific experience of Switzerland than to the general arguments which, as things now stand in the United Kingdom, are producible against and in favour of direct intervention by the electors in acts of legislation. He will also find it convenient to consider the operation of the Referendum in England, not as a check on legislation generally, but as a veto solely on changes in the Constitution, or, at any rate, on laws affecting the fundamental institutions of the State, such as the poor-law.[10]

Two obvious objections lie against the introduction of the Referendum into England.

The Referendum diminishes the importance of Parliamentary debate, and thereby detracts from the influence of Parliament.

That this must be so admits of no denial; a veto, whether it be exercised by a king or by an electorate, lessens the power of the Legislature whereof the Bills are liable to be vetoed. When Elizabeth refused her assent to half the Bills of a session, the two Houses possessed nothing like the legislative authority which they exercise under Queen Victoria, who, during her reign of more than fifty years, has never refused assent to a Bill passed by Lords and Commons. If ever the electors obtain authority to reject Bills passed by the Houses, the Houses will lose their legislative supremacy.

---

[10] The Poor Law Amendment, colloquially known as the New Poor Law, replaced the system of poor relief that had been in place since the Elizabethan era. It was seen as a hallmark achievement of philosophic radicalism and political economy. Its key premise was that the Old Poor Law, which had required individual parishes to maintain the poor, disabled, and unemployed, had been overly expensive and counterproductive, and that therefore the conditions for receiving relief had to be made "less eligible." Consequently it introduced, among other provisions: a requirement of labor in workhouses for able-bodied men to receive support; a reduction in relief for single mothers; separation of married couples and segregation of sexes in the workhouses; and the erection of a national Poor Law Commission to coordinate and inspect the local boards administering the program.

Debates which are indecisive can never possess the full importance, or interest, attached to discussions which result in final decisions.

Though the truth of the allegation that the Referendum would diminish the authority of the Legislature is undeniable, its practical importance may well be exaggerated; under any system similar to that which exists in Switzerland, no law could be passed without the full assent of Parliament. The Referendum, as already pointed out, does not enable the electors to pass laws at their own will. It is a mere veto on such legislation as does not approve itself to the electorate. Debates in Parliament would in any case possess immense importance. The certainty of an appeal to the people might add to the reality, and increase the force, of Parliamentary argument. No one out of Bedlam supposes that the results of a division are greatly, if at all, affected by the speeches which are supposed to convince the House. Sudden efforts of rhetoric, dexterity in the management of debate, astuteness in the framing of an amendment, may on rare occasions (generally to the damage of the country) affect the division list. But even the outside public can conjecture, before a debate has begun, what members will vote for or against the Government; and a "Whip" can venture upon predictions, having far more of certainty than is generally ascribed to conjecture. If it were certain that the ultimate fate of a measure, say for the disestablishment of the Church, would finally turn not upon the votes of members of Parliament, but upon the votes of outsiders who never took part in the hollow and artificial system of warfare waged at Westminster, it is conceivable that speakers in Parliament might address themselves to the task of convincing an unseen, but more or less dispassionate, audience; it is conceivable (wild though the idea appears) that power of reasoning might become a force of some slight moment even in practical politics. Swiss experience does here a little help us. There is nothing to show that the Federal Assembly lacks weight or respectability; it compares favourably enough with the Sovereign National Assembly which makes and unmakes the Ministries and controls the destiny of France. That "sovereignty of Parliament," moreover, which Parliamentarians defend against popular control is, though a legal fact, something of a political fiction.[11] Worshippers of power instinctively discover where it is that their idol has its shrine. Oratory, rhetoric, reasoning, and adulation

---

[11] Dicey had already made use of the distinction between legal sovereignty and political sovereignty in the first edition of the *Law of the Constitution* (see esp. Lecture II).

are nowadays addressed by politicians to the electors. The electorate is king; the Referendum might turn out little more than the formal recognition of a fact which exists, even while men shut their eyes to its existence.

An appeal in matters of legislation from Parliament to the people is (it may be urged), on the face of it, an appeal from knowledge to ignorance.

This objection to the Referendum has weighed heavily with Maine and thinkers of the same school. Its weight cannot be denied, but may be lessened by more than one reflection.[12]

This line of attack on the principle of an appeal to the people is an assault upon the foundations of popular government. It establishes, indeed, what no one denies, that nations, which have not reached a certain stage of development, are unfit for democratic institutions, and that democracy is a form of government which, at best, is marred by grave deficiencies. But if, for the sake of argument, we concede that every charge which reasonable men have brought against popular sovereignty can be substantiated—and this is to grant a good deal more than truth requires—the concession does not support the inference that the Referendum is of necessity an evil. For the matter to be determined is not whether democracy be or be not an admirable form of government, but, the quite different question, whether in democratic countries, like France, England, or Switzerland, a veto by the electors on the legislation of a democratic Parliament, especially when such legislation changes the Constitution, may not, on the whole, have salutary effects. The Referendum is but a veto, and, for the purpose of the present article, a veto only on the alteration of fundamental laws. But were this appeal to the people imported from Switzerland to-morrow, and made, what no careful thinker would at present advise, applicable to every kind of law, it would not compel the passing by Parliament of a single Act which Parliament might deem impolitic. Parliament could still maintain an institution such as, say, the poor-law, of dubious popularity, but of undoubted wisdom. What Parliament could not do (supposing the Referendum were applicable to the poor-laws) would be to develop still further sound, though unpopular, principles in the administration of relief for the poor. This incapacity would be an evil. Unfortunately it is an evil which already exists. A modern Parliament may possibly maintain wise

---

[12] On Maine, see page 46, note 28 above and the later appearances on pages 127–35, 186, 205–6. Dicey consistently sets up Maine as his foil on the question of the referendum.

legislation enacted by the bold statesmanship of a less democratic age, but hardly in harmony with prevalent sentimentalism. But no modern Parliament will pass laws known to offend the general sentiment of the electors. This state of things may, or may not, be lamentable; it will not be rendered worse by recognising its existence. It is an error to imagine that there is great danger in taking from Parliament theoretical authority certain never to be exercised in practice. Against this delusion it behoves us to be specially on our guard. The weakness of English statesmanship is to retain names whilst sacrificing realities; the Crown has been stripped of real authority, whereof the maintenance might have been beneficial to the nation, by Ministers who would have resigned rather than deprive the Crown of a single nominal prerogative. Nor is it certain that the independence of members of Parliament, if such independence has still any real existence, would decline in proportion to the increase in the legislative authority of the people. A member might defy the whims of local busybodies, or the fanaticism of benevolent associations, if he knew that his conduct might ultimately be ratified by the visible and unmistakable approval of the nation.

No doubt the Parliamentary opponents of the Referendum have in their minds an idea which does not often in modern times find distinct expression in their speeches. They think, and not without reason, that electors well capable of determining who are the kind of men fit to be members of Parliament, are not capable of determining what are the laws which members of Parliament should pass or reject. This idea, as we all know, has been expressed in various forms by Burke, and by writers whom Burke influenced.[13] Its substantial truth is, subject to certain reservations, past dispute, but its applicability to the circumstances of to-day is open to the gravest question. The House of Commons has ceased to be a body of men to whom the electors confide full authority to legislate in accordance with the wisdom or the interests of members of Parliament. It is really a body of persons elected for the purpose of carrying out the policy of the predominant party. It is not the fact that voters choose a respectable squire or successful merchant because they know him to be a worthy man, and trust that he will legislate more wisely for them than they could for themselves; they

---

[13] The *locus classicus* is Burke's famous speech to the Electors of Bristol of 3 November 1774.

elect a member—a worthy man, if they can get him—because he pledges himself, more or less distinctly, to vote for certain measures and to support certain political leaders. Elections are now decided for or against the Ministry according as the majority of the electors are Unionists or Gladstonians. It is idle to fancy that what the voters consider is simply, or mainly, the prudence, capacity, or character of their representative.

Full weight must be given to the arguments against the Referendum, but it is equally necessary to examine fairly the grounds on which a fair-minded man may advocate the introduction into England of the popular veto on constitutional changes.

These grounds are, when stated broadly, twofold.

First, the Referendum supplies, under the present state of things, the best, if not the only possible, check upon ill-considered alterations in the fundamental institutions of the country.

Our Constitution stands in a peculiar position. It has always been from a legal point of view liable to revolution by Act of Parliament. But this liability has till recent times been little more than a theoretical risk. From 1689 down to, roughly speaking, 1828, the fundamental laws of the land, though not unchangeable, were never changed. The customs and feeling and opinion of the age, no less than the interest of the classes who alone exercised effective political authority, all told against innovation. The idea of constant Parliamentary activity in the field of legislation was unknown to Englishmen till near the era of the Reform Act. Faction was as violent under George the Third as under Victoria; it was far more vicious and cruel in the last century than at present. But parties did not seek power by proposing alterations in the fundamental institutions of the land. Serious statesmen did not, the moment they quitted office, discover some new principle whereof the adoption was to achieve the main object of restoring its advocates to power, while it incidentally changed the composition of the electoral body. A century ago every one admired the far-famed Constitution of England, and the advocacy even of admitted improvements repelled rather than attracted the classes whose goodwill conferred success on politicians. It were far easier in 1890 to abolish the House of Lords than it would have been in 1790 to disfranchise Old Sarum.[14] The change or amendment of the Constitution was till recently a slow and

---

[14] On Old Sarum, see page 11, note 11.

laborious process. For nearly half a century before the passing of the Roman Catholic Relief Act, every argument against the penal laws had been laid before the public. It took forty years more to drive into the minds of Englishmen the unanswerable objections to the exclusive maintenance of a Protestant Establishment in Ireland.[15] Reform, free trade, and every important change in national laws or habits, has till recently been the fruit of agitation as long as it was laborious. This agitation was an evil in itself and the parent of evils, but it was the visible sign of the strength of the barriers opposed to innovation. The state of the world has now entirely altered. The authority of the Crown, the influence of the nobility, our old party system grounded on aristocratic connection, the predominance of a prudent and moneyed middle-class, are matters of the past. The barriers which used to limit the exercise of unbounded authority by a Parliamentary majority are all broken down. What is more serious, change has become the order of the day. An age devoid of the genuine revolutionary enthusiasm which a century ago carried away the best minds in Europe, is also devoid of the conservative instincts or passion which saved England from succumbing to the fanaticism or violence of the French Revolution. Everything is now deemed changeable, and there is nothing from the Crown downwards which Parliament cannot legally change. The experience of 1886 has taught the country one lesson which will be remembered when the agitation for Home Rule is at an end. A Bill which in effect repealed the Act of Union with Ireland might conceivably have become law without the country having ever expressed assent to a change amounting to a constitutional revolution. The measure, moreover, which might have been carried in 1886, is one which, as regards its most important provision, is now in 1890 neither advocated nor defended, by Gladstonian Home Rulers. A calm critic, indeed, may doubt whether the Bill of 1886 would not lose its one merit by the omission of the clauses which excluded Irish members from the British Parliament. With this matter we need not concern ourselves. The noteworthy point is that in 1886 Parliament might have passed a law which, if reproduced in the same form in 1890, would assuredly be vetoed on an appeal to the people. Here we come to the root of the whole matter. Englishmen have, in accordance with our curious system of bit-by-bit reform, at last established a

---

[15] As noted above, the Roman Catholic Relief Act which removed the civil and political restrictions on Catholics was passed in 1829 after a long campaign, and the Church of Ireland, formerly united to the Church of England, was disestablished in 1869.

democracy without establishing those safeguards which in avowedly democratic commonwealths, such as the United States or Switzerland, protect the Constitution from sudden changes, and thus ensure that every amendment in the fundamental laws of the land shall receive the deliberate sanction of the people; the object, be it noted, of these safeguards is not to thwart the wishes of the democracy, but to ensure that a temporary, or factitious, majority shall not override the will of the nation.

The time may come when Englishmen may borrow from America the constitutional provisions which, by delaying alterations in the Constitution, protect the sovereignty of the people. But to frame a written and rigid Constitution is not the work of a day or of a year. Whether in England such a polity when framed would answer its purpose, is, moreover, a question not to be answered without most careful consideration. Meanwhile the Referendum, which might be introduced with comparative ease, and, what is equally important, might be introduced as an experiment, supplies the very kind of safeguard which all true democrats feel to be required. It is an institution which admirably fits a system of popular government. It is the only check on the predominance of party which is at the same time democratic and conservative. It is democratic, for it appeals to and protects the sovereignty of the people; it is conservative, for it balances the weight of the nation's common sense or inertia against the violence of partisanship and the fanaticism of reformers. This check has one preeminent recommendation, not possessed by any of the artful, or ingenious, devices for strengthening the power of a Second Chamber, or placing a veto in the hands of a minority. Its application does not cause irritation. If the Lords reject a Bill people demand the reform of the Peerage; if the French Senate (a popularly elected body) hesitates to approve a revision of the Constitution, the next scheme of revision contains a clause for the abolition of the Senate. Popular pride is roused, voters are asked to make it a point of honour that a measure, which an aristocratic or select Chamber has rejected, shall be carried. A Bill's rejection turns into a reason for its passing into law. Should a regular appeal to the electors result in the rejection of a Bill passed by Parliament, this childish irritation becomes an impossibility. The people cannot be angered at the act of the people.

Secondly, the Referendum tends to sever legislation from politics.

That this separation is in itself desirable is a matter almost past dispute. It were hard to find, I will not say valid arguments, but even plausible fallacies, in favour of the position that the passing of an important law should depend upon circumstances, which have no necessary connection with the nature or the terms of the enactment. It cannot, to take an example from recent Swiss legislation, be reasonable that a law, restoring the penalty of capital punishment for murder, should be passed, or rejected, because of the popularity or the unpopularity of the politicians by whom the measure is proposed. The Referendum is a distinct recognition of the elementary but important principle that in matters of legislation patriotic citizens ought to distinguish between measures and men. This distinction the Swiss voters have shown themselves fully capable of drawing. They have, as already pointed out, rejected legislative propositions made to them by leaders of whose policy on the whole they approved. Whoever studies with care Adams' account of the Referendum will think it doubtful whether, on the whole, the Swiss people have not shown a good deal of sound sense in the use of their legislative veto. Let it be granted, however, what is more than possible, that the electors have in some cases exhibited less enlightenment than their representatives. Still it is difficult to exaggerate the immense benefit which in the long run accrues to a people from the habit of treating legislation as a matter to be determined not by the instincts of political partisanship, but by the weight of argument. The Referendum is, or may be, an education in the application of men's understandings to the weightiest of political concerns—namely, the passing of laws—such as is absolutely unobtainable by voters, who have been trained to think, that their whole duty as citizens consists in supporting the Conservative or the Radical party, and in their blind acceptance of every proposed enactment which happens to form part of the party platform.

The Referendum, however, it is sometimes suggested, will, if introduced into England, be at best but a useless innovation. English politics, it is argued, are already subject to the predominant influence of party. Voters will always adhere to their party programme, and the men who, at a general election, will give a Tory, or a Liberal, vote, would, on a Referendum, unhesitatingly support any law carried through Parliament by Lord Salisbury or by Mr. Gladstone.

This reasoning undoubtedly contains an element of truth. The party system would for a long time, at any rate, often vitiate the working of the Referendum. But there is not the least reason to suppose that the result of an appeal to the electors of the United Kingdom on the question whether they would pass, or reject, a particular law, would always have the same result as an appeal to the constituencies, at a general election, on the question whether they would send up to Parliament a Conservative or a Liberal majority.

76

The differences between the two appeals are most important. The electors voting for members in different constituencies are a very different body from the electors voting *en masse* throughout the United Kingdom. The persons, in the second place, who vote at an election, and who would vote on a Referendum, need not necessarily, and indeed would not probably, be exactly the same. There exist, it may well be supposed, large bodies of electors who, while taking little part in current politics, especially in places where they happen to be in a minority, would record their votes with regard to a given law of which they knew the importance, and which was the subject of their strong and deliberate approval or condemnation. The question lastly submitted for decision at an election is of a totally different kind from the question submitted for decision on a Referendum. It is one thing to be asked which of two men, for neither of whom have you any liking, shall represent you, or misrepresent you, in Parliament, and another to be asked whether you approve of a law, say for disestablishing the Church of England, or for repealing the Act of Union with Ireland. There is at least nothing absurd or irrational in the anticipation that citizens who did not care to answer the first inquiry at all might answer the second with a peremptoriness and unanimity surprising to politicians. No phenomenon is more curious than the divergence which, in all countries enjoying representative institutions, is apt to exist between Parliamentary opinion and popular convictions. Even as things now are, careful observers conjecture that measures, which it were hardly possible even to propose in Parliament, might not displease the electors, whilst proposals which command strong Parliamentary support might not stand the ordeal of a popular vote. Small would be the support which Parliament would give to one of the most salutary reforms conceivable—the reduction of the number of seats to be filled both in the House of Commons and in the House of Lords. Yet there is no reason for asserting that the people of the United Kingdom would object to a change which reduced the Houses of Parliament to something like the size of the Houses of Congress. Every year the likelihood increases that Parliament will grant the electoral franchise to women. Yet even those who, in common with the present writer, look with no disfavour on this reform, may gravely doubt whether it would, on a Referendum, command the approval of the electorate. There always have been, and there are, questions which interest politicians, but hardly interest the people. No historian would pledge himself to the assertion that, between 1832 and 1865, the electors cared deeply for the reform of Parliament. Yet during that period statesmen promised, or produced, more than one Reform Bill. We all know that the so-called religious question has in the hands of politicians impeded efforts to establish or extend popular education. Yet well-informed persons will sometimes assert that ordinary parents look with great indifference on a controversy which excites bitter contention among the members, of all parties, by whom these parents are represented. From whichever side the matter be looked at, the conclusion becomes more than probable that the results of a Referendum would, occasionally at least, be utterly different from the results of a general election, and that the electors, when consulted on the advisability of passing a definite law, might break through the bonds of party allegiance to follow the dictates of their own prejudices or common sense.

The popular veto on constitutional changes which freed electors from bondage to the party system might also promote the straightforwardness of English statesmanship. As things at present stand, the position of a statesman, forced to surrender a policy which he feels does not approve itself to the nation, is full of awkwardness. We all admit that a political leader must, sooner or later, shape his course of action in conformity with the will of the country. No one blames Peel for his loyal acceptance of the Reform Act; no one now thinks the worse of Lord Derby for having in 1852 acquiesced in the national resolve to maintain free trade.[16] Unfortunately, legitimate changes of conduct are apt under our present system to bear the appearance of dubious changes in opinion. It may often be a doubtful matter whether on a particular subject the country has, or has not, pronounced a final verdict. As the tenure of office is, or may be, immediately connected with a Minister's success in carrying a given Bill through Parliament, there is great difficulty in his renouncing legislation proposed by himself, when he finds the country will not support his Bill, without his at least incurring the charge of undue tenacity in clinging to office. The reference of a particular law, say a Parliamentary Reform Bill, to the people for approval or rejection, would greatly increase the freedom, and improve the moral position, of the Minister who advocated the measure. If the Bill were accepted, things would stand exactly as they do now when a Bill finally passes, into an Act. If it were rejected, the Minister could, like a member of the Swiss

---

[16] On Peel's and Derby's acceptances of the defeats of policies for they had long fought, see page 51, note 30.

Council, accept the rejection as a final expression of the nation's will. It would soon be felt that he might with perfect honesty pursue the course which would now be taken by a member of the Swiss Council. He need not pretend that his opinion is altered; he might say openly that he still, as a matter of opinion, thought his Reform Bill wise and politic. But he might also say that it was a matter on which the nation was the final judge, and that he accepted the nation's decision. In all this there would be no pretence at conversion; there would simply be a pledge as to conduct. The Minister might, if still supported by Parliament, continue to administer the affairs of the country as honourably as Peel held office after the passing of the Reform Act, or as a servant of the Crown in the days of Elizabeth remained in the service of the Queen even though her Majesty had, on some high matter of state, rejected his advice.

The modification in the doctrine of Ministerial responsibility which would, certainly, sooner or later, be caused by the introduction of the Referendum, must, to all devotees of the system of government by party, seem a fatal objection to the suggested innovation. Of speculations which have some family similarity to the ideas propounded in this article, my friend Mr. Morley (whose zeal for party takes me by surprise) warns us that they "must be viewed with lively suspicion by everybody who believes that party is an essential element in the wholesome working of Parliamentary government."[17] To this suspicion all, who call attention to the merits of the Referendum, are, it is to be feared, obnoxious. The plain truth must be stated. The party system, whatever its advantages, and they are not insignificant, is opposed to the sovereignty of the people, which is the fundamental dogma of modern democracy. That system throws the control of legislation first into the hands of a party, and then into the hands of the most active or the most numerous section of that party. But the part of a party may be, and probably is, a mere fraction of the nation. The principle of the Referendum, on the other hand, is to place, at any rate as regards important legislation, parties, factions, and sections under the control of the national majority. The creation of a popular veto is open, it must be frankly admitted, to grave

---

[17] John Morley, *Walpole* (London, 1889). Morley, a prolific Liberal editor and journalist and, from 1883, Liberal MP and minister, had held quite similar views to Dicey until the 1880s, when he supported Home Rule and remained faithful to Gladstone. In the passage from which this quotation is taken, Morley was not investigating the referendum but condemning those who celebrated collaboration by "the chief men of both parties" in order to remove partisan considerations from "some great act of State."

objections. The consideration, however, which, more than any other, may commend it to the favourable attention of thoughtful men, is its tendency to revive, in democratic societies, the idea which the influence of partisanship threatens with death, that allegiance to party must in the minds of good citizens yield to the claims of loyalty to the nation.

Let none of my readers suppose that my object in writing this article is directly, or decisively, to recommend the adoption in England of the Swiss Referendum. My object is simply to show that there is much more to be said for, no less than against, the popular veto than English thinkers are generally ready to admit. The time approaches when we may import from the United States the "Constitutional Convention," which in the domain of politics is by far the most valuable result of American inventiveness. The time has come when we ought all to consider the possible expediency of introducing into England that appeal to the people which is by far the most original creation of Swiss democracy.

4

The Defence of the Union (1892)

What are the principles which ought to guide Unionists in the defence of the Union?

This is the inquiry to which I propose to supply an answer. My purpose is not to make any startling or novel suggestion, but to recall public attention to considerations, regarding the defence of our national unity, so obvious that their truth hardly admits of dispute, so trite that they hardly seem to need restatement, yet so constantly overlooked at the present moment, and so likely to be disregarded in the heat of the impending conflict, that they demand emphatic reiteration.

Three principles ought to govern, as on the whole they have hitherto governed, the action of Unionists.

First.—Unionists must spare no legitimate effort whatever to win the general election.[1]

To insist upon this point may seem childish or pedantic. We are all, it will be said, arming for the political campaign; what need then of saying that we must struggle for victory? The reply is easy. It is that hundreds of Unionists fail to grasp the momentous character of the impending conflict. Much current talk implies that a Gladstonian victory, if it be not an overwhelming one, will be of no great importance. "A Gladstonian majority," it is argued, "if gained at all, must in any case be a narrow one; it will consist of factions filled with mutual distrust, not to say hostility, and so opposed to each other on matters both of feeling and of principle, that it will be impossible for them to frame any measure of Home Rule

---

[1] This article was released a few months prior to the July 1892 general election. Dicey's preferred result did not occur; Gladstone returned for his fourth and final premiership. The Liberals won fewer seats than the Conservatives but entered into government by relying on support from the Irish Nationalist bloc.

on which they could agree, or which, if by any possibility they could come to an agreement, could be carried through the House of Commons. If on return to office Mr. Gladstone delays to bring forward a Home Rule Bill, he will lose all credit for statesmanship. If he proposes any definite scheme he will, as in 1886, rent his party in twain; his Irish allies will reject any plan which does not go a good deal further than the Bill of 1886 towards securing Irish independence; his English supporters will pass no Bill which does not ensure to the Imperial Parliament far greater authority than was secured by the Bill of 1886. The Irish members must be retained at Westminster or relegated to Dublin. A measure which retains them cannot be supported by Liberals who see that the one compensation offered to England for the Parliamentary independence of Ireland is the exclusion of Irish members from a part in the debates at Westminster, whilst a measure which deprives Irish members of their seats in the English Parliament cannot be supported by scores of Gladstonians, who have pledged themselves up to the lips to the retention of the Irish members at Westminster, as a pledge and sign of the legislative supremacy reserved to the Imperial Parliament." Some Unionists press this line of argument so far as to wish that if the Unionists cannot gain a large majority, Mr. Gladstone may return to office with a small majority of say fifteen or twenty members. His return to nominal power will, they fancy, be the end of his real authority; a few months will show that he is powerless, and strip him for ever both of weight and of popularity.

This is the kind of loose talk—the result of loose thinking—which is doing an infinity of damage to Unionism. It saps the energy of Unionists and keeps them living in a fool's paradise; for the whole line of argument I have described is, plausible though it sounds, utterly misleading. It is based on a whole mass of either disputable or demonstrably false assumptions.

Whether the Opposition will at the next general election obtain a majority at all is a matter of the most doubtful speculation. There is every ground for energy, there is no ground whatever for want of heart or hope, on the part of Unionists. But should the next election result in a Gladstonian triumph, it is at least as likely to produce a large as a small majority of Separatists.[2] Vast bodies of democratic voters tend to sway

---

[2] Separatist was not a label that most Home Rulers would accept for themselves, as many denied that Home Rule entailed Ireland leaving the Empire. To Dicey, however, Home Rule was not a stable solution and would inevitably lead to Irish Independence if granted.

strongly towards any side to which they incline at all. The plausibility of the prediction that any majority, whether Unionist or Gladstonian, must be a small one arises from the conviction, which undoubtedly is well founded, that there are thousands of electors, among both parties, who cannot now be shaken in their opinions. A great orator or a great statesman might at the present moment rouse the enthusiasm and stimulate the energy of his followers; he could hardly hope to make many converts from the ranks of his opponents. It is not, however, on the votes of men of fixed convictions that the immediate issue of the political contest turns. A change, in many constituencies, of a few hundred votes, or less, from one side to the other, the rally round Mr. Gladstone of Liberals who in 1886 never went to the poll, the action, in short, of a comparatively small number of voters, who may be described as waverers, might under conceivable circumstances give the Separatists a considerable Parliamentary majority. Grant, however, for the sake of argument, that neither party can by possibility obtain a majority of more than from twenty to thirty votes. Such a majority, if in favour of Separation, might work, and probably would work, untold evil. It is idle to argue from notorious differences of opinion and feeling which, under the pressure of defeat, would, break the Opposition to pieces, that the Separatists, when cheered by victory, could not agree upon a policy of Home Rule. Success is a great pacificator. Home Rulers, if victorious in 1892 by however slender a majority, would know that the success of their policy, if achievable at all, must be achieved then and there. They would come to terms of agreement for the simple reason that concord would be a necessity; they would be compelled either to agree or, as a party, to perish. Should a Bill be framed which satisfied English Gladstonians, Irish Nationalists would, we may be sure, accept it. They would do so for a very valid reason; they would know that no better opportunity for effecting the ends they desire would ever present itself. In the attempt to dissolve the Union, the first step, they would rightly feel, is everything. The creation of an Irish Parliament claiming a legal right to speak in the name of the Irish people would give Nationalists not indeed all they desire, but the certain means of obtaining it. Were such a Parliament endowed only with the right of regulating gas, electricity, water-works, and such trivial matters, which is pretty nearly all the authority that the present Separatist member for Rossendale was, in his astuteness or his simplicity, willing to concede to a body claiming to represent Ireland as a nation, still the existence of a so-called national Parliament on College

Green, though wielding powers no greater than those of a vestry, would be the virtual repeal of the Act of Union, and would involve the moral defeat of Unionism.[3] There is not an Irish agitator who does not know that, though to create an Irish Parliament is a matter of infinite labour, there would be, comparatively speaking, no difficulty in extending the authority of an Irish Parliament if once the electorate of Great Britain had acquiesced in its existence. Suppose, however, that Mr. Gladstone should elect rather to satisfy the aspirations of Mr. Healy, Mr. Davitt, or Mr. Redmond, than to gratify the very modest ideas of Home Rule entertained by the respectable rank and file of his English supporters.[4] Suppose that a Home Rule Bill, say, the measure of 1886, deprived by the retention of Irish members at Westminster of its one benefit for England, should be so drawn as to ensure the support of Irish Nationalists. What reason have we to suppose that moderate Gladstonians would refuse to swallow a nostrum which in their hearts they may thoroughly dislike? None whatever. They have already done many things which it might be supposed would have offended their judgment or their conscience; they have condoned or palliated boycotting; they have, to say the least, never denounced the plan of campaign; they have made light of criminal conspiracy. Yet from a moral point of view the apology for criminals condemned by the Special Commission must have been, one would suppose, far more painful to Moderates like Lord Herschell than would be the acceptance of a very extensive measure of Home Rule.[5] In 1886 Liberals, who throughout their lives had detested or denounced the policy of Home Rule, were free to follow their own convictions. Yet in the main the bond of party—a very different thing, I must in fairness add, from considerations of self-interest

[3] Dicey is referring to John Henry Maden, who had won just weeks prior a fiercely contested by-election to take a seat that had previously belonged to the Liberal Unionists. College Green had been the site of the Irish Parliament prior to the Act of Union.

[4] Timothy Healy, Michael Davitt, and John Redmond were "extreme" Irish nationalists and republicans, although they differed among themselves on several points. By "respectable" English backers of Home Rule he had in mind figures like John Morley.

[5] The Plan of Campaign, organized by Healy and left-wing Nationalists, coordinated the refusal to pay rents to Anglo-Irish and often absentee landlords, and involved significant violence. The term *boycotting* had only recently been created, referring to the organized social ostracism of a land agent (surname Boycott) for an Anglo-Irish aristocrat. The Special Commission on Parnellism and Crime of 1888–9 had been set up in response to a (forged) document showing the leader of the Irish Nationalists expressing support for the assassination of two British government officials in Dublin. Farrer Herschell, 1st Baron Herschell had been, and would again be soon after the 1892 General Election, Lord High Chancellor under Gladstone.

—was found stronger than the tie of principle. In 1892 or 1893 all freedom of action will have gone from the Gladstonians, they will have been sworn in to party allegiance; their triumph, if it be achieved, will have been due to party discipline, loyalty to colleagues, self-interest, the passion for victory, the longing to end once and for all a tedious controversy, the unbearable humiliation of confessing that they have been dupes, some of the best no less than some of the worst of human feelings, all the natural impulses of partisanship will tend in one direction.[6] The predominant sentiment of the moment will be that no man must flinch in the hour of battle. Gladstone will be dictator. The sole mandate of any cogency imposed by Gladstonian electors upon their representatives will be the mandate to accept any Home Rule Bill whatever which is endorsed with the name of Gladstone.

If any critic thinks my anticipation of the probable attitude of Gladstonians after an electoral victory untrustworthy, and fancies that Gladstonian Liberals, if dissatisfied with their leader's scheme for Home Rule, will for the first time break from their party, let the objector reflect that it would be quite possible to avoid for the moment putting the party loyalty of Moderates to too severe a test. The immediate passing of a Home [Rule] Bill would not be a necessity. Other modes of promoting the cause of separation might easily be discovered. A small Gladstonian majority might find it difficult—though I doubt the difficulty turning out in fact so great as it appears—to carry a measure of Home Rule through the House of Commons. But such a majority could certainly pass a resolution pledging the House of Commons to the principle of Irish parliamentary independence. No person returned as a Gladstonian member since 1886, no person elected to Parliament in 1892 or 1893, on whatever terms, as a supporter of Mr. Gladstone, could with honesty or with decency refuse to vote in favour of such a resolution. It might be, and probably would be, drawn in terms so vague as to remove the possibility of conflict between the hostile groups which would constitute the Gladstonian majority. The effect, however, of a resolution in favour of granting an independent Parliament to Ireland must not be measured by the moderation or the ambiguity of its language. Whatever its terms, its meaning would be understood by the whole world, and its effect would be enormous. Should the House of Commons once sanction the

---

[6] This run-on sentence appears in this fashion in the original.

principle of disunion, a blow of incalculable weight would have been struck at the unity of the nation. Disastrous have been the results flowing from the adoption of Repeal as the policy of an English party, far more disastrous effects would flow from the sanction of Repeal by a body which could legally speak in the name of the people of England.[7] The House of Representatives have never possessed in the United States half the constitutional power, or a tithe of the traditional authority, which in England the course of history has conferred upon the House of Commons. But if the House of Representatives had, during the War of Secession, passed a resolution in favour of dissolving the Union, it may well be doubted whether the forces of the Northern States could have been effectively employed for the suppression of the slave-owners' rebellion.[8]

It argues, again, simplicity or ignorance to suppose that even the immediate passing of Home Rule resolutions is needful for the triumph of Separatists. The formation of a Gladstonian Cabinet means that the government of Ireland will be handed over to the enemies of England. Nominal authority indeed may be placed in the hands of the most respectable among our opponents. Lord Spencer or Lord Aberdeen, Mr. Morley or Sir George Trevelyan may hold office; any one of them who likes to undertake the task, or all of them together, may put the United Kingdom into liquidation, and wind up the connection between Ireland and Great Britain. But whoever be the occupants of the Castle, the real governors of Ireland would be Mr. Healy, Archbishop Walsh, Mr. William O'Brien, Mr. Dillon, and Mr. Davitt.[9] Men found guilty of criminal conspiracy, priests who have connived at boycotting or who have promoted it, politicians who have objected to no kind of violence which was not directed against themselves or their partisans, lawyers who have never respected the law unless it could be in some way turned against their opponents, would, if Mr. Gladstone should ever return to

---

[7] "Repeal" here refers to repeal of the Act of Union of Britain and Ireland, on which see Chapter 3, note 5.

[8] Dicey had been fervently pro-Union during the American Civil War. The equation of Irish Nationalism with the Southern cause was a trope among Unionists.

[9] On Morley, see note Chapter 3, note 17. The 5th Earl Spencer, Lord Aberdeen, and George Trevelyan had all been high-ranking Liberals with responsibilities for Irish affairs. Dublin Castle was the seat of the British administration in Ireland. On Healy and Davitt, see page 84, note 4. William O'Brien and John Dillon were both Irish MPs and nationalists/land reformers; William Walsh was the Catholic Archbishop of Dublin and (a source of some conflict with the Vatican) a proponent of nationalism and agrarian radicalism.

office, guide the administration, nominate the judges, direct the police of Ireland. This practical instalment of Home Rule would go a good way to arrest the possible opposition of Nationalists to the moderation of Mr. Gladstone's legislative proposals. It would farther break down the spirit of Loyalists. The working of the Land Purchase Act would, under such a state of things, become impossible;[10] every magistrate who, in spite of popular clamour, has enforced the law of the land; every farmer who, in the midst of dishonest or terrorised neighbours, has manfully paid his rent; every tenant who, in defiance of the National League or the leaders in the Plan of Campaign, has under the sanction of the law purchased or leased land offered to him by a boycotted landlord; every constable who has performed his duty to the State—every one, in short, high or low, rich or poor, who has respected the law, and has obeyed the rules of loyalty and justice, confident in the power and the will of the English people to protect honest men in the exercise of their just rights —would find himself the victim of injustice and persecution, and would feel that honesty and manliness had turned out folly, and that he had been betrayed by the country which he trusted, and had been made subject to the tyrants whose power he had ventured to defy. It is idle to suppose that such an experience of wrong would not produce its natural effects. Grant, for the sake of argument—and this is granting a great deal more than the facts warrant—that a Gladstonian Government, if supported by only a small majority, could under no circumstances continue to exist for more than half a year, yet six months of misrule would be enough to undo all the good which has been painfully obtained by six years of just and legal government. Destruction is far more rapid than construction. It may well be doubted whether a few months of injustice would not make it impossible to restore for years to come in Ireland the authority of ordinary law, and the machinery of constitutional government. Nor does the matter end here. It is indeed my firm conviction that a Unionist minority, if firmly bound together, could by its strenuous resistance ultimately render abortive any attempt of Separatists to tear asunder the union between Great Britain and Ireland. But who dares count on the unbroken steadfastness and absolute discipline of the whole Unionist party under circumstances of defeat? I yield to no man in my

---

[10] Dicey is referring to legislation, passed in response to agrarian agitation against the Anglo-Irish landlord class, that would establish regulations for Irish tenants to buy land and set terms for government loans to purchasers.

respect for the Unionist leaders, whether they be Conservatives such as Lord Salisbury and Mr. Balfour, or Liberals such as the Duke of Devonshire and Mr. Chamberlain;[11] no party has ever clung more firmly to its principles, or has exhibited a higher tone of public spirit than have the rank and file of the Unionists. But a party consists of men of unequal judgment and of unequal force of character. If nothing succeeds like success, nothing fails like failure. Defeat begets quarrels and favours intrigue. The discipline of an army is never strengthened by a repulse. Should the Gladstonians obtain a decided success, there would inevitably be found Unionists to begin dreaming of compromise. But to Unionism compromise is death. Then, too, would begin the day of intrigue. But political manœuvring is the degradation of public character, and the moral reputation of the Unionists is the true source of their strength.

Unionists, moreover, ought to be stimulated to the most energetic action, not only by the thought that defeat involves the risk of fatal disaster, but by the knowledge that success, however moderate at the next General Election, is equivalent to permanent victory. There is no real reason why the Unionists should not substantially maintain the position they already hold. Suppose, however, that their success should fall far below their deserts, and that they should secure a majority of from twenty to thirty members, or even less. This would not enable them to constitute a strong Government; a Ministry which could count on nothing more than a bare working majority could not carry through any grand scheme of improvement. But from a Unionist point of view, the retention of a small working majority would be a decisive victory. The strength no less than the weakness of Unionists is that they are a party of defence. If the next election returns them to power, but for the time diminishes their resources, their right course clearly will be to enter on a defensive campaign. They will not need to attempt anything new,

---

[11] On Salisbury, see page 37, note 24. Arthur Balfour was one of the most prominent Conservative politicians, particularly on Irish questions, having served as Chief Secretary for Ireland from 1887 to 1891; he would serve as Prime Minister from 1901 to 1905. Something of a philosopher himself, he was the brother-in-law of the great moral philosopher Henry Sidgwick, himself a disaffected Liberal turned Unionist. The 8th Duke of Devonshire, for most of his career known as Lord Hartington, had once been a leader of the Liberal party but split with Gladstone over Home Rule. Joseph Chamberlain had been a leader of the radical-democratic wing of Liberalism but likewise left the party in opposition to Home Rule.

but they will find it easy to perform their one essential duty—the maintenance of our existing political institutions. The tactics of defence, if honestly pursued, would, it is probable, be crowned with speedy success. The members of the Opposition have been held together by hopes of victory. The elation of triumph might for a time weld incongruous and discordant factions into something like a disciplined force. Disaster of even a moderate kind would break up a body which has not, we may feel sure, been kept together without considerable difficulty. Mr. Gladstone's second defeat would be his last; every one would feel that a policy which could not be executed under the sanction of his name and under the favour of his popularity, had become an impossible policy. The English members of the Opposition would, it may be anticipated, after another defeat renounce Home Rule. But this renunciation would render impossible the alliance with Irish Nationalists. It is, in short, as certain as anything of the kind can be that a Unionist victory at the General Election would, before six years more had elapsed, dissolve the forces of the Opposition. Irish difficulties, and it may be feared Irish misery, will tax the resources of British statesmanship long after every leading politician now living is in his grave. But a defeat of Home Rulers at the polling booths in 1892 would put an end to the political significance of the present Home Rule agitation. From whichever side, in short, a thoughtful man looks at the matter he is driven to the conclusion which, though often disputed, is suggested by the most ordinary common sense, that the impending political contest is of paramount importance, and that it behoves all Unionists to fight with the energy of men bent with their whole hearts on the attainment of victory.

Secondly.—Unionists must stand together, and stand by the principle of Unionism.

The absolute necessity of the union of Unionists is admitted by all who have at heart the integrity of the nation. There are, however, to be found many able and honest defenders of the Union, who fail to perceive all that is involved in this admission. Unionists are bound together by one common object and one common principle; their common aim is to avert the disintegration of the United Kingdom; their common principle is that the maintenance of national unity overrides every other political consideration. One Unionist may be an ardent supporter of the connection between Church and State, another may believe that the country would gain by the disestablishment of the Church; one man may believe that temperance should be enforced by law, another may hold that individual freedom is of more consequence than national sobriety.[12] These and other points of disagreement have nothing to do with the tie by which Unionists are bound to one another. They are linked together by the conviction that the matters on which they may disagree are of far less significance than the maintenance of that national unity as to which they are heart and soul at one.

Their position is in principle exactly the position occupied from 1861 to 1864 by the Northerners whose arms and sacrifices maintained the national existence of the United States. Among the supporters of the Union were to be found Republicans and Democrats, Protectionists and Free Traders. No one was ever so foolish as to contend that there was any inconsistency in a Protectionist and a Free Trader fighting side by side in the armies of the Union. So it would be if England were threatened with foreign invasion. Liberals and Conservatives alike would feel that in the face of this peril party differences sank to nothing. This is exactly what Unionists do feel at the present crisis. To many honest Gladstonians the candid recognition of the Unionist attitude is an impossibility. That this is so should afford no matter for surprise. Politicians who have persuaded themselves that Home Rule is, at the very worst, only a harmless experiment, cannot believe that their opponents see in the triumph of Mr. William O'Brien, of Mr. Dillon, of Mr. Davitt, and of Mr. Davitt's friend, that eminent Christian and distinguished patron of dynamite, Mr. Ford, a more ignominious, and, in the long run, a more ruinous disaster than would be the defeat of a British army by France or Russia.[13] What may cause some wonder is that Unionists do not always fully realise their own position. The unity of the United Kingdom is their watchword, their object, and their bond of union. No doubt agreement in zeal for the supremacy of the nation has been found by degrees to involve agreement on many other matters. Unionists are by their creed compelled to place the will of the nation above the demands of party. Unionists, recognising as they do, the law as the voice of the nation, are compelled, happily for themselves, to support the equal enforcement of law against every person, and against every

---

[12] The temperance movement was a major force in politics at the time and was associated primarily with the Liberal party.

[13] Patrick Ford was Irish by birth and had come to America as a child during the potato famine. He ran the *Irish World* newspaper which advocated political violence by Nationalists and in particular the use of (recently invented) dynamite against high-profile targets in Britain and Ireland.

class. They perceive, further, that national unity is menaced by the existence of any legitimate cause of complaint which arouses discontent among any large section of the population. They have attempted therefore, as notably in the case of the Land Purchase Act, and are ready to attempt, the removal of every proved grievance which can be abolished by legislation. Unionists also are coming slowly to recognise the all-important truth, that in a democratic age, the only sure method for preserving either the supremacy of the law, or the authority of the nation, is the candid and complete acceptance of democracy. These and other sentiments flowing from the fundamental principle of Unionism, combined with the habit of common action, are fusing Unionists of every stamp into a party of true Nationalists; the progress which has been made in this direction may be seen in the constantly increasing popularity of Mr. Balfour. Still the fact remains that the firm faith in the political integrity of the nation, and the conviction that its maintenance is, at this moment, of more importance than the carrying out of any social or political reform, are the foundation on which rests the whole policy of Unionism.

This fact at once condemns any policy of bids and dodges. You cannot bribe men into love of country: payment is fatal to patriotism. The suggestion that Unionists can go into the market and in effect say to the working men of England: "Stand by the country and we will reward you by passing measures, say, the Eight Hours Bill, which most of us believe to be injurious to yourselves and unjust to others," embodies a policy condemned, if by no other consideration, then, by its futility.[14] It is certain to fail; the party of genuine and intelligent conservatism (in the true sense of that much abused term), no less than of high public morality, cannot in a rivalry of promises compete with the recklessness of new Jacobinism. Unionists are bound over to respect for legal rights. How can they outbid opponents ready to override legal rights in deference to the exigencies of popular sentiment? Note, too, that for every doubtful ally to be gained by reckless pledges Unionists must lose ten sure friends prepared to rally round statesmen who, while they offer to carry out even difficult reforms, pledge themselves to the principle that

---

[14] Advocacy for the legislative mandate of an eight-hour workday was prominent in the labour movement of the late nineteenth century in the UK as elsewhere in Europe. Dicey opposed the policy as an interference with liberty of contract and a contravention of the laws of political economy.

even the removal of abuses shall be subject to the rules of common fairness. No doubt it sounds not a little old-fashioned to express a belief in the permanent influence of public morality and of fixed principle. But it needs no very profound acquaintance with history to feel convinced that moral faults rather than political errors have caused the fall of great parties. The supreme duty, then, of the Unionists, as it will be found in the long run their truest political interest, is to carry high the flag of the Union. There is not the least reason why Unionism should prove inconsistent with the planning and execution of large reforms, both social and political. One consideration, however, must not be dropped out of sight. The obtrusion on the public of schemes, however meritorious in themselves, which have no connection with Unionism, involves for the moment—though for the moment only—two dangers. It tends to disunite the defenders of the Union; it tends still more to confuse the minds of the electors. The difficulty of the day is to make men, who are many of them new to the use of political power and unaccustomed to political speculation, perceive all the dangers latent in a tremendous constitutional change, which, ill-advised and perilous in itself, is pressed on the acceptance of the country by means far worse than the innovation they are meant to promote. It is therefore of primary consequence that every elector should know that the Unionist leaders hold the maintenance of the Union to be the one thing absolutely necessary to the welfare of the country.

But how can it be expected that electors should see the supreme importance of maintaining the greatness of the nation if Unionist statesmen appear to be occupied at the moment with other questions than the maintenance of the Union? It is, in short, of vital import that at the next election, as in 1886, the one clear issue brought before the electors should be union or separation. On such an issue Unionists are certain to obtain a favourable verdict. Gladstonians see that this is so, and, wisely enough from their point of view, leave no stone unturned to prevent the one clear question—whether the unity of the nation shall or shall not be preserved—being submitted to the judgment of English and Scotch electors. In Ireland, indeed, these tactics are useless; every man and woman there knows well enough what is at stake. All this is a broad hint to the Unionists as to the course which wisdom requires them to pursue. It is tiresome, I admit, to harp continuously on one string; but it is a matter of the clearest duty and the plainest expediency to force at all costs upon the electors a decision for or against the maintenance of the

Union. Let it further be noted that such a course of action is sure of its reward. Even were the Unionists defeated, which, on the issue of Unionism, is all but impossible, the return to Parliament of a large minority, sent there with no mandate but the command to save the nation from disintegration, would, under proper management, be fatal to the policy of Home Rule.

Thirdly.—Unionists must heartily accept democracy, and save the unity of the nation by appealing from the clamour of a mob, or the intrigues of a party, to the deliberate voice of the people.

The necessity and the wisdom of reliance on the democracy sounds to many Conservatives a hard doctrine, yet to any man who looks facts in the face its truth is as clear as day. The existing English constitution is a democracy, masked under the forms of a regal aristocracy. The majority of the electors are the sovereign power; their deliberate will, when once expressed, is irresistible, and meets with no resistance. No one supposes for a moment that the Crown or the Peers would refuse to grant a Parliament to Ireland when once it should be plain that a decisive majority among the citizens of the United Kingdom had approved the policy of Home Rule. This supremacy of numbers, which is the true note of a democratic society, need, in the mind of a thoughtful man, excite neither enthusiasm nor aversion. The one essential thing is to recognise its existence, and to acknowledge frankly that a democratic constitution while it has merits which ought never to be underrated, has also defects which it is a mission of prudent statesmanship as far as possible to diminish or guard against. Among these defects lies the risk that a party which has obtained a slight or temporary majority may, by means of intrigue or violence, usurp the power of the nation. In avowed democracies, such as the United States or the Swiss Confederation, steps, more or less effective, have been deliberately taken to guard against this kind of usurpation. The fundamental laws of the State have been placed beyond the reach of a mere Parliamentary majority. Let us suppose that the citizens of the United States or of Switzerland were equally divided for or against some far-reaching change in the constitution, say the abolition of a second chamber. It is quite certain that under these circumstances no change could take place. We may go a good deal further than this, and assert that in both these democratic Republics the constitution could not be fundamentally altered, unless a very decided majority of the people deliberately approved of the specific innovation, say, the abolition of the bicameral system, and held it to be for its own sake desirable. In England it is otherwise. The very notion of a fundamental law is foreign to our political conceptions. It is within the authority of Parliament to introduce any change whatever into the constitution. The significance of this fact is concealed by the maintenance of ancient forms, which possess little remaining reality. These fictions of the constitution are often harmless, and sometimes useful. Their existence, however, produces one evil. It leads Englishmen to mistake sham for real checks on reckless innovation. The miscalled veto of the Crown and the, more or less fictitious, legislative independence of the House of Lords look like securities against the tyranny of a party. But the one is obsolete, the other is unreal. The House of Lords may indeed, as I shall show, exercise a most salutary and decisive authority as protector of the rights of the democracy, but the exertion of the legislative authority left to the House of Lords is liable to be grossly misrepresented, and to be treated as opposition to the will of the people when it is really the safeguard of popular sovereignty. It is at any rate quite possible, under our present constitutional arrangements, that a party which commanded a majority in the House of Commons might, unless our statesmen acted both with skill and vigour, carry through fundamental and irreparable changes which were not sanctioned by the deliberate will of the nation, and were not desired even by a bare majority of the electors. This danger cannot be warded off by any attack on democracy; it cannot be circumvented by any dodge, however ingenious; but it may be met by a loyal appeal to the essential principles of democracy, by calling upon the people to see to it, that no faction or combination of factions pass a measure which, like a Home Rule Bill, would radically change our whole system of government without having obtained the deliberate and undoubted sanction of the people of the United Kingdom. The means by which to assure a *bonâ fide* appeal to the people are not hard to find. What is needed is firmness, doggedness, and courage, in insisting upon their being used. It is worth while to point out, in the merest outline, one or two of these methods which are available and will be effective, because they are in harmony with the spirit at once of true conservatism and of true democracy.

The Unionist leaders would do well to lose no time in making the redistribution of seats, on thoroughly democratic principles, a main plank—to use a convenient piece of American political terminology—of their party platform. There is little real unfairness in the violation of the so-called principle summed up in the phrase, "one man, one vote."

But the fact that one citizen should have more votes than another, is, in a democratic State, an anomaly which—though it is for the moment justified by its slightly counterbalancing the unfair effect of other far more serious anomalies—is, in the present state of English opinion, certain to excite discontent. The course of wisdom is not to fight for a conservative advantage, if such it be, but to get rid at one stroke both of this and of other anomalies in our electoral system which are opposed to democratic principle or sentiment. The whole United Kingdom suffers from the over-representation of Ireland and Wales, and the under-representation of England. That Englishmen should have less than their fair share of power is an anomaly which is condemned not only by the abstract principles of democracy, but, what is of far more consequence, by every consideration of obvious expediency. The substantial defence of democratic government is that—at any rate, in modern Europe—population is a test, though a very rough one, of power and capacity. In the United Kingdom, at least, London, Lancashire, the North of Ireland, and the like, are the centres of life and intelligence. England, after all, contains a greater portion of the talent, the vigour, the worth of the State than does any other division of the United Kingdom. That this is so arises not from any special merit of Englishmen, but from the fact that to England and to London are irresistibly drawn men of capacity from every part of the kingdom. A system which gives to Ireland in Parliament more than the weight of the Metropolis is self-condemned. No political philosopher and no sincere democrat can openly defend a scheme of representation which gives to the five thousand electors of Galway, Kilkenny, and Newry three times the weight in the House of Commons of the sixteen thousand electors of Wandsworth. On this matter I need, however, say little. The whole subject is admirably handled by Mr. St. Loe Strachey in the *National Review* of last month.[i] It may be, however, allowable to suggest to Liberals like Sir George Trevelyan, whose political conscience has become so morbidly sensitive to the least infringement on the principle of "one man, one vote," that the phrase, "one vote, one worth," sounds at least as well as their

---

[i] See "One Man One Value." By St. Loe Strachey. *National Review*, No. 108, p. 789. [Strachey's article was actually titled "One Vote, One Value" (*National Review* 18 [1892]: 89–98). Strachey cited evidence that England had twenty-three fewer seats than it would have had on an allocation strictly proportional to population, with Wales having three more and Ireland twenty more than population alone would have dictated.]

favourite formula, and has at the present moment a good deal more of true political significance. One further observation is worth making. A national government should make it a primary object of its policy to provide by legislation for the automatic redistribution of seats from time to time, say, every ten years, in accordance with the growth or change of the population. No doubt I shall be told that, for some reason or other, such an arrangement is impossible. My reply is, that it exists and works with perfect ease in France. This answer will, I know, not avail me much. It is the pleasant custom of English controversialists, whatever be their political party, to assert that arrangements—*e.g.*, the registration of the title to land—are impossible, whilst everybody knows that these arrangements are in actual existence in other countries.

Unionist statesmen, again, should, and can, insist that no Home Rule Bill shall pass into law until it has received the deliberate—I might almost say the formal—sanction of the people.

This is a duty which, whatever be the result of the general election, the Unionists will certainly have the power to perform. Suppose, to illustrate my position, that the Gladstonians should obtain a majority at the General Election, and should thereupon bring into the House of Commons the Bill of 1886, modified only by the retention at Westminster of the whole or of some part of the Irish members. Every step must under these circumstances be taken to ensure, by any method of Parliamentary tactics which approves itself to our leaders, that the whole details of the Bill, the viciousness of its principle, and the dangers threatened by its passing into law should be made known to every elector. Everything, I may add, should be done to show that the Unionists will take no part whatever in the modification of a scheme which they hold to be essentially vicious. What may be the best end for securing this result depends wholly upon the circumstances of the day, one may say of the hour. The essential thing is that the whole responsibility for tampering with the unity of the nation should visibly rest on the Separatists. It is not the business of men who disbelieve entirely in the policy of Repeal to aid moderate Home Rulers in resisting the extreme demands of exacting allies. It may possibly be most desirable that all England should see the true character of the measure which alone can satisfy Parnellites or anti-Parnellites.[15] With these

---

[15] Charles Stewart Parnell was an Irish MP, leader of the Nationalist movement and the Irish Parliamentary Party, and founder of the Land League. In 1890 (two years prior to this essay) the discovery of a long-running affair precipitated his fall from leadership of

matters, however, there is no need for the moment to concern ourselves. The tactics of Parliamentary warfare depend upon the circumstances of the moment, and must be left in the hands of Parliamentary tacticians.

Suppose, however, that the calamitous day should dawn when, in spite of Unionist opposition, a Home Rule Bill passes the House of Commons. This is the point at which the power of Unionists would revive. Be they few or many in the House of Commons they could at any moment, by the action of the House of Lords, compel the submission of the Bill to the judgment of the electors before it becomes the law of the land. The obvious way of achieving this result is of course for the Peers firmly and on principle to refuse their assent to the Bill until a dissolution followed by a general election has given the electors an opportunity of pronouncing for or against the specific measure sanctioned by the House of Commons. It is, however, quite possible that under our present system even a general election might not make clear that the people really assented to the proposed innovation, and it is at least worth consideration whether under conceivable circumstances the House of Lords might not well refuse to pass the Bill unless a clause were added providing, in effect, that the Bill should not come into force unless and until the question whether the Bill should become law or not had, say, within three months, been submitted to the electors of the United Kingdom and a majority of the voters had been obtained in its favour. This introduction of the referendum into English politics, which has been already suggested by the present writer,[ii] would be, it must frankly be admitted, open to criticism, both legitimate and illegitimate. All that need here be said is that the referendum is one of those institutions which is in its principle democratic and in its working conservative; that it exists in Switzerland, that at this very moment the Government of Belgium proposes to introduce it into that country in a form suitable to a constitutional monarchy, and, lastly, that the principle, though not the name, of the referendum is known to every State, or to nearly every State, of the American Union.[iii] What might at any rate make it well worth

the movement and caused a split in the party, with most deserting him. He died several months after the publication of this essay.

[ii] See "Ought the Referendum to be introduced into England?" CONTEMPORARY REVIEW, April 1890, p. 489. [Chapter 3 of this collection.]
[iii] See "Law-making by Popular Vote; or, The American Referendum." By Ellis P. Oberholtzer. *Annals of the American Academy*, vol. ii. No. 3, p. 36. [Oberholtzer was a journalist and historian. The thrust of his essay was that the referendum and other

consideration whether such a formal appeal to the people ought not to be made before any measure of Home Rule finally passes into law, is that such a formal appeal would put the conduct of the House of Lords in its true light, and show that the object of the Peers in for the moment rejecting a measure which they did not approve was not to resist the will of the people, but simply as to act as the guardians of the national sovereignty. This is a matter on which it is impossible to lay too much stress. The House of Lords has neither the power nor the right to overrule the voice of the country; the House therefore ought never on any important question to claim more than a suspensive veto. But the House has the power, and therefore is in duty bound, to see that no measure affecting the unity of the nation shall become law until it has received the deliberate sanction of the citizens of the United Kingdom. It is well to make our minds quite clear as to the grounds which make the rejection by the House of Lords of any Home Rule Bill which can be passed by the next Parliament an imperative duty. The House is the guardian of the constitution; it is not the business of the Lords to avert changes, even though these changes be rash innovations, which their lordships thoroughly condemn. It is the business of the Lords, as in their default it would be the business of any authority in the State which could legally accomplish the object, to see that a faction does not usurp the rights of the nation. The House in fulfilling this duty performs a strictly democratic function, for it safeguards the supremacy of the people.

Two arguments may be advanced against the intervention of the House of Lords.

The question of Home Rule, it may be said, has now been before the country for six years. If in 1892 or in 1893 the electors should return a Gladstonian majority this would be a clear intimation of their wish to establish an independent Parliament in Ireland. The Peers, if they reject the measure which embodies this policy, will be guilty of defying the people of England; it is idle for the Peers to argue that they are protecting the rights of the electors when they refuse to obey the representatives who are entitled to speak on behalf of the electorate.

This argument will no doubt, should the House of Lords ever be called upon to reject a measure of Home Rule, be put forward with all

devices of direct popular lawmaking were of even deeper historical lineage in the United States than in Switzerland, and that one could expect them to keep proliferating for the foreseeable future.]

the force that can be given to it by rhetoric and passion. It is, however, in itself worthless. Even were the Bill to be passed in 1893 by the House of Commons the identical measure proposed to and rejected by the House and the country in 1886; even had the Bill of 1886 been invariably put forward by the Opposition as the embodiment of their Irish policy; even should the present Opposition regain power—if they ever happen to regain it—solely as the advocates of Home Rule; even under these circumstances, which are the strongest conceivable in favour of at once passing the Gladstonian Home Rule Bill, it would still be reasonable that a plan involving, by the admission of its supporters, the most far-reaching consequences, and endangering, in the opinion of its opponents, the power and the welfare of the country, should be once more submitted to the electors for their approval or rejection. But every one knows that none of the conditions which might be strong presumptions in favour of at once putting into force Mr. Gladstone's Home Rule policy exist, or now can by any possibility exist. The measure tendered to the nation will not be the exact Bill of 1886. One of that Bill's characteristic provisions—the retirement of the Irish members from Westminster—has been rejected by the mass of Gladstonians.[16] No leader of the Opposition has told us, or will tell us, or probably can tell us, what will be the outlines of any future scheme of Home Rule. All we know is that, whilst some Home Rulers look favourably on a gigantic scheme of Federation which is to affect England, Scotland, and Wales no less than Ireland, others show a disposition to reduce Home Rule in Ireland nearly to the dimensions of extended local self-government.

Meanwhile the members of the Opposition have gained such success as has fallen to them, not by the unceasing demand for Home Rule, but by favouring or acquiescing in all the various, and sometimes inconsistent, cries which may chance to please any section of the electorate. These tactics deserve neither praise nor blame; they are perhaps the inevitable result of the vices which attach to our existing party system. From a wire-puller's point of view they present great advantages. They have, however, this inherent defect: they deprive the Gladstonians, should they return to office, of any right, either moral or constitutional, to claim that their next measure of Home Rule, when at last revealed, has

---

[16] The 1886 First Home Rule Bill included a provision for the withdrawal of all Irish representation in Westminster. The Second Home Rule Bill of 1893, on the other hand, would indeed provide for the retention of Irish members of the Commons.

received the sanction of the majority of the electors. All we know is that the electors rejected decisively one scheme for virtually repealing the Act of Union. We have no proof whatever that in 1893 or 1894, they may not be willing to reject another and quite different scheme. Nor would the state of things be essentially changed were the Gladstonians now to produce their plan of Home Rule in a definite form. Whatever happens between this time and the meeting of the next Parliament, the question of Home Rule has been far too much complicated with other issues to make it possible to accept the result of the next election as a final and decisive verdict of the country in favour of a definite scheme for giving Ireland Parliamentary independence. It is impossible for me, in common honesty, to stop here. What might have been the case had a plan of Home Rule, supported by the whole Opposition, been under the consideration of the country for the last five or six years it is useless to determine; there is no good in speculating upon the effect of events which have not happened. But the plain truth is, that in any case no plan of Home Rule ought to become law which has not, at the very lowest, been sanctioned in its details by the result of an election taking place after the plan has been passed as a Bill through the House of Commons.

To see that this is so, let us look at the matter from another point of view. Should a Home Rule Bill—say, in 1893—be carried through the House of Commons, it either would, or would not, in reality, command the approval of the electors. On either supposition, there could be no valid objection to laying the measure before the electorate. If the Gladstonians should be right in their estimate of popular opinion, the election of a new Parliament would, in all probability, determine the matter at issue. There would at worst be a delay of, say, three or four months in putting the scheme of Home Rule into execution. No man who is not a slave to partisanship can believe that this delay would be of vital consequence. The worst evils it could by any possibility produce would be as nothing compared with the irreparable calamity of carrying a measure intended to pacify Ireland in such a manner as permanently to irritate the majority of Englishmen, because they felt they had a right to suspect that the change they detested had not really been sanctioned by the nation. Common prudence should warn statesmen not so to repeal the Act of Union as to excite among large masses of Englishmen a sense of wrong as deep as was excited among large numbers of Irishmen by the methods used by our forefathers for carrying the Act of Union. Suppose, however, what, till the matter is tested, must always remain a fair supposition, that the future Home Rule Bill of 1893, if ever it comes into existence, should not command the approval of the electorate. What are the arguments by which any sincere democrat can defend the refusal to submit the measure to the approval of the electors? I must leave it to the ingenuity and boldness of Sir William Harcourt, Mr. Morley, Sir George Trevelyan, and Mr. Labouchere to find avowable reasons in favour of the paradox, that the representatives of the people have a right to revolutionise the constitution against the will of the people whom they profess to represent.[17] Let no one try to get out of the difficulty by saying that we must assume the majority of the House of Commons to represent the people. You cannot meet facts by reliance on constitutional fictions.

The rejection of an important Bill passed by a newly-elected House of Commons, it will be argued, will expose the House of Lords to risk of destruction.

To this argument there are two short and valid replies. The first is that the risk, great or small, ought to be run. If the House of Lords cannot ensure that no serious change in the constitution shall be carried out without an appeal to the people, then the second chamber has become all but avowedly useless, and will soon become manifestly contemptible. But inutility and contemptibility are not guarantees for the existence of any institution whatever. The second reply is that the supposed risk is imaginary. The rejection of a dangerous innovation, with a view to consult the nation, must be accompanied with a pledge that the innovation shall be accepted when once all fair doubt has been removed of the nation having approved a change which may still not commend itself to the Peers. Let this be made clear, and there will not be the remotest reason to fear the anger of the people. The members of the House of Commons will no doubt rage. Parliamentary majorities burn with anger when reminded that Parliamentary majorities derive their authority and power from the support of the nation. Fox and Burke were eminent statesmen and sound constitutionalists, but they, and the majority whom they led, would gladly, had they really possessed the power, have

---

[17] These four were all leading promoters of the Liberal position on Home Rule. On Morley and Trevelyan, see page 79, note 17 and page 86, note 9 respectively. Harcourt had previously been Home Secretary and would be Chancellor of the Exchequer in Gladstone's administration that would begin later in the year. Labouchere was an anti-imperialist radical who had been one of the earliest prominent English politicians to endorse Home Rule (Dicey had been commenting on Labouchere's support since the early 1880s).

impeached Pitt for appealing from the violence of a majority formed by an immoral coalition of discordant factions to the voice of the electors.[18] But in 1783, the electors themselves showed no anger at an acknowledgment of their own power. Human nature will remain in 1893 much what it was in 1783. The electors of England entertain no idolatrous reverence for the House of Commons; they will feel no lasting or even temporary displeasure at any party who submit to the final arbitrament of the electorate, the gravest political question which for more than half a century has occupied the attention of the nation.

---

[18] On Pitt the younger, see page 9, note 9. Charles James Fox was one of the most prominent late-eighteenth-century Whig statesmen, and Burke was a Whig MP. After the close of the American War of Independence, George III wished to be rid of the Whigs and selected Pitt to head the government, but Fox and the Whig majority blocked all government action. When the king dissolved parliament Pitt and the Tories won a resounding victory.

5

The Referendum (1894)

I.

Ought the Referendum to be introduced into England?

In 1890 this question was raised in a leading periodical.[i] The enquiry received little attention and no answer. The nature and the very name of the Referendum were then unknown to English statesmen.

Four years have wrought a vast change. The Referendum we all now know is an institution under which no proposal for changing the constitution of a country can become law until it has received the direct approval of the citizens. The institution, though hitherto unfamiliar to the inhabitants of England, is well-known to numbers of the English people; it exists, though not under the name of the Referendum, in most of the States of the American Union.[ii] Sir William Harcourt's abuse and Mr. Balfour's approval are signs of the time. In periods of revolution, like the present, men live fast. The speculative question of 1890 may, it is likely enough, be transformed into the popular demand of 1895 or 1896. The Referendum is the People's Veto; the nation is sovereign, and may

---

[i] See *Contemporary Review*, April, 1890. [Chapter 3 of this edition.]

[ii] See *Referendum in America*, by E.P. Oberholtzer, with which read *Etablissement et Revision des Constitutions en Amérique et en Europe*, by C. Borgeand.

I have, it will be observed, treated the Referendum as a veto on constitutional changes. I am, of course, aware that it may be used, and is used, as a veto on ordinary legislation. [This is a misprint, the author is actually Charles Borgeaud, *Etablissement et Revision des Constitutions en Amérique et en Europe* (Paris, 1893.) Oberholtzer's *Referendum in America: A Discussion of Law-Making by Popular Vote* (Philadelphia, 1893) was an expansion of the article cited in the previous chapter and a prelude to what would be the definitive American study of the subject: *The Referendum in America, Together with Some Chapters on the Initiative and the Recall*, second edition (New York, 1912).]

well decree that the constitution shall not be changed without the direct sanction of the nation.

Whence comes this turn of public opinion? It flows in the main[iii] from a keen perception of the evils which infect our present Parliamentary system and a conviction that these evils might be mitigated by the exercise of a national veto.

The defects of Parliamentary Government as now practised in England result from the unchecked though temporary supremacy of any Party which can obtain a majority in the House of Commons. They may be summed up under four heads.

The supremacy of a Parliamentary majority, or, to use more popular though less accurate language, of the House of Commons, forbids the invention of any means for securing from attack the very bases of the Constitution. In democratic countries, such as the United States or Switzerland, the articles of the Constitution are in a strict sense the law of the land. They cannot be altered, they cannot even be menaced by the small and temporary majority of a representative assembly. The people of these Republics know that such a majority, however fairly elected, may misrepresent the will of the nation; they know and acknowledge that the foundations of the State must rest on some support firmer than the transitory wishes of a majority of the people. Under our modern English Constitution we cannot secure—witness the experience of 1893 —that the House of Commons shall even debate the gigantic constitutional innovations which it is prepared to enact.[1] The sovereignty of Parliament, I may be reminded, excludes any distinction between the articles of the Constitution and ordinary laws. The sovereignty of Parliament, I reply, is a very different thing from the supremacy of the House of Commons, and influences, I add, which have lost their power have, until recent times, in practice though not in law, maintained a distinction between laws which affect the Constitution and laws which deal with matters of everyday life. Till 1893 no statesman dreamt that a majority of from 30 to 40 warranted the attempt to dissolve the Union between Great Britain and Ireland.

---

[1] Gladstone had gotten the bill through the Commons by use of the guillotine (then a very new device; see page 124, note 19 below) to overcome Unionist opposition during the debate stages. The bill was then defeated in the Lords.

[iii] It is attributable also in part to the profound distrust in representative bodies which moulds the opinion and even the legislation of countries so different from one another as Switzerland, France, the German Empire, and the United States.

Our present scheme of government again, while it ultimately refers every question to the decision of the electors, is so worked as to prevent the electors from deciding any question on its intrinsic merits. The art of Party warfare is turning into the art of bribing and confusing the voters. The absurdity of supposing or asserting that the fair and reasonable method of obtaining a national verdict on the question whether Ireland shall be given a separate Executive and Parliament is to mix this enquiry up with the whole number of political problems raised by the Newcastle Programme, is too patent to need exposure.[2] The judge who should direct a jury that they could not properly give a verdict upon one most difficult case, unless they at the same time gave a verdict on twenty others as difficult, would not be allowed to remain a day longer upon the Bench. But the behaviour which would argue madness in a judge when asking for the verdict of a jury, is considered the wisdom or astuteness of politicians when appealing to the verdict of the country. Nor is this confusion of issues caused solely by the unscrupulosity of statesmen. The English form of Parliamentary government inevitably confounds questions of persons with questions of principle. Half, at least, of the voters who came to the poll at the last General Election meant to vote that Lord Salisbury or Mr. Gladstone, as the case might be, should be Premier, and expressed a very indirect opinion against or in favour of Home Rule. The other half were perplexed both in thought and conduct by being called upon to decide at once the two totally different questions, whether Mr. Gladstone ought to be Premier and whether the Act of Union ought to be repealed. The position of every elector was a false and absurd one, though habit has blinded us to its falsity and absurdity; for it is in the strictest sense preposterous that a man cannot support Mr. Gladstone's candidature for the Premiership of which he approves, without supporting the Home Rule policy which he condemns, or cannot, on the other hand, support Lord Salisbury's foreign policy, without sacrificing that concession of Home Rule to Ireland which he conceives to be an act of justice.

The artificial supremacy again of a Parliamentary majority, occasionally at any rate, deprives large minorities of their due political influence. Nobody supposes that the Irish representation fairly represents the Irish

---

[2] The Newcastle Programme was a landmark Liberal party declaration of 1891, arguably the first modern British party manifesto, stating Liberal commitment to a number of radical positions on issues of land reform, political equality, and church–state relations.

people. The Protestants constitute roughly about a fourth of the population; they are represented by less than a fifth of the Irish Members.

The last, the most subtle, and by far the most dangerous of the evils attributable to our present system is that it stimulates instead of mitigating the influence of Party. No one, of course, supposes that partisanship can be banished from politics. Few are the sensible men who believe that the public life of modern England can dispense with some kind of Party organization. Parties are an evil, but in the estimation of most persons a necessary evil. The reasonable complaint is not that parties exist, but that the course of events has been allowed by statesmen to increase all the evils of partisanship. If parties are to conduce to the benefit of the country, every patriotic man must with scrupulous care observe two conditions of political warfare. The first condition is that respectable leaders should not tolerate the violation of the ordinary rules of fairness and of public morality. The second condition is the practical recognition of the principle that allegiance to the nation always at a crisis overrides the demands of Party loyalty, or what is really the same thing, that there are certain matters which politicians of every school must agree to treat as of more importance than political victory. To this doctrine respectable men, whatever their political creed, will presumably in words assent. No English statesman will maintain that for the sake of placing Liberals or Conservatives in office he may rightly impede the action of the National Executive, lower the character of Parliament, excite the mutual animosities of classes, or give aid and comfort to conspirators. We all agree that the country has paramount claims upon our loyalty. But as it appears to thousands of Englishmen, the conditions of salutary political conflict have of recent years been violated. The tolerance by men otherwise entitled to esteem of slanders or abuse which they themselves would never utter, the attempts by statesmen who have themselves served the Crown to weaken the servants of the Crown when engaged in a desperate contest with crime and violence, the toleration or palliation of boycotting by politicians whom we must believe to be themselves incapable of acts of oppression and lawlessness, the intimate alliance of a whole English Party with a body of men found guilty of criminal conspiracy and of inciting to sedition and the commission of crime, are things which politicians ignore, but which have made a lasting impression on thoughtful and moderate men who stand outside politics; the suppression of Parliamentary debate by a predominant Party at the very moment when vital constitutional changes ought to have received the most ample consideration, can hardly have passed away from the not very retentive memory of the English democracy. But it is not the violence alone of partisanship which deserves notice and censure. What is at least equally important and deplorable is the condition of sentiment which Parliamentary conflicts produce. The predominance of a majority in the House of Commons, depending as it does upon the maintenance of Party discipline, engenders even among politicians of good intentions the delusion that the one virtue of public life is Party loyalty; the charge of having deserted Mr. Gladstone seems, in their eyes at least, as serious an accusation against a statesman as the charge of having betrayed the interests of his country. The belief that the triumph of a particular political connection is essential to the prosperity of the country soon turns into the conviction that persons who do not belong to this political connection cannot count as part of the nation. Party becomes everything, the Nation sinks to nothing.[iv]

These are the patent defects of Parliamentary Government as it exists in England; they constitute the new political disease known in foreign countries as "Parliamentarism." No man of sense can expect that any piece of constitutional mechanism will be a panacea for the maladies of the State. But for reasons which can be briefly assigned the introduction of the Referendum may be expected to moderate, if not to cure, the evils of Parliamentarism.

First.—The Referendum may undoubtedly be so used as to establish a clear distinction between laws which effect permanent changes in the Constitution and ordinary legislation.

Suppose, for example, that Parliament passed an enactment which may be termed the Referendum Act, providing that no Bill which affected, *e.g.*, the rights of the Crown, the constitution of either House of Parliament, or the Acts of Union, should become law until it had been submitted to the electors of the United Kingdom for their approval or disapproval, and had obtained the assent of the majority of the actual voters. Such a Referendum Act would make every man of intelligence throughout the country at once realize the difference between any

---

[iv] As I write this article I observe that here and there a so-called Liberal M.P. suggests the practical abolition of the House of Lords by an exercise of the Prerogative. The suggestion is absurd, but it is not the less significant. It betrays the existence, perhaps the prevalence, of that worst of revolutionary delusions that a faction may rightly usurp the authority of the nation and override the law of the land.

ordinary law and the fundamental laws of the realm. He would understand what now many men do not perceive, that it is one thing to pass a
Merchant Shipping Act which may be repealed or amended next year,
and quite another thing to abolish an institution such as the House of
Lords which can never be restored, or to establish an Irish Parliament
which, except at the cost of a civil war, can never be abolished. The
Referendum Act would directly secure the fundamental laws of the
country from sudden assault. This result, moreover, would be attained
in the simplest and the most effective manner. For the Referendum, or
the People's Veto, is an institution which is in absolute harmony with the
democratic principles or sentiment of the day. It violates no democratic
conviction, it constitutes the nation itself the guardian of the rights of the
nation. Add to this the consideration that the Referendum would greatly
diminish the importance of merely personal questions. Under the proposed system it would be possible, at least, for the national rejection or, it
may be, the national approval of a change in the Constitution not to
involve a change of Government. Let us suppose, for the sake of
example, that a measure for abolishing the House of Lords were submitted by Mr. Gladstone and his colleagues to the nation for its sanction,
and that this sanction were refused. The rejection of the Bill need not, if
the Gladstonians were still a majority of the House of Commons, involve
the retirement of the Ministry. Ministers might with perfect propriety
retain office. It would clearly appear that the nation wished Mr.
Gladstone to administer the affairs of the country, but did not wish to
repeal the Act of Union. There would be nothing degrading in a statesman's submission to the deliberately expressed will of the country. Any
man may bow without loss of self-respect to the commands of the nation.
No one blames Peel for acquiescence in the Reform Act; no one blames
the Protectionists for having ultimately accepted the national verdict in
favour of Free Trade.

Secondly.—The Referendum would ensure that in matters affecting the
constitution the country always came to a decision on a clear and plain issue.

That this would be the effect of the Referendum is patent; that this
effect would be beneficial is past dispute. It is impossible for any honest
or clear-headed man to maintain that it is an advantage that the electors,
who are the true sovereign of the country, should not clearly understand
the effect of their votes. The Referendum, moreover, just because it
places a clear issue before the country, is a guarantee—and under
conceivable circumstances, may be a much needed guarantee—against

reaction. As things now stand it is possible that gigantic revolutions may be the result of mere Parliamentary intrigue, and may be legally enacted without ever having received the sanction of the country. Yet changes which the nation has not really sanctioned have no moral claim to permanence, and can never be safe against the influence of reaction. Suppose, for example, that a Home Rule Bill, or a Bill giving the Parliamentary Suffrage to women, were passed to-morrow by the present Parliament in consequence of some private arrangement or compromise come to by the leaders of the two great political parties. Who is the man who can warrant that both or either of these measures had not been passed in defiance of the wish of the nation? Yet, if even the suspicion of national disapproval existed, neither of these measures could be free from the risk of reactionary change. It is to innovators or reformers, at least, as much as to Conservatives, that the Referendum should commend itself. Unwarranted innovation produces revolutionary reaction.

Thirdly.—The Referendum of its own nature gives due weight to the wishes of all voters.

Under the present condition of affairs, neither the Unionist minority in Ireland nor the Home Rule minority in England exerts its rightful influence. This evil may or may not be capable of mitigation by measures other than the Referendum. On this point I express no opinion: all I maintain is that the Referendum, as regards any measure to which it is applied, gets rid of this defect in our scheme of representation. If the question, Should the Home Rule Bill of 1893, or a measure like it, pass into law? could be put to every elector throughout the United Kingdom, each man's vote would have its due weight. The Unionist minority in Ireland and the Separatist minority in England would each exhibit its true strength.[v]

Fourthly.—The Referendum places the nation above parties or factions.

---

[v] I have assumed, for the sake of argument, what I am not prepared to concede, —namely, that a measure affecting the Act of Union with Ireland can be justly carried by a mere majority of the electors of the United Kingdom. The Act is not only a law but a treaty, and a treaty cannot in fairness be altered without the assent of all the parties thereto; that is to say, in this case, without the consent of the majority of the electors of Great Britain and Ireland respectively, and perhaps of England, Scotland, and Ireland respectively. This opinion is no novel paradox invented for the occasion; it was in principle maintained more than a century ago by Bentham (see *Fragment on Government*, Chap. IV., s. xxxvii., *note*). [Jeremy Bentham, *A Fragment on Government*, ed. J.H. Burns and H.L.A. Hart (Cambridge, 1988), 102–3.]

This is its highest recommendation. The existence of an appeal to the country reminds us all that when orators have exhausted their rhetoric and Members of Parliament have given their vote the final decision of the nation's destiny must be referred to a more august tribunal than the House of Commons, or even than Parliament. Sentiment plays no small part in public life, and thinkers who appreciate the force of moral feeling will attach great importance to the formal acknowledgment of the nation's supreme authority. But the advocates of a direct appeal to the people need not base their advocacy solely on the tendency of such an appeal to stimulate sound national feeling. They can show that the Referendum increases the authority of the nation as compared with the power of parties or sections, and this in two very practical ways. The Referendum, in the first place, by compelling electors to vote on a single issue of profound importance, leads them on this one occasion at least to follow their own convictions rather than their Party connections. Men who vote at an ordinary General Election for a particular Member who advocates a Party programme must in general vote with reference to the interests of their Party. Every elector, therefore, for the sake of measures for which he cares much supports other measures for which he cares little or nothing: A swallows a Home Rule Bill because he wishes for an Eight Hours Bill: B, with great difficulty, supports an Eight Hours Bill because he wishes Ireland to have Home Rule: whilst C, who cares neither for restrictions on the hours of labour nor for Home Rule, votes in effect for a Home Rule Bill and an Eight Hours Bill because he is a zealous advocate of Local Option.[3] It is probable that were each measure separately submitted to each elector each would vote only for the measures which he actually approves: A would reject Home Rule; B would reject the Eight Hours Bill; and C, while rejecting both the Home Rule Bill and the Eight Hours Bill, would vote only for the establishment of Local Option. The Referendum, in the second place, would bring men to the ballot-box who now hardly vote at all. Some of the most intelligent and most unbiassed members of the community who rarely take part in Parliamentary Elections would vote for or against a definite proposal,

---

[3] A local option is a referendum in which residents of a locality decide on a policy question. At the time Dicey was writing, using the term *local option* without specification further referred to the subject of liquor sales; as part of the Newcastle Programme the Liberals supported allowing localities to decide by popular vote whether to permit the sale of alcohol. The local option in reference to alcohol was in wide use across the Atlantic.

say a Bill for the abolition of the House of Lords. Abstention from electoral contests is always a dereliction of civic duty. Still human nature being what it is, abstention is often a natural, if not a pardonable, offence. A Gladstonian of Birmingham hardly cares to vote against Mr. Chamberlain. Unionists at Cork who cannot by any possibility return a representative of their own way of thinking shrink from coming to the polling booths. When once a single issue is submitted to the judgment of the people the whole aspect of affairs will be changed. Let us keep to the case of Home Rule. When a Home Rule Bill is submitted to the judgment of the electors every man will know that he must act then and there. Every Unionist who dreads the rule of Mr. Healy, every Nationalist who desires an Irish Parliament, must acknowledge the occurrence of a final crisis. The men who are most indifferent when minor issues are confusedly placed before them will rise, it is to be hoped, to the requirements of this great occasion. Party connections, personal preferences, or individual fancies must surely lose their influence when every man is called upon both to hear and to pronounce the verdict of the nation.

The advantages of the Referendum may possibly be outweighed by more than compensating evils. The consideration of the objections which may be fairly urged against the People's Veto must however be reserved for another occasion.

6

Will the Form of Parliamentary Government Be Permanent? (1899)

The prevalent faith in the permanence of Parliamentary government rests on two facts of most unequal significance.

Of these the first, and by far the most important, is the endurance and the success of the English constitution.

The English Parliament has existed more or less under its present form for more than six centuries, and as one generation has succeeded another generation the power of two Houses, and especially of the House of Commons, has increased until at last they have become the center of our public life.

The impressiveness of this fact is increased by the knowledge that the position, the influence, and the character of the English Parliament has varied from age to age. For this variation establishes the capacity inherent in representative government for adapting itself to the changing circumstances of different eras. This is just one of those phenomena which impress the imagination. The constitution, which in a certain sense took its present form under Edward I., has been found to suit times as different from the age of the Plantagenets as from our own, and step by step, as the power of England has increased, so the constitution has proved itself capable of expansion.[1] The constitution has been flexible enough to admit of the incorporation of Wales with England, the union of England and Scotland, and the union of Great Britain

---

[1] Edward I called the first parliament in 1275. Edward I was of the House of Plantagenet, from which all English monarchs were taken from 1145 to 1485 and between branches of which the War of the Roses was fought in the fifteenth century.

with Ireland.[2] A system, moreover, framed originally for the government of part of a small island, has by a course of almost unconscious adjustment developed so as to meet the wants of a large empire, and the body which was originally the Parliament merely of England, has come to control in different manners and in different degrees colonies and dependencies whereof some, such as Victoria or the Canadian Dominion, have attained to virtual independence, and others, such as the whole Indian Empire, are in truth governed by officials who in the last resort take their orders from a Parliamentary committee. Nor can the severest censor deny that English constitutionalism has, if judged by its fruits, been crowned with extraordinary success. Parliament, no doubt, has committed the grossest errors, but the same thing may be said of every government which has ever existed; the smallness of the wisdom which is employed upon and suffices for the ruling of the world has become proverbial. In the United States, at any rate, is it at all likely that the incapacity and want of foresight displayed in colonial affairs by George the Third and his people will be underrated, — though it may still remain a question to be solved only by the history of the future whether the folly and incompetence of Presidents may not in the long run prove as disastrous as the ignorance and arrogance of Kings? But when the blunders of Parliament are weighed against the achievements of the English people, candid critics will own that a large balance stands to the credit of constitutional government. For England under, if not by virtue of, her constitution has in every age come safely through storms in which other nations have made shipwreck. The constitution, in which must be included our whole judicial system, kept alive the traditions of freedom throughout the anarchy of the War of the Roses and prevented the turbulence of aristocratic factions from destroying the vitality of the people. National prosperity under the Tudors was due, it may be asserted, to the crown rather than to the two houses. But this assertion, even if its truth be granted, does not substantially detract from the services rendered to the country by representative institutions. For the existence of Parliament either checked the tyranny of the crown, or directed

---

[2] Wales was incorporated into England via the Laws of Wales Acts 1535–42, Scotland and England were united in 1707, and, as mentioned above, Great Britain and Ireland were united in 1800. As glimpsed in Chapter 9, Dicey repeatedly expressed the conviction that the Union with Scotland was the finest act of statesmanship in British history. Despite his staunch Unionism, he had many more reservations about how the union with Ireland was effected.

despotic power into channels in which its exercise, while it increased the authority of the King, favoured the welfare of the nation. Under the Parliamentary system of England the country went with success through the social and ecclesiastical revolution which we call the reformation, and suffered not one tithe of the miseries which crushed the hope of establishing religious freedom in France and deferred for generations the unity and the prosperity of Germany. That the constitution enabled the nation to resist the despotism of the Stuarts and ultimately to establish the reign of religious toleration is patent to every student.[3] A matter which is less observed, and therefore deserves more attention, is that English constitutionalism restored the public morality which had been shaken by the revolutionary movements of the seventeenth century. Compare the age of Walpole with the age of Peel.[4] Mark the gradual revival of high public spirit which had taken place during the intervening period. From such a comparison it is impossible not to conclude that, whatever the defects of the unreformed Parliament, there was something to be found in the institutions of England which not only allowed but encouraged an improvement in the general character of public life.[5] Parliamentary constitutionalism, lastly, carried the country triumphantly through the conflict with Jacobinical and Imperial France, and during the long peace which ensued procured for England without the evils of revolution all the beneficial reforms which on the Continent have been attained (if at all) at the cost of violence and injustice.[6] No one, then, can wonder that the combined stability and flexibility of English institutions should have made a lasting impression on the imagination of the modern world.

The second great fact on which rests the faith in representative government is the extension of the Parliamentary system throughout the whole of the civilized world.

---

[3] In the Glorious Revolution of 1688, James II, the fourth of the Stuart kings and a Catholic, was deposed and the Protestants Mary II and William III seated on the throne at the invitation of parliament. In the following year the Act of Toleration was passed which granted rights of religious worship, although not political rights, to Protestant dissenters.

[4] On Walpole and Peel, see page 38, note 25 and page 51, note 30, respectively. Walpole was famous for his use of patronage and "corruption" to hold together his parliamentary majority and shore up support for the Hanoverian monarchy against the claims of the Stuarts.

[5] "Unreformed" refers to the period before the 1832 passage of the First Reform Act.

[6] Dicey is referring to the conflicts known as the French Revolutionary and Napoleonic Wars, which ran from 1792 to 1815. That England was a "land of reform" in contrast to the foreign lands of revolution was one of the central tropes of British thought in the long nineteenth century.

This system of government has now been adopted by all the states of Europe except Russia and Turkey; it prevails, speaking broadly, in every country which has drawn its civilization from European sources; it has at last invaded even the far East. The extraordinary, not to say excessive, imitativeness of the Japanese has enabled them to create, as it were at one stroke, a copy or a caricature of modern constitutionalism.[7] They have their constitutional King, their Cabinets, their Ministerial majorities, their Opposition, and their Obstructives, and have reproduced the flaws as accurately as the beauties of popular government in its latest shape. Whether this importation of the political wares of Europe into an Eastern country will turn out for the benefit of Japan, time alone can show; but the adoption of the forms of constitutionalism by an Eastern race utterly devoid of Parliamentary traditions is conclusive evidence that to the men of to-day representative government appears to be an essential characteristic of a civilized or progressive state.

This state of opinion is perfectly natural, yet there exist considerations which may suggest a doubt whether its soundness is established by the facts on which it admittedly rests.

The constitutional history of England, in the first place, is exceptional, not to say anomalous, and any careful reasoner must be on his guard against applying to the inhabitants of other lands lessons drawn from the experience of Englishmen. One example among a score which lie ready to hand is enough to illustrate my meaning. The insular character of the country has saved the liberties of England from destruction. It is difficult to see how they could possibly have struck deep root or been gradually extended on the European continent, or indeed in any country exposed to the attacks of powerful neighbors and hence compelled to strengthen the authority of the executive and ultimately to keep on foot a large standing army. At the present moment it is hard to realize how insignificant were the armed forces of England during the period when Parliament laid the foundations of its authority. At one crisis, indeed, the protection of English freedom necessitated the creation of a standing army and submission to the unlimited power of a successful general. This attempt to use military force on behalf of Parliamentary freedom was made under the most favourable circumstances; Cromwell was by training a civilian, his soldiers were republicans. But the experiment

---

[7] The Meiji Constitution of 1889 diminished the political power of the emperor and established a constitutional monarchy with separation of powers.

ended in failure. Supremacy of the army was found incompatible with respect for the liberties of Englishmen, and the Restoration was even more the victory of the Parliament than of the crown.[8] The United Kingdom now maintains armed forces which a past generation would have considered, and not without reason, a menace to civil liberty. But British armies now exist for the protection of the whole British Empire, and for this purpose they are not large, and a navy is a force which, except in the rarest cases, cannot be used as the means for effecting revolution. Parliament, moreover, — and this is, after all, the main point, — has now become an essential part of English institutions and the whole English people have been thoroughly imbued with Parliamentary ideas and Parliamentary traditions. The most vigilant friends of freedom therefore are assured that they may now witness with indifference the creation of armies far more numerous than the regiments which under Cromwell defied and dissolved Parliaments. There is no need to illustrate my point further. It is clear that both the annals of England and the experience of other countries during the last hundred years make it in the highest degree doubtful how far English institutions can with success be transplanted to countries of which the development has been utterly different from the exceptional history of England; it assuredly were rash to assume that English experience proves Parliamentary government to be a form of polity adapted to the wants of every civilized people.

This proof is, it is supposed, afforded by our second great fact, namely, the expansion of Parliamentary government throughout the world.

Any thinker, however, who has learnt how immense is the influence in human affairs of imitativeness will hesitate to conclude that the rapid growth of a fashion proves its fitness to meet a given want. In politics fashion is omnipotent. Parliamentary government has during the last half century become fashionable, and the nations who one after another have adopted representative institutions have acted from the natural desire to imitate neighbours whose prosperity or power they admired. Japanese statesmen have perceived that Europe is strong. They wish to be like Europeans; they have adopted the political dress which is fashionable in

---

[8] After the English Civil War which saw the deposition and execution of the Stuart monarch Charles I, the victorious general Oliver Cromwell instituted the Commonwealth, which was grounded in military support. After Cromwell's death the regime fell apart and Charles I's son was called upon to assume the throne, beginning the Restoration period which lasted until the Glorious Revolution. Dicey wrote extensively about the political and constitutional history of the Commonwealth.

Europe, just as they have many of them put on tail coats and tall hats. In each case they have wished to look like Europeans. They have acted exactly as did the Franks or the Lombards when they adopted the titles or the laws existing in the Roman Empire. If the desire to acquire Western habits had prevailed in Japan at the time when Louis the Fourteenth was the most admired of European potentates, Japanese statesmen would have organized an administration modelled on the administrative system of France; they would have followed the fashion of Paris rather than of London.[9] The sequacity of human nature is not after all peculiar to any one race or country. The statesmen of modern Spain, Italy, or Mexico have under different forms followed the prevalent fashion of their day. Whether the constitution of a country should be a Parliamentary Monarchy, a Centralized Republic, or a Federal Commonwealth has in many cases been determined not by any rational conviction that a particular kind of government was adapted to meet the wants of a given people, but by the unconscious desire of constitution makers to follow the reigning fashion of their day, which in its turn depended upon the predominant prestige of England or of France, or of the United States.

A political invention, however, it may be said, — and Parliamentary government is nothing else than a more or less recently invented piece of political mechanism, — is like other products of human ingenuity, such, for example, as the steam-engine or the electric telegraph, adopted in one country or another in part at least because of its proved utility. The wide diffusion, therefore, of parliamentary institutions affords a presumption of their being found of advantage by the nations who adopt them.

This remark is obviously true; its force, however, is diminished by two reflections. The political fashion, in the first place, in which we are concerned is, historically speaking, of recent origin. In 1788—the year before that meeting of the French States-General which opened the revolutionary drama[10]—Parliamentary institutions were, broadly speaking, the exclusive possession of the English people. They existed only in England or in countries which were or had been colonies or dependencies of England. In Denmark and in Sweden, indeed, Parliaments had at

---

9 The Lombards and the Franks were the Germanic peoples who succeeded to dominance in Italy after the fall of the Roman Empire. Louis XIV was King of France from 1643 to 1715 and the archetypal absolute monarch of *ancien régime* Europe.

10 The Estates General was a representative assembly, called by the King, of the three "orders" or "estates" of France: the clergy, the nobility, and the third estate. It was convened by Louis XVI in 1789 after having been dormant since 1614.

dates which were then still recent been powerful, but in these countries they had been, or were about to be, abolished, and in each case the triumph of the crown was due to the favour of the people. There has, in the second place, been nothing more remarkable than the constant fluctuations of popular sentiment in regard to the advantages of Parliamentary constitutionalism. The French Revolution was a movement directed against social inequality and political despotism and naturally kindled enthusiasm for the best known and most successful form of popular government. At one moment therefore it seemed reasonable to anticipate that the Parliamentary system might be established in the leading states of Europe. This expectation was disappointed. Napoleon invented a new form of enlightened despotism more opposed to that freedom of discussion which is the very soul of Parliamentary government than were the monarchies which were destroyed or shaken by the Revolution. His fall brought English constitutionalism into vogue, but neither the overthrow of Napoleonic Imperialism nor the triumph of England did as much as might have been expected to propagate the faith in Parliamentary freedom. Consider the state of Europe in 1845. In several important countries, as for example, in France, in Belgium, and in the Spanish Peninsula, were to be found constitutional monarchies which reproduced at any rate the onward forms of English freedom. In some of these countries the reproduction was far more nominal than real. Still, in 1845 the realm of liberty, as that term is understood in England, has been extended, but against this gain must be set the supremacy of despotism in Italy and practically throughout the whole of the Austrian Empire.[11] Turn now to the year 1858. We shall find that the revolutions of 1848, though most of them futile, had in one or two countries, notably in Piedmont and in Switzerland, established a permanent form of Parliamentary government. But progress had been balanced by retrogression. In France the Empire had been re-established, and however odious the treachery of the *coup d'état*, re-established with the acquiescence if not with the active approbation of the French nation.[12] But the

[11] The Austrian Empire under the Hapsburgs then covered much of central and eastern Europe including northern Italy.
[12] Since 1848 Louis-Napoleon Bonaparte had been president of the French Second Republic. However, according to the Republican constitution presidents were restricted to a single term. After an effort to alter the constitution failed, Louis-Napoleon staged a *coup d'état* on 2 December 1851. In the next year a new constitution and the establishment of the Second Empire were established in two plebiscites.

Empire, whatever its other characteristics, was, and always will be, the negation of Parliamentary government. Throughout the Austrian dominion the rule of despotism had been strengthened and the constitutional rights of Hungary had been destroyed. The date of 1858 is worth notice; it marks the end of an age. In 1859 the war which partially liberated Italy opened something like a new era. Since that year Parliaments have been reintroduced or re-established in almost every European state. Still this fact, important though it be, does not entitle us to disregard the changes of public opinion in regard to Parliamentary government. They prove the possibility, at any rate, that a nation which, in accordance with the fashion of the day, has adopted, may, as the fashion alters, surrender a Parliamentary system of government; it cannot claim to stand on the same level as any invention which has so manifestly benefited mankind that it will not, or rather cannot, be given up by those who have once experienced its advantages.

The belief, then, in the permanence of the Parliamentary form of government rests, after all, on a narrow and uncertain basis of historical fact; it is founded, as we have seen, first, on the admitted success of the British constitution, and next, on the experience of something between fifty and a hundred years.

Against the force of these two facts is to be placed a phenomenon of which, whatever its permanent importance, no candid observer can deny the existence.

Faith in Parliaments has undergone an eclipse; in proportion as the area of representative government has extended, so the moral authority and prestige of representative government has diminished.

That this is so must be patent to any man old enough to remember the condition of opinion as late even as the middle of this century. When the revolutions of 1848 gave to reformers or revolutionists an unexpected though transient opportunity for putting their theories into action, there arose in one European country after another the demand for a "constitution," a word which in those days invariably included the introduction, or the extention, of Parliamentary government. The truth is that at that date there was not a friend of the progress of freedom throughout Europe who did not believe that the extension of representative institutions of one kind or another throughout the civilized world would confer the greatest benefit on mankind. On this matter, and perhaps on this matter alone, English statesmen, such as Macaulay, Palmerston, or Gladstone, agreed not only with continental Parliamentarians, such as

Cavour, but also with revolutionists of the most different types, such, for instance, as Lamartine, Kossuth, or Mazzini.[13] Compare now this universal faith which marked the middle with the skepticism which marks the close of the nineteenth century. From every part of the world is heard criticism or censure of Parliamentary institutions. They may all be summed up in the one word, "Parliamentarism." It is an un-English term, though it can now make good its claim to the wide if not indiscriminate hospitality extended by Dr. Murray's dictionary to any word, however uncouth, which has been used by any scribbler who purports to write the English language.[14] It is of continental origin and expresses an idea which has till recently been foreign and almost unnatural to Englishmen, namely, the moral breakdown of Parliamentary government.

It were easy to cite proofs of the discredit, though it may well be only temporary discredit, into which Parliamentary constitutionalism has fallen. The increasing rigidity and minuteness of American constitutions, the Referendum of Switzerland, — which, by the way, exists in reality though not in name, in all but every State of the American Republic, — the proposals for elaborate schemes of proportional representation, the

---

[13] Thomas Babington Macaulay was a leading Whig statesman and one of the most successful men of letters of the early-/mid-Victorian periods. Henry John Temple, 3rd Viscount Palmerston was a conservative Whig-Liberal Foreign Secretary and Prime Minister of the middle third of the century. Camilo Benso, Count of Cavour was, as Prime Minister of Sardinia, a leader of Italian unification. Alphonse de Lamartine was a famous poet-historian and a key figure of the 1848 Revolution. Lajos Kossuth was a Hungarian revolutionary who sought to establish an independent democratic Hungary in 1848. Giuseppe Mazzini was a father of the Italian revolutionary and nationalist movements.

[14] The dictionary which Dicey is lampooning here is the *Oxford English Dictionary*, which was in the midst of the nearly four-decade-long publication in installments of the first edition. Dicey's jibe is intriguing for several reasons. First, James Murray, the *OED*'s editor, was Dicey's neighbor in Oxford, and the two were, at least on one notable occasion, in an acrimonious relationship: Dicey objected that Murray's initial plan for his Scriptorium (the central office, so to speak, of the great lexicographical project) was destroying the view from his house. As a result, Murray sunk the scriptorium a few feet, which made it an insalubrious working environment. Second, Dicey's contempt for the inclusion of parliamentarism remarkably anticipates the entry for the word by a half-decade. The relevant fascicle (*P-Pennached*) only appeared at the end of 1904, and serious work on the letter *P* had not commenced and would not commence until 1903. In the end Murray did indeed treat the word, as Dicey had feared, in a neutral way and not as a foreign importation betokening loss of faith in representative institutions. (The first edition of the *OED* defined parliamentarism simply as "a parliamentary system of government.") Dicey was not alone in his frustration with the *OED*'s policy of inclusiveness and perceived lack of discrimination between good English words and usages in poor taste.

denunciation of the party system by brilliant and weighty writers who express in language which few men can command sentiments which thousands of men entertain, all bear witness to the widespread distrust of representative systems under which it, occasionally at least, may happen that an elected Parliament represents only the worst side of a great nation. But it is needless to produce evidence of a state of opinion of which few observers will deny the existence. For my present purpose the important matter is to define its causes.

These causes may be summed up under three or several different heads.

First. The general adoption of representative government has of necessity robbed Parliaments of much of their prestige.

As long as the countries which possessed representative legislatures were few and, as it happened, prosperous, it was easy to attribute their well-being to their admirable constitutions and to believe that any people would prosper who acquired the right to be their own lawgivers. It was easy also for every enthusiast to believe that a Parliament which represented the people would enact every law by which the people would benefit, or in other words every law which the reformer or philanthropist himself thought beneficial.[15] These pleasing anticipations which at revolutionary crises have unduly influenced the judgment even of wise and experienced men were doomed to disappointment. Now that every country has its Parliament and countries still differ greatly in prosperity, we know for certain that representative institutions cannot insure national good fortune. Parliamentary legislatures, again, represent the folly no less than the wisdom of their electors and their legislation is often simply a record of human stupidity. A law, moreover, which is approved by one reformer is opposed to the firmest convictions of another; there never has been and never will be a law-giving body, be it King, Parliament, or popular assembly, the laws whereof do not offend at least as many persons as they conciliate.

Secondly. Some of the blessings which persons who could not be called optimists reasonably expected from the extension of popular government have not in fact been conferred upon the nations which of modern times have enjoyed representative institutions.

Take as an example of this the case of Italy. Not much more than forty years have passed since the best and wisest men throughout every

---

[15] Dicey is undoubtedly mocking, among others, his younger self and the "academic liberal" set among which he then ran.

country in Europe hailed with delight and hope the new birth of the Italian people. Every one had noted that under the most unfavourable circumstances Italy, though torn in pieces by foreigners and held in intellectual darkness by priestly tyranny and persecution, could still produce men of high genius and undoubted patriotism. The expulsion of foreigners and the introduction of civil and religious liberty would, it was confidently supposed, give new life to Italy, and enable her to form citizens who might in heart and intellect be the guides of modern Europe. Italy has now become as free as any country in the world; she is ruled, and has been wholly ruled for more than twenty-five years, by a freely elected Parliament, convened by a constitutional monarch who has been absolutely loyal to the constitution, yet the hopes of the friends of Italy have been disappointed. They have been doomed to witness a historical paradox. The rule of the foreigner, of the despot, and of the priest gave birth to Italians whose names history will not easily forget; Italian freedom and independence have produced, as far as the outer world can see, nothing but politicians who for the most part may be happy to reflect that the insignificance which deprives them of contemporary fame may protect them from posthumous infamy. Where are the successors of Cavour, of Mazzini, of Garibaldi, or of Manin?[16] Assuredly they are not to be found on the seats of the Parliament at Rome. No sane man, let me add, can wish for the restoration of despotism or doubt that Italy contains, as she always has contained, men of genius and greatness. But there are many observers at this moment who, unreasonably enough it may be, doubt whether Parliamentary constitutionalism of the modern type is likely to bring what is best and noblest in Italy to the service of a country which certainly needs the guidance of leaders endowed with wisdom and honesty. Add to this that Italy is not the only country in which representative government has of recent years failed to foster the best fruits of freedom.

Thirdly. The circumstances of modern life divest representative assemblies of dignity.

Publicity is a necessity, but it is also the bane of public life. It were easier for Englishmen to admire the House of Commons, and I conjecture for American citizens to admire the House of Representatives, were it not possible to read the daily records of Parliamentary or Congressional debates. There are certainly few works containing information of any

---

[16] On the first three listed, see note page 30, note 12 and page 120, note 13. Daniele Manin was a leader of the revolutionary movement in Venice.

worth whatever which in point of dreariness can rival the pages of Hansard. On the whole, the world has gained by the existence of a free press, and yet the instinctive hostility of the House of Commons to reporters was not in every way unreasonable. The newspapers inevitably display to the world the paltry and undignified side of Parliamentary government. There is no valid ground to suppose that the amount of talent to be found among English Members of Parliament at the end of the nineteenth century is less than can be discovered among their predecessors at the end of the eighteenth century. But there is one great difference. Every Member of Parliament, whatever his talents, is now more or less before the world. We all know the weak sides of our great men, and what is perhaps even worse, the utter commonplaceness of our second-rate and third-rate politicians. At the end of the last century the few men who were known to the mass of the nation were leaders, and these leaders never came before the public in undress. Even fifty years ago, Lord Palmerston could jeer at Mr. Bright for "starring it in the provinces."[17] The jest was even then a little out of date; it would now be unmeaning. To "star it in the provinces" has for the last twenty years or more been a main occupation of every public man from the premier downwards who was, or aspired to be, a leader.

Fourthly. Recent years have revealed the liability of Parliament to two weaknesses or diseases, the existence of which was not noted even by an observer so acute as Bagehot.[18]

The first of these maladies is the tyranny of minorities. We now know that by means of obstruction a determined minority may thwart the will of a majority and undermine at once the authority and efficiency of a legislature. This disease, it is true, can, as we also know, be checked by its proper remedy, but the closure, which is as yet the only discovered safeguard against obstruction, is from the point of view of a Parliamentarian such as Bagehot, nearly as bad as the malady it cures. For the closure puts an end to that free debate which is essential to

---

[17] By "starring it in the provinces" was meant the "demagogic" routine of holding large public rallies in order to cultivate a mass political base, rather than restraining one's political speech to the confines of Westminster.

[18] Walter Bagehot, essayist, banker, and editor of the *Economist*, authored among other important works *The English Constitution* in 1867, which was credited with cutting through outdated abstractions and providing a realistic account of Britain's fundamental institutions. Dicey regarded Bagehot with something close to veneration and sought to emulate him in several ways, including his comparative approach to the study of constitutions and his combination of commentary on current events with broader historical and philosophical reflection.

government by discussion,[19] and the possibility of dispensing with discussion suggests at least the idea which is fatal to the moral authority of Parliament, that Parliamentary debate is in itself of no great value.

The second of these diseases is the failure of a Parliament fairly elected by fairly formed constituencies to represent, even on matters of importance, the wishes of the nation.

This is a risk against which you will find little or no warning in the pages of the older writers on the constitution, such as Hallam, Freeman or Bagehot.[20] Yet the possibility of such failure has now become notorious. Whenever the citizens of an American State reject changes proposed by a constitutional convention, whenever the people of Switzerland on a Referendum veto laws passed by the Federal Assembly, whenever a newly elected English House of Commons condemns by a decisive majority a bill which has been passed by a House of Commons which has just been dissolved, it is patent that representative bodies have misrepresented the wishes of their electors. Let it too be noted that this failure on the part of a representative assembly to perform its main function need not arise from any treachery or misconduct on the part of its members. The Swiss people have again and again re-elected to seats in Parliament the very men whose legislation the Swiss people have refused to sanction. On the merits or defects of direct legislation by the people it is for my present purpose unnecessary to pronounce any opinion whatever. All that is here insisted upon is that the possibility of a representative body failing to represent the persons who elected it detracts from the authority of a Parliament.

Lastly. Parliaments have suffered in credit because they have of recent years been set to do work for the performance of which an assembly is by its nature unfit.

This is assuredly true of the ancient Parliament of England. The aim of the reformers who at the end of the last and in the early part of the present century extolled the merits of representative government was in the main to destroy all the monopolies and privileges which hampered the exercise of individual freedom. Now for purposes of destruction a

---

[19] "Government by discussion" is another homage to Bagehot, although the latter was not alone in using the phrase. The closure (or "cloture" in American usage) and the guillotine are motions for limiting or terminating debate. They were still new at the time of writing, having been introduced in the 1880s in response to the obstruction tactics of Irish MPs.

[20] Henry Hallam was one of the towering Whig historians of the first half of the nineteenth century. On Bagehot and Freeman, see page 123, note 18 and page 30, note 13, respectively.

popular assembly is the best of instruments. The Long Parliament by two short ordinances abolished the English Monarchy and the House of Lords.[21] The National Assembly of France in one night's sitting destroyed all the remnants of feudalism, and if "the St. Bartholomew of Abuses," as a French historian has named the 4th of August, 1789, did not in reality make as clean a sweep as the Assembly desired of the *ancien régime*, the partial failure was due to the impossibility of reforming the land laws of any country without constructive legislation which replaces the laws which you abolish by some new and better system.[22] Nor is it revolutionary assemblies alone which are good at destruction. To repeal the penal laws which oppressed the Catholics, to do away with every form of Protection, to disestablish the Irish Church, were feats which lay well within the competence and were admirably performed by the Parliament of the United Kingdom.[23] There is no reason to suppose that Parliamentary capacity for destruction is a whit lessened. If the demand of the age were still a demand for destructive legislation, the Parliament of England would prove as efficient as ever. A change, however, has gradually come over the spirit of our times. Modern reformers have, at any rate for the last quarter of a century, called for constructive legislation which it is supposed will meet the needs of the country and render happier the life of the masses. We have passed, or we have partially passed, and this almost unconsciously, from the creed of Individualism to the creed of Collectivism.[24] This new form of faith imposes upon a representative assembly the very work which a large representative

---

[21] The Long Parliament was in session from 1640 to 1660, that is, for the Civil War and the Interregnum. In 1648 Cromwell's army purged it of members opposed to trying King Charles. In early 1649, the "Rump" Parliament, consisting of the remnant that survived Pride's Purge, abolished both the monarchy and the House of Lords.

[22] The phrase was that of the liberal historian François Mignet. On 4 August 1789, in a fit of collective exuberance, the National Assembly declared the entire feudal system abolished. The details, naturally, took a while longer to work out.

[23] Dicey is referring here to the laws on Catholic Emancipation (1829), the repeal of the Corn Laws (1846), and the disestablishment of the Irish Church (1869), respectively.

[24] Dicey would put this periodization into canonical form a few years later in his *Lectures on the Relation of Law and Public Opinion*, which postulated that English legislation had passed through three periods in the nineteenth century: reaction and stagnation after the French Revolution in the first couple of decades; Benthamite, classical-liberal individualism in the long middle decades of the century; and then a turn toward collectivism and state interference toward the end of the century. He had already delivered this thesis at Harvard a few years earlier, and indeed elaborated it more or less fully in a series of articles in *The Nation* in the mid-1880s.

assembly is not well fitted to perform. The declining belief in the doctrine of *laissez-faire* connects naturally with the fall in the credit and moral authority of Parliament.

If there be any truth in these reflections, we arrive at results which, though far removed from the field of practical politics, may have a certain speculative interest. The belief that the Parliamentary system, as it now exists, is likely to be permanent, is based, we find, on certain real and important facts, which, however, afford a narrow and insufficient foundation for the conclusion rested upon them. It becomes clear again, on the other hand, that during the latter part of the nineteenth century the prestige of Parliamentary government has declined. This loss of credit or moral authority is due (it is submitted) to definite causes of very varying importance. To what extent these causes are likely to continue in operation and how far they may be removed or counteracted, is one of those questions on which a prudent thinker will do well to pronounce no definite opinion, but leave it to the consideration of intelligent readers.

7

The Referendum and Its Critics (1910)

1. *The Referendum in Switzerland.* By Simon Deploige, advocate. London: Longmans, 1898.
2. *Popular Government.* Four essays. By Sir Henry S. Maine. London: Murray, 1885.
3. *The Crisis of Liberalism: New Issues of Democracy.* By J.A. Hobson. London: P.S. King and Son, 1909.
4. *By the People. Arguments and Authorities for Direct Legislation, or the Initiative and the Referendum. Direct Legislation Record.* By E. Pomeroy and others. Newark, N.J. (Published quarterly.)
5. *The American Commonwealth.* By James Bryce. Two vols. Third edition. London: Macmillan, 1893.
6. *The Reform of the House of Lords.* By W.S. McKechnie. Glasgow: MacLehose, 1909.

In 1880 the name of the Referendum was unknown to Englishmen. In 1885 Maine revealed to his countrymen the existence in Switzerland of this 'most recent of democratic inventions.' His 'Popular Government' was marked by all his brilliancy of style. It lacked something of his usually sound judgment. It was nothing else than a clever diatribe against democracy. To Maine the Referendum was merely a *reductio ad absurdum* of democratic doctrine. No man of half his ability could in 1910 treat this constitutional invention after Maine's manner of supercilious superiority. The lapse of twenty-five years has worked a revolution in public opinion. The name of the Referendum is now on the lips of every person interested in political theory. The general nature of the institution is pretty well understood. The Referendum is perceived to be the formal acknowledgment in matters of legislation of the nation's veto. Under whatever shape it exists we all now know that the Referendum is the

127

application of the following principle, namely, that—if for convenience I may use English parliamentary terms—no Bill of serious importance, e.g. a Bill changing the constitution of either House of Parliament, shall pass into law or become an Act of Parliament until and unless it has been submitted to, and received the sanction of, the electors who vote on the question, whether such Bill shall or shall not become an Act of Parliament. This Referendum, or appeal to the people, or national veto, aims at achieving one or both of two compatible objects, namely, first, that a Bill of importance shall not, even though passed by both Houses of Parliament, become an Act or law of the land against the deliberate will of the nation; and secondly, that when a legislative deadlock arises through the one House of Parliament passing and the other rejecting a given Bill, the deadlock shall be terminated by such Referendum, or appeal to the electors as aforesaid, on the question whether the Bill shall or shall not become an Act of Parliament. The fact is, as is now well known, that, even when Maine wrote, the institution was not peculiar to Switzerland. It derives its name from that country, but it had long existed, if not in name yet in reality, in all the States of the American Commonwealth. The Referendum now forms part of the institutions of the Australian Commonwealth. It has been introduced into that new polity under the Constitution Act passed by the Imperial Parliament.[1] At this time of day an institution which only amused or amazed Maine can no longer be treated as merely an absurd though legitimate deduction from fallacies which, as he held, vitiated the whole theory of popular government. Like other constitutional contrivances which have stood the test of time, the Referendum is the product of circumstances and experience. Lecky was no Radical. But he foretold, as early as 1896, that the idea embodied in the Referendum was destined to exert a wide influence, and might be used to temper the defects of parliamentary government.[2]

---

[1] Dicey is referring to the Commonwealth of Australia Act 1900, which itself had been preceded by a series of referenda in Australia approving the core of the constitutional text. Following the Swiss model, it established the amendment of the constitution by a system of double majority referendums – that is, an amendment was ratified only if it received a majority of individual voters nationwide and a majority vote in a majority of the states.

[2] W.E.H. Lecky was an Irish Protestant historian. Like Dicey, he considered himself a liberal but ardently defended the Union and entered the Commons for the Unionist party. Dicey is referring here to Lecky's *Democracy and Liberty*, 2 vols. (London, 1896), a somber work which predicted many ills from modern democracy including socialist expropriation and advocated the referendum (as well as proportional representation, with which Dicey had less sympathy).

His forecast has been completely justified by the event. The Referendum at this moment arouses the attention and excites the hope of many reformers. But their approval of a democratic institution is not due to any increased enthusiasm for the principles preached by Rousseau and at one time adopted throughout the Continent of Europe by all Republicans. Even in France the principles of 1789 have lost much of their popularity.[i] Englishmen turn their eyes towards the Referendum because the last thirty years have gradually revealed to all candid observers some unsuspected weaknesses of parliamentary government. Obstruction has robbed the English House of Commons of half its dignity. The closure and the guillotine (necessary though they may be) have destroyed that free and rational debate which was once supposed to be the soul of the representative system. With unfettered debate has all but vanished the liberty of voting. Lowell's 'Government of England' demonstrates with arithmetical certainty that the rigidity of party discipline has increased year by year.[3] Hence has perished, or is perishing, the silent authority exercised between 1832 and 1870 by the more moderate members of the House of Commons. No two statesmen ever differed more widely than Peel and Palmerston; they both however understood the House of Commons created by the Reform Act of 1832. Each of them exerted untold influence by his capacity for conciliating the actual, if not always the nominal, support of the moderate men of all parties. The crushing defeat of 1832 did not prevent Peel from reconstructing the Conservative party by 1835.[4] He pursued with consummate skill a policy which was more attractive to moderate Whigs than the ideas— some of them very sound ideas—advocated by the Whig leaders, and which was more acceptable to sensible Tories than the high Toryism

---

[3] A. Lawrence Lowell, *The Government of England*, 2 vols. (New York, 1908). Lowell was, along with Woodrow Wilson, the most influential American political scientist of the late nineteenth/early twentieth century. He was a correspondent of Dicey and served as president of Harvard University.

[4] In the general election of 1836, Peel's first as leader of the party, Conservatives picked up a great number of seats but fell short of a majority. It was not until 1841 that Peel's Conservatives could next form a government.

[i] See especially Chardon, 'L'Administration de la France: Les Fonctionnaires.' [Henri Chardon, *L'Administration de la France: Les Fonctionnaires* (Paris, 1908).]

of Lord Eldon.[5] Palmerston, at the height of his power, was in reality the representative of moderate opinion. He was the most popular leader of the Liberals. He was preferred by many Conservatives to Disraeli. The triumphs of Peel and of Palmerston do not now admit of imitation. Party discipline has created a machine which overpowers the independence of individual members. In 1893 the electorate of the United Kingdom, taken as a whole, detested the Home Rule Bill carried through the House of Commons by Mr Gladstone.[6] The measure was never supported in that House by a majority of more than about forty members. No historian will doubt that many English Liberals regarded with anything but liking the Bill pushed through the House by their votes. Yet the faithful forty stood firm. They were not independent legislators, they were the trained soldiers of their party. But who can doubt that, but for the establishment of household suffrage, the conviction of independent members of Parliament would have made it impossible for a majority of forty to have passed through the House of Commons a Bill which proposed to revolutionise the constitution of the United Kingdom? Nor does the lesson of 1893–1895 end here. The events of those years show that in the matter of Home Rule the deliberate will of the country was expressed, not by the representative and elected House of Commons, but by the hereditary and unelected House of Peers. An assembly freely chosen by the electors may fail then to represent the nation. This is the truth which was first forced home upon Englishmen in 1895. It is a truth which the exercise of the Swiss Referendum impresses on every student of constitutional history. This detected weakness in the working of representative government is the portentous addition to political knowledge supplied by the recent annals of democratic progress throughout the civilised world. It is the knowledge of this weakness which is yearly gaining in England adhesion to the principle of the Referendum from

---

[5] Eldon was the Tory Lord Chancellor at the head of the effort of the nineteenth century's first three decades to quell civil unrest and clamp down on radical movements in the wake of the French Revolution; characteristically, he boasted that he had "prosecuted more libels" than any Attorney-General in British history. In the *Lectures on the Relation of Law and Public Opinion* of five years earlier Dicey had treated Eldon as the epitome of "reaction" and "Old Toryism," the first of the three periods through which public opinion had passed on his telling since the French Revolution.

[6] On the Government of Ireland Bill 1893 or Second Home Rule Bill, see page 99, note 16. The Bill passed the Commons 301–267 before being rejected by the Lords 41–419.

statesmen of the highest character and of the widest experience. Hear, for example, these words of Lord Rosebery:

> 'There is nothing I should rejoice at as much as any reference of that kind [i.e. an appeal to the people for assent or negation of the Budget], if there were any constitutional means of obtaining it without mixing it up with other issues foreign to it, and which may directly impair the directness and validity of the decision. If you had the Referendum in this country—and I for my part believe that you will never arrive at a final solution on questions of difference between the two Houses without some form of Referendum—I should vote for it on this occasion.'[ii]

The spread of a new belief inevitably excites the increased opposition of those who do not become its converts. The idea of the nation's veto is abhorrent to Liberal-Conservatives, to Parliamentarians, and to Revolutionists, especially if they be Socialists.

The criticism of a Liberal-Conservative is still best expressed in a classical passage from Maine's 'Popular Government':

> 'I do not undertake' (he writes) 'to say that the expedient [of the Referendum] has failed [in Switzerland], but it can only be considered thoroughly successful by those who wish that there should be as little legislation as possible. Contrary to all expectations, to the bitter disappointment of the authors of the Referendum, laws of the highest importance, some of them openly framed for popularity, have been vetoed by the People after they had been adopted by the Federal or Cantonal Legislature. The result is sufficiently intelligible. It is possible, by agitation and exhortation, to produce in the mind of the average citizen a vague impression that he desires a particular change. But, when the agitation has settled down on the dregs, when the excitement has died away, when the subject has been threshed out, when the law is before him with all its detail, he is sure to find in it much that is likely to disturb his habits, his ideas, his prejudices, or his interests; and so, in the long run, he votes "No" to every proposal. The delusion that Democracy, when it has once had all things put under its feet, is a progressive form of government, lies deep in the convictions of a particular political school; but there can be no delusion grosser. . . . All that has made England famous, and all that has made England

---

[ii] Lord Rosebery's speech in House of Lords, 'Times,' November 25, 1900, p. 6; and 'The Lords' Debate on the Finance Bill,' published by 'The Times,' p. 75.

wealthy, has been the work of minorities, sometimes very small ones. It seems to me quite certain that, if for four centuries there had been a very widely extended franchise and a very large electoral body in this country, there would have been no reformation of religion, no change of dynasty, no toleration of Dissent, not even an accurate Calendar. The threshing-machine, the power-loom, the spinning-jenny, and possibly the steam-engine, would have been prohibited. Even in our day vaccination is in the utmost danger; and we may say generally that the gradual establishment of the masses in power is of the blackest omen for all legislation founded on scientific opinion, which requires tension of mind to understand it, and self-denial to submit to it.'[iii]

The essence of Maine's attack is that in his eyes the Referendum constitutes an appeal from knowledge to ignorance, from enlightenment to prejudice. His reasoning is surely not without force. But its effect is reduced, if not annihilated, by considerations which, even when he wrote, he overlooked, or by facts which in 1885 might well escape his notice. By his own admission the Referendum is the most powerful check hitherto invented on the inconsiderate or foolish action of democracy; no one has a right to complain of an effective bridle that it is not a spur. Maine reasons with considerable effect against democracy. But he does not even attempt to show that where democratic government is established the representatives of the people are sure or even likely to be in all circumstances far wiser or more patriotic than the electors themselves. Still less does he prove that where party government is, as in England, fully developed, an elected House of Commons will display the wisdom or the independence assuredly possessed by some, though by no means the whole, of its members. He does not, as in 1886 was natural, even recognise the danger, which every one now knows to be a very pressing one, that representatives of the people may, consciously or unconsciously, place the interest of their party far above the welfare of the nation, or come *bona fide* to believe that the welfare of the nation can be absolutely identified with the success of a particular party. Maine's feeling when arguing apparently against the Referendum, but in reality against the supremacy of numbers, was that the House of Commons is certain to be far more trustworthy than the mass of the electors. Yet Maine himself had no profound belief in the wisdom of Parliament. He had attacked

---

[iii] Maine, 'Popular Government,' pp. 96–98; conf. 41, 67. [Dicey alluded to these passages earlier on pages 45–6.]

with vigour the abolition by Parliament of the old East India Company.[iv]
He admired, not without reason, the rigidity to be found in the
Constitution of the United States. He assuredly distrusted the party
system. But, with all his rare gifts, he seems, as a politician, to have lacked
the sense of reality. He never perceives what is the true question at issue
between the advocates and the opponents of the Referendum. The point
in debate is whether the English democracy now established in power
requires to be spurred on towards rapid legislation by the factitious and by
no means always disinterested agitation that forms the life of the party
system, or rather needs some strong check on the tendency to yield at once
to the prevalent idea, sentiment, or passion of the moment. The aristocratic Parliament destroyed by the Reform Act of 1832 was, at any rate
towards the end of its existence, too little disposed to move with the times.
The middle-class Parliament which determined the destiny of the country
between 1832 and 1866 was in many ways checked from, if not always
indisposed to, vehement action. The traditions of an earlier time, the
influence of statesmen such as Palmerston, Russell, and Gladstone, who
had been trained during the existence of the unreformed Parliament, the
ideas prevailing among the English middle class itself, were all guarantees
against sudden or imprudent action.[7] The electorate between 1832 and
1866, and their representatives, erred rather by a dislike for any bold and
decisive policy than by the disposition to violent and hurried action even
when carried through under legal forms. The parliaments of that era
listened to the warning, again and again repeated by men such as
Bagehot, that sound action is the fruit of long and hesitating thought,
and that delay in attempting the solution of difficult political problems is
worth the price, immensely heavy though it sometimes is, of permitting on
all important subjects lengthy discussion to precede energetic legislation.
Maine, oddly enough, distrustful though he was of democratic

---

[7] 1832 was the date of the First Reform Act, and 1867 of the Second Reform Act. This mid-
century period between the two Acts is sometimes referred to as the heyday or classical
age of parliamentary government in Britain. Lord John Russell was, like Palmerston and
Gladstone, a parliamentarian whose service extended from before the First to after the
Second Reform. He was eventually a Whig-Liberal Prime Minister, succeeding
Palmerston in the latter capacity.

[iv] See 'Maine: Life and Speeches,' pp. 15–17. [M.E. Grant Duff, *Sir Henry Maine: A Brief
Memoir of His Life, with Some of His Indian Speeches and Minutes* (New York, 1892). Dicey is
alluding to Maine's opposition to what became the Government of India Act, 1858, which
replaced the rule of the East India Company with direct control of British India by the
British government. John Stuart Mill also wrote memorably in the company's defense.]

government, seems at any rate, when he criticises the Referendum, to have dismissed from his mind the idea that representatives elected by democratic constituencies might, especially when under the influence of a party machine, be inclined towards violent action and need the restraint imposed by some sort of veto. His whole charge against democracy seems to be that a popular government is not necessarily a progressive form of government. Admit, without hesitation, that this is so. Admit that during many periods of English history democratic institutions would have arrested salutary reforms. Admit, what is probably true, that, as Maine urges, the existence of a national veto would, at certain periods of English history, have delayed progress, and, to take two of his most striking illustrations, have prevented the toleration of Dissent, and the adoption of an accurate Calendar. From these concessions the indisputably sound conclusion follows, that there have been many times when, and that there are now many countries where, the establishment of democratic institutions would have been, or be, madness. But this conclusion hardly tends to prove that in all cases and in all circumstances a flourishing democracy would act wisely in entrusting unrestrained legislative power to its elected representatives. Nor do the annals of modern Switzerland bear out Maine's assumption that progress is impossible where the veto of the electors can stop the legislative action of a representative assembly. No man of candour and knowledge will maintain that the Swiss have not from time to time erred in rejecting laws laid before the electorate by the Federal Assembly. To a foreign critic the errors committed are not very patent, and seem not very numerous. But it were folly to claim for the Swiss people an infallibility or even an unvarying good sense which certainly cannot be ascribed to the English Parliament. Maine's reference to vaccination in the celebrated passage already cited from his 'Popular Government' has turned out infelicitous. True it is that 'even in our day vaccination is in the utmost danger.' This may be a valid argument, as far as it goes, against popular government. But then is the enforcement of vaccination at all safe when left to the sole control of Parliament? What are we to say for the childish deference now paid in this matter to the conscientious objector?[8] Is it not at least arguable that a system of compulsory

---

[8] Widespread resistance to vaccination was a common source of anxiety among *fin de siècle* and Edwardian liberal writers, for whom it raised vexing questions about the scope of liberty.

vaccination, when once in working order, could be less easily upset in a country where a retrogressive change could not, owing to the existence of the Referendum, come into force unless such change were sanctioned by the majority of the electorate, than in a country such as modern England, where a government still commanding a parliamentary majority, but trembling at the result of each by-election, might purchase transitory success by abject submission to the commands of a fanatical minority of anti-vaccinators? The simple truth is that the experience of Switzerland tells, on the whole, in favour of the Referendum. Switzerland makes constant use of the new democratic invention, and Switzerland is not an unprogressive country, whilst the democratic government of Switzerland is armed with far stronger weapons for resistance to Socialism than is the parliamentary government of England. But, on the other hand, fairness requires the admission that the constitution, the traditions, the whole cir-cumstances of Switzerland, differ so widely from those of England that no candid advocate of the Referendum can, from the success of the Referendum in Switzerland, predict with confidence that it would work beneficially in England. What can fairly be urged on that point is this: In the opinion of many competent judges, one source of our constitutional difficulties is to be found in the increasing power of the party system, and the Referendum certainly does, in favourable circumstances, put a check on the power and the development of the machinery of partisanship. However this may be, Maine's criticism on the Referendum is for the most part irrelevant. He exposes the weaknesses of democracy, he does not show that they are increased rather than diminished by the institution of a national veto.

The objection of parliamentarians generally takes one of two forms.

The first form is summed up in the statement that a general election performs substantially in England the part of a Referendum in Switzerland. From a general election, it is said, you may in substance, though not in so many words, obtain the expression of the nation's will on the leading measures submitted, or to be submitted, by a government to the consider-ation of the country. This contention has one grave defect: it does not correspond with the facts of English public life. At times, no doubt, though the occasions are rare, an election may constitute an almost direct appeal to the people on the question whether a particular Bill shall pass into law? It then is a sort of informal Referendum. One instance of such an informal appeal to the people is to be found in the 'leading case,' to use legal phraseology, of the Great Reform Act. It was passed in 1832 to the cry of 'The Bill, the whole Bill, and nothing but the Bill.' No man of competent knowledge doubts that it received the assent of the nation. But in 1832 the peculiar course of events placed the electors in a position very like that occupied by the people of Switzerland when asked under a Referendum to accept or reject a constitutional change which has been formally passed by the Federal Legislature. There have been one or two other crises in which a general election has been a rough kind of Referendum. But these instances of a genuine and definite appeal to the people are rare, and the further development of the party system is making them year by year rarer. At the very best a general election confuses a question of persons with a question of measures. How is a reasonable man to vote squarely and fairly when forced to answer, by one and the same vote, two quite separate enquiries, namely, first, whether he prefers Mr Asquith as Prime Minister to Mr Balfour, and secondly, whether he does or does not wish for the destruction of the House of Lords?[9] But when we take a general election, not at its best, but at its worst, it turns out to be for all practical purposes nothing like a Referendum. As the party system is now worked in England, a general election lays before the electorate a huge number of incongruous and confused issues on the whole of which it is absolutely impossible for the ablest and most temperate of electors to give a satisfactory reply; for note in passing that the voter has practically no other means of giving a verdict on the issues which he is supposed to determine than the very awkward and indirect one of voting for either a supporter or an opponent of the Government. Put the last point aside and let us consider for a moment a few among the numerous questions raised at the general election of January and February last. Had the House of Lords a constitutional right to reject a Finance Bill passed by the House of Commons, and reject it on the ground that it was condemned by the people? Was the Finance Bill, or Budget, in itself a just and wise measure? Is the policy of Tariff Reform preferable to the policy of Free-trade? Ought the House of Lords to be left unchanged, to be mended, or to be ended? Ought Home Rule to be granted to Ireland? Ought women to be admitted to the parliamentary franchise? These are a few among the most important of the enquiries to which a puzzled elector was supposed to give an answer. The perplexity of the situation was increased by the fact that neither the party leaders nor the candidates for a seat in Parliament would or could make up their minds, or at any rate state plainly, what was the main issue on which the electors were called upon to

---

[9] On Balfour, see page 88, note 11. H.H. Asquith was the leader of the Liberal party and Prime Minister (from 1908 to 1916).

decide. The voter was told at one time that the matter in dispute was whether Free-trade was more beneficial to the nation than would be Tariff Reform. At another moment he was informed that the sole subject worth consideration was whether the House of Lords had or had not unconstitutionally invaded the rights of 'the Commons'—an expression, by the way, which meant sometimes 'the privileges of the House of Commons' and sometimes 'the rights of the people.' The man about to give a vote was in reality in a position as grotesque as would be the situation of a juryman who, being called upon to find a given prisoner 'guilty' or 'not guilty,' was told by the judge at one moment that the man in the dock was being tried for murder, and at another moment that he was being tried for larceny. An artificial system perverted by the arts of partisanship led to confusion worse confounded, of which the effects are too serious for jocosity, but the absurdity too ridiculous for anything but laughter. The Ministry went to the country, as the expression goes, on the strength of the so-called 'People's Budget.'[10] It had been approved in the House of Commons by large majorities. The Peers appealed to the people against a Finance Bill which was no real Finance Bill but an attempt to work a social revolution by the authority, not of Parliament but of the House of Commons alone. The Ministry obtained at the general election a majority of some 124 votes. The question of the Budget seemed settled. The fact soon, however, became as clear as day that the coalition which supported the Government could hardly hold together. It became equally clear that while all Unionists had denounced, every member from Ireland, whether a Unionist or a Nationalist, detested the Budget. The indisputable result was that, in regard to the Budget, the will of the nation was represented, not by the representative and elected House of Commons which passed the Finance Bill, but by the non-representative and hereditary House of Peers which refused to let the Finance Bill become an Act of Parliament. The People's Budget has been rejected by the people.[11] No bribe which leads Irish

---

[10] The Liberal People's Budget, devised by then Chancellor of the Exchequer Lloyd George, included heavy taxes on land and inheritance, as well as other tax hikes, for the sake of funding novel social programs. It was rejected by the House of Lords in 1909 despite a convention against the Lords rejecting "money bills," leading to a general election in which the Liberal party defended their budget and attacked the Lords' powers, which in turn led (after yet another general election) to the Parliament Act 1911, which is the subject of the next chapter.

[11] This is something of a tendentious interpretation, but it was the case that the Liberal party had won a majority neither of votes nor seats and thus had to rely on the support of

Nationalists to accept for the moment financial proposals which all Ireland abhors, will deprive of their true meaning facts which no man can dispute. The general election of 1910 will remain for ever a satire upon the attempt to identify a general election with a Referendum.

The objection of parliamentarians to any form of national veto often assumes another and a different form.

The electors, it is urged, are able to decide whether a particular man is likely to be a wise and patriotic member of Parliament; they may even perhaps determine whether a particular leader, say in one age Chatham, in another Peel, in a third Palmerston, is the man most fit to be Prime Minister; the electorate or particular electors, in short, may form a sagacious judgment on personal character; but the opinion of the electors on matters of policy or legislation is hardly worth having. The duty, therefore, of a voter is to support a good man as his representative, or even to give a vote in favour of a Minister whom a large part of the nation admires; but when this is done an elector has fulfilled the whole of his duty and ought to leave the management of affairs in the hands of the excellent men who, on account of their public and private virtues, have obtained seats in the House of Commons. This, one is often told, is the principle which not only ought to govern, but does govern, the choice and the position of English members of Parliament. The principle sounds a fine one. The notion of a country ruled by all its best and wisest citizens, chosen for seats in Parliament solely on account of their conspicuous virtues and of their statesmanlike prudence, must, it would seem, meet with general approval. Unfortunately, the picture of a House of Commons consisting of good men to whom absolute power has been confided by wise electors, though it embodies some slight elements of truth, never really represented the nature of the English Parliament in any age. It is an absurdly false representation of the English House of Commons as it now exists. It is absolutely inconsistent with the actual working of our party system. In the present year of grace members of Parliament are and must be elected in England, not, of course, without reference to personal character and ability, but chiefly because they represent a party to which certain electors belong, and because they are in the main prepared to obey the directions of the leaders of that party. It was assuredly neither want of

---

Labour and the Irish Nationalists, the latter of which drove a hard bargain to ensure the introduction of a Home Rule Bill as the price for their support of the Budget.

high character nor lack of marked and parliamentary ability which has, to the loss of the nation, closed to Mr Harold Cox and to Lord Robert Cecil the entrance into the present House of Commons.[12] In plain truth, the principle of the Referendum, by whatever name you call it, has for many years past been claiming a place among the ideas which make up the ruling maxims of English constitutionalism. No man can speak with more authority on any question of constitutional theory or practice than Mr Bryce. Listen to words published by him some seventeen years ago:

'A general election' (he writes), 'although in form a choice of particular persons as members, has now practically become an expression of popular opinion on the two or three leading measures then propounded and discussed by the party leaders, as well as a vote of confidence or no confidence in the Ministry of the day. It is in substance a vote upon those measures; although, of course, a vote only on their general principles, and not, like the Swiss Referendum, upon the statute which the Legislature has passed. Even, therefore, in a country which clings to and founds itself upon the absolute supremacy of its representative chamber, the notion of a direct appeal to the people has made progress.'[v]

His language is characteristically moderate. He in words overrates somewhat the superficial likeness between a Referendum and a general election, but he clearly recognises the fact that the nominal supremacy of the representative Chamber was, even in 1893, becoming in practice qualified by the notion of a direct appeal to the people. What was partially true in 1893 has become completely true in 1910. The time has arrived for the formal recognition of a principle which in fact, if not in theory, forms part of our constitutional morality.

Another and essentially different objection to the Referendum tells for much with parliamentarians. The Referendum, it is urged, must 'tend to paralyse any acute sense of responsibility in parliamentary life; members of the House of Commons might justify their ill-considered or interested votes on the ground that the last word rested with the people, who must accept the first responsibility.'[vi] This criticism merits attention, but its importance may well be exaggerated. The 'acute sense of responsibility'

---

[12] Cox and Cecil left the Commons in the January 1910 general election. They were both free traders with notable intellectual reputations, Cox in the Liberal and Cecil in the Conservative party. Cecil, son of the Prime Minister Salisbury, would later win the Nobel Peace Prize for his work in forming the League of Nations.

[v] Bryce, 'American Commonwealth,' 1, 466, 467.   [vi] McKechnie, p. 90.

attributed to the House of Commons is at the present moment not very easily discerned by an impartial observer. True it is that timid members of Parliament who, as the expression goes, are sitting on the fence, may try to shift the burden of decision from themselves to the people. But this is, after all, a less evil than the constant attempt to escape responsibility for dubious policies by placing the obligations of partisanship above duty to the country. The Referendum will be an untold blessing if it revives a sense of responsibility to the nation. The proper solution, further, of many, though assuredly not of all, political questions does, we must remember, rightly depend upon its being in accordance with the real will of the nation. If ever it should be clearly ascertained that the vast majority of the electors of the United Kingdom were opposed to the maintenance of the political union between England and Ireland, or had become zealots for bestowing parliamentary votes upon women, not the sternest opponent of Home Rule, or of Woman Suffrage, would in most cases deny the necessity for establishing a Parliament at Dublin or for the registration of women among parliamentary voters. Such concession on the part of Unionists or of opponents of Woman Suffrage would be no superstitious homage to the moral authority of the *vox populi*, but a simple acknowledgment of the fact that, under any form of popular government, it is an impossibility, and therefore not a duty, to maintain institutions which are permanently condemned by the will of the people. The Referendum gives expression to the will of the people, and under any form of popular government the people must be treated as the sovereign, and entitled to obedience.

But it is from revolutionists or Socialists inspired by the fanaticism of partisanship, rather than from Conservatives or Parliamentarians, that comes the most vehement of all the attacks on the Referendum. Let my readers weigh for a moment the following extracts from a political tract of no great merit, entitled 'Against the Referendum.'

> 'The Referendum would work steadily to the disadvantage of the Liberal Party.'
>
> 'It must surely be obvious that there would never be a sufficient number of voters enthusiastic enough about any one reform to carry it in the teeth of the formidable opposition that would make itself felt through the Referendum. When the people vote at an election, they vote for a number of reforms, both social and political; the man who cares for one may be quite indifferent to another. The keen educationalist may have given no thought to licensing reform; the zealous advocate of old-age pensions may detest Home Rule.'

'Imagine now that some great reforming measure, on which a Liberal Government has received a clear mandate from the country, has been rejected by the Lords, and that the rejection is accompanied with a demand for the Referendum. Would not money be spent like water by all those interests which imagined themselves assailed? Would not a thousand glozing orators be launched upon the constituencies, picking holes in the proposed legislation, seeking to arouse the basest and most selfish interests? Would not the antireforming press exhaust itself in malignant falsehoods calculated to deceive the people? And when the Bill—the child, perhaps, of the wisest and most enlightened brains in England—had been contemptuously flung out by a small but sufficient majority, what would be the position of the Government which was responsible for the defeated measure?'[13]

This rant may all be summed up in one sentiment uttered some years ago, in a more or less public debate, by a speaker who inclined apparently towards Socialism. 'The people are too stupid to be entrusted with the Referendum.' And rant, which is of little value in itself, is of great importance as an indication of prevailing opinion. The author, whoever he be, of 'Against the Referendum,' betrays a belief by no means uncommon, that the constitution and the powers of government itself exist in a country such as England, not for the sake of giving effect to the will of the nation, but in order to secure the power and authority of a party. No doubt the fanatics of partisanship are often from their own point of view sincere patriots. A partisan of the higher type believes that the triumph of his own ideas will be the salvation of the country. He believes further that the victory of his convictions depends upon office being obtained by the party to which he belongs. Such a one may be a genuine enthusiast, he may call himself a Liberal or a Democrat. He has, whatever his virtues, no right to either title. He disbelieves in liberty if granted to his opponents. He disbelieves in the supremacy of the nation unless the nation has come round to his own faith. Such a man is, as things at present stand, likely enough to be a Socialist. And though it is quite true that many Socialists are as fair-minded as their opponents, yet there exists a real reason why a certain kind of intolerance is likely to be found in connexion with Socialism. A Socialist may really be a democrat

---

[13] Dicey is referring to material which had originally been published serially in the nonconformist Liberal newspaper *The British Weekly* and which is distilled in Jane T. Stoddart and Robertson Nicholl, *Against the Referendum* (London, 1910), cited later on page 206, note xxxvii.

in the sense of being one who wishes that the powers of the State should be used for the benefit of the whole people. He may be a Liberal in the sense that he is willing to use parliamentary institutions for the attainment of socialistic ends. But for all this there exists, as many thinkers hold, an essential inconsistency, which is gradually becoming visible to every one, between the ideals of Socialism and the ideals of Democracy. Socialism tends towards the authoritative government of experts;[14] Democracy tends towards the promotion of general prosperity through the protection of individual freedom and the stimulating of individual energy. In any case 'Against the Referendum' affords an argument of untold weight in favour of a national veto to men who feel that the Referendum is the strongest of protections against the pressing danger of the despotism of partisanship.

All opponents of the Referendum—Conservatives, Parliamentarians, Socialists, and that omnipotent 'man in the street,' of whom we hear so much and know so little—dispose of an innovation which they depreciate or detest by the one dogmatic plea that 'the Referendum will not work in England.' The boldness of this assertion is to half the world a guarantee of its self-evident truth, whilst its vagueness and ambiguity add to the difficulty of its confutation. Hence it is worth while to expose the hollowness of a dogma which rests upon slight, if any, basis of argument.

The plea that the Referendum will not work in England has at least three different meanings.

It may import that in this country it is impossible to establish by means of legislation an institution which will attain the objects for the sake of which the Referendum has been introduced into countries where it works effectively. Now these objects are, as has been already pointed out, twofold.

The first and the primary object of the Referendum is to ensure that the laws passed by a representative Assembly or Parliament shall be in conformity with the deliberate will of the nation; this is the main use of the Referendum under the Federal Constitution of Switzerland. But it is certain that the Imperial Parliament could, if supported by the electors, easily carry through legislation which would greatly diminish, if not

---

[14] It is likely that Dicey here has in mind the Fabian socialists, an influential group which advocated a gradualist, reformist, and technocratic socialism and had significant influence on the young Labour party.

entirely get rid of, the risk of any law being enacted by Parliament which, though it fell in with the wish of a predominant party, was opposed to the deliberate will of the electors, that is, of the nation. The simplest method of attaining this end would be to pass a Referendum Act. Such a statute should contain two main provisions which I do not attempt to reduce to the technical language of parliamentary draftsmanship. The first provision should be that no Bill which repealed, changed, added to, or otherwise affected the Acts enumerated in the Schedule to the Referendum Act should, even though passed by both Houses of Parliament, become an Act of Parliament, i.e. a law, unless and until such Bill had been submitted to, and received the sanction of, the majority of the electors voting on the question whether the Bill should become an Act of Parliament. These scheduled Acts should at first, at any rate, be few in number, and should in any case be statutes of the highest importance, such, for example, as the Act of Settlement, the Union with Scotland Act, 1707, the Union with Ireland Act, 1800, and the various Parliamentary Reform Acts.[15] Among such scheduled Acts ought to be included the Referendum Act itself. The second provision of the Referendum Act should be that any Bill, or so-called Act, passed by both Houses of Parliament and assented to by the Crown, which, whilst affecting any one of the scheduled Acts, had not been sanctioned by and on an appeal under the Referendum Act, should be held invalid by every court of law throughout the British Empire. Our supposed Referendum Act would clearly, as regards any enactment whatever included in its Schedule, e.g. the Act of Union with Ireland, make an alteration impossible without an appeal to the people. The Referendum Act would further in no way diminish the need for obtaining for every Bill whatever the sanction of both Houses of Parliament and of the Crown. It would do nothing more than require for any Bill affecting the statutes scheduled in the Referendum Act the sanction, not only of Parliament, but also of the electorate. Such an Act therefore provides the appropriate means for preventing legislation pleasing to a party which for a time possesses a parliamentary majority, but opposed to the permanent will of the nation.

[15] The Act of Settlement of 1701 established the Hanoverian line of succession to the throne and stipulated that future monarchs must be Protestant. On the other Acts named, see respectively, Chapter 6, note 2; Chapter 3, note 5; Chapter 7, note 7; and Chapter 8, note 6.

A Referendum Act, it is sometimes urged, would, after all, as long as the sovereignty of the Imperial Parliament is acknowledged, be futile, for Parliament could clearly evade the Referendum Act by adding to any Bill which affected any scheduled Act (e.g. the Act of Union with Ireland) words exempting the Bill from the operation of the Referendum Act. This criticism is worth notice. It is verbally sound, but in reality it is, except in one possible case, without force. The electors may be trusted to resent an attempt to deprive them of legal power ensured to them by the Referendum Act. No party leader will risk this resentment. The Referendum Act will be less subject to change, except by way of extension, than any enactment in the statute book. In one exceptional state of circumstances, and in one alone, the Referendum Act might in fact be overridden by Parliament. If the safety of the country imperatively demanded rapid and immediate legislation, Parliament might assuredly, with the approval of all loyal citizens, escape from the bonds of the Referendum Act, just as, at the present moment, if the safety of England is at stake, a Government may break, and ought to break, the law of the land, and rely on an Act of Indemnity to cover conduct which, though technically criminal, is dictated by the necessity of protecting the State against imminent peril, e.g. of foreign invasion.[16] The latent sovereignty of Parliament is in truth an argument, not against, but in favour of the Referendum. It preserves to the English Constitution that degree of flexibility which, in the changing circumstances of the world, cannot be absolutely sacrificed without imperilling the welfare of the United Kingdom.[vii]

It is then, in reality, past a doubt that in England, as elsewhere, a Referendum can by proper legislation be created which will secure for

---

[16] An act of indemnity, to use Dicey's own definition, is "a statute, the object of which is to make legal transactions which when they took place were illegal, or to free individuals to whom the statute applies from liability for having broken the law." This class of acts was integral to Dicey's theorization of the rule of law: to Dicey's mind, a society which upheld "the supremacy of law" would not grant broad discretion to government officials to act as they saw fit in emergency settings, but would instead keep ordinary law in place wherever possible and release from liability actors whose deeds were seen, with the benefit of the crisis having passed, to have acted as the public good warranted.

[vii] The Swiss Constitution itself in effect allows the necessity for a Referendum to be in effect dispensed with by the Federal Parliament in the case of laws 'of an urgent nature,' and leaves to the Parliament the sole and final decision of the question whether a given law is of an urgent nature. (See Federal Constitution of Switzerland, Art. 89.)

the country one of the main objects for the sake of which a Referendum is called into existence.

The second object of a Referendum—the main purpose, indeed, for which it exists in the Commonwealth of Australia—is the termination of the kind of deadlock which sometimes arises when the two Houses of Parliament differ as to the passing of a given law. There is, it is suggested, some difficulty in determining how in this case the Referendum ought to be brought into play. The simplest, though certainly not the only method suitable for this purpose would appear to be the passing of an Act which should give to either House of Parliament, on any occasion when the House of Lords and the House of Commons could not agree as to the passing of a particular Bill, the legal right to demand that the Bill should be made the subject of a Referendum, or an appeal to the electors, and that the result of such appeal should decide whether the Bill should or should not become an Act of Parliament. There is, it is submitted, no reason whatever to doubt that an Act of Parliament, though it might necessarily contain some rather complicated provisions,[viii] could easily be drawn which would make it possible to terminate a legislative deadlock of the kind referred to by the use of the Referendum. And, if this be so, there is not the least ground for the assertion that a Referendum might not be introduced into England which would so work as to secure for the country the second object for the sake of which the institution exists. But, even to earnest advocates of the Referendum, it may appear a question still open to discussion whether it be expedient to use the Referendum as a means for removing legislative deadlocks arising from disagreement between the two Houses of Parliament, and this for the following reasons: (1) We have as yet a comparatively small amount of experience as to the success of the Referendum when used for this purpose; (2) the Referendum, nominally used merely to remove a parliamentary deadlock, might occasionally, though not often, operate, not as a check upon, but as an incitement to, hasty legislation; (3) the end proposed might be attained by a different and possibly better method. The experience of the French Senate suggests that, if the House of Lords were improved or reformed by being reduced for legislative purposes to, say, 300 persons, the kind of legislative deadlock might be removed by an enactment that the two Houses, if they could

---

viii See Commonwealth of Australia Constitution Act, s. 128 and s. 57.

not finally agree as to the passing of a Bill, should sit, debate, and vote together as one assembly, and that the vote of such assembly should determine whether the Bill should or should not pass.[17]

The assertion that the Referendum will not work in England may again mean that it is impossible to provide with us the almost mechanical means by which the electors may vote 'Aye' or 'No' on the question whether a given Bill shall become an Act of Parliament. This statement needs no elaborate refutation. A mode of voting which is practised with success in Switzerland, in almost every State of the American Commonwealth, and in the Commonwealth of Australia, can assuredly be successfully practised in England also. Among Englishmen of otherwise sound sense there exists a curious habit of asserting that institutions which flourish abroad cannot be made to work in England. A sensible solicitor will tell you that the sale and purchase of English land does not admit of simplification. He treats as of no importance the fact that the sale of land in France is carried out with an ease unknown to sellers or purchasers of land in England. Let the principle of the Referendum be once accepted by Englishmen as sound and the difficulties of putting it into practice will vanish.

The statement, lastly, that the Referendum will not work in England may mean that the creation of the nation's veto is inconsistent with the further development, and even to some extent with the actual working, of party government as now understood among Englishmen. This is profoundly true; but then we shall find that, to the advocates of the Referendum, its recommendation to a great extent lies in its tendency to correct the defects and to check the further development of a party system which they believe is working injury to the nation.

Before stating the arguments in favour of making trial in England of an institution abhorrent to Conservatism, to parliamentarianism and to dogmatic Socialism, it is well to note two circumstances which tell in favour of giving a trial to a novel proposal. The first of these circumstances is that the change advocated is one of those very rare constitutional innovations which may be the object of real experiment. In this it differs from proposals to give parliamentary votes to women, or to place the government of Ireland in the hands of an Irish Parliament, guided by an Irish executive. Common-sense tells us that either of these steps, when once taken, can never be retraced. With the Referendum it is

---

[17] Under the French Third Republic the Senate indeed had 300 members, all of whom (in contrast to the more powerful Chamber of Deputies) were indirectly elected.

otherwise. There is not the remotest reason why it should not be tried in some special case, and then, if it be found not to answer, never be tried again. The second circumstance is that the national veto is perfectly compatible with any other change, such as the reform of the House of Lords, or the adoption of proportional representation, which may commend itself to thinkers or statesmen. The experiment of the Referendum can certainly be tried without peril. The direct reasons in favour of such trial may be broadly summed up under two heads:

First: The Referendum makes it possible, in a way which in England it is now impossible, to get on any matter of real importance a clear and distinct expression of the will of the nation.

The Referendum submits to the electors a clear and distinct issue to which Englishmen can give as decided an answer as the Swiss. It may be absolutely decisive one way or the other of the matter on which the opinion of the nation has been obtained. Let the question, shall a Bill giving parliamentary votes to women either be accepted or rejected by the undoubted majority of the electors of the United Kingdom, and we may be certain that the question which now harasses, though it certainly does not excite, the country, will be for a considerable time set at rest.

The Referendum is the only check as yet suggested strong enough for its purpose. A reformed Second Chamber might possess a veto more powerful than any check on legislation possessed by the present House of Lords, but the authority of the very best constituted Second Chamber would be far less potent than the authentic voice of the nation. The strength of the Referendum lies in its being at once a conservative and a democratic check on the power of any party which, though supreme in the House of Commons, did not in reality represent the settled will of the English people. It is easy for a disbeliever in democracy to find forcible arguments against the newest democratic invention. But the genuine democrat is estopped from denying the validity of a direct appeal to the people. The democrat who prefers the verdict given on the confused issues raised by a general election to the verdict of electors who are consulted on a separate, limited, and distinct issue, is driven to the absurdity of maintaining that he will hear with deference the decision of Philip drunk, but will refuse attention to the decision of Philip sober. A democratic institution may, I fully admit, be a faulty and an undesirable institution; my sole contention is that, if you wish to place a check on rash or impolitic legislation, that check is strongest which falls in with the democratic belief and sentiment of the age. The Referendum further, as applied to the United Kingdom, provides for the equal representation of every part of the United Kingdom. The predominant partner will, if we create a national veto, for the first time exert his legitimate and beneficial authority. The Referendum, further, cannot so easily as can the vote of the electorate be perverted from its proper use by the ingenuity and unscrupulousness of party managers. They will do their best, or their worst, to subject the national veto to the control of the 'Machine.' They will sometimes succeed; but, on the whole, they will find it difficult to coerce or to corrupt the majority of the electorate.

Secondly: The Referendum, and the Referendum alone, holds out the hope that some limit may be placed on the ever increasing power of the party system.

Thus the action of the nation's veto will of itself revive a recognition of the now far too little respected authority of the nation. Even party managers and wirepullers will be forced to remember that they owe obedience to the will of the country when the nation on a critical occasion utters with its own voice its undoubted command. The Referendum again may give a new freedom to all persons who take part in public life. A voter may feel himself delivered from bondage to the despotism of party spirit when he finds that he may vote against a measure which he condemns without voting for the expulsion from office of Ministers who command his approval. The possibility of a Government remaining in office when the country disapproves of some measure which Ministers recommend to the electors for acceptance, seems a strange thing to Englishmen of to-day, though it was perfectly familiar to their grandfathers, who had again and again seen Pitt, the most powerful of Prime Ministers, forced to acquiesce in the defeat of his proposals, and to acquiesce without a thought of resigning in consequence. And to a Swiss citizen it seems at least as strange that Ministers who propose a measure to which the country does not assent should of necessity cease to be the servants of the nation. To him it appears the most natural thing in the world that, when once the will of the nation has been pronounced, statesmen should obey the national command and continue to render loyal service to the country. If once Englishmen adopt, not only the Referendum, but also the spirit in which the Referendum is worked in Switzerland, some other changes of considerable benefit to England might ensue. An administrator, whose talent and character every one respects, might remain in a Cabinet without agreeing with every measure advocated by the Government. There does not appear in the nature of things to be any clear reason why a Chancellor of the highest legal eminence should not remain a member of a Cabinet though he does not agree with all the political views of his colleagues. No doubt this suggestion is foreign to the customs of the English Constitution as they now exist. It is alien to party government as at this moment carried on in England. But it is opposed to no rule either of honesty or of common-sense. The nation would gain a good deal, though party organisation would be weakened, if officials, such as the Lord Chancellor or the Secretary for Foreign Affairs, who ought to possess very special aptitudes, and ought not to be very ardent partisans, did not necessarily go out of office with every change of Cabinet. The Referendum would certainly facilitate the continuous employment in successive Cabinets of men who, whilst holding a particular office, such as that of the Chancellorship, acted rather as experts than as men who shared the political opinions held by their colleagues. The existence of the national veto might, lastly, give new honesty—a thing certainly much wanted—to the public life of our country. The party system introduces into the working of the constitution a host of shams and fictions; but shams and fictions inevitably foster insincerity. The fiction (for it is nothing better) that the members of a Cabinet always act together in perfect agreement leads at times to studied misrepresentation, which, as it hardly deceives the public, ought not, perhaps, to be characterised as mendacity. A Minister, again, is often not only driven to support a policy from which he partially dissents, and which he accepts in reality because it is approved of by the nation, but is also induced to pretend, which is a pure evil, that he heartily agrees with measures which his judgment condemns. The Referendum would at any rate lessen the need for constitutional pretences. There is nothing disgraceful or dishonest in a statesman obeying the commands of the country. The dishonesty begins when he pretends that he approves every order which he obeys. There is, of course, no doubt that if the Referendum once took root in England it would give rise to changes in the working and in the morality—if I may use the expression—of the Constitution. Hence parliamentarians who hold that the Constitution is working admirably, naturally object to any fundamental change in its character.

On this point it may be allowable to cite words written some twenty years ago:

> 'Of speculations which have some family similarity to the ideas propounded in this article, my friend Mr Morley (whose zeal for party takes me by surprise) warns us that they "must be viewed with lively suspicion by everybody who believes that party is an essential element in the wholesome working of parliamentary government."[ix] To this suspicion all who call attention to the merits of the Referendum are, it is to be feared, obnoxious. ... The party system, whatever its advantages, and they are not insignificant, is opposed to the sovereignty of the people, which is the fundamental dogma of modern democracy. That system throws the control of legislation first into the hands of a party, and then into the hands of the most active or the most numerous section of that party. But the part of a party may be, and probably is, a mere fraction of the nation. The principle of the Referendum, on the other hand, is to place, at any rate as regards important legislation, parties, factions, and sections under the control of the national majority. The creation of a popular veto is open ... to grave objections. The consideration, however, which, more than any other, may commend it to the favourable attention of thoughtful men, is its tendency to revive, in democratic societies, the idea which the influence of partisanship threatens with death, that allegiance to party must, in the minds of good citizens, yield to the claims of loyalty to the nation.'[x]

The language here cited is as true in 1910 as in 1890—perhaps truer. To contented parliamentarians in office it naturally seems that all is going on for the best under the best of all possible Constitutions, and that the Referendum is as odious as it is unnecessary.[18] But a different view may as naturally present itself to observers who stand quite outside parliamentary life and have taken no hand in the party game as played at Westminster. Such men are no more dogmatic democrats than is Lord Morley. But to them it seems that evils which in 1890 were latent

---

[18] This is, like Voltaire's *Candide*, a play on the theodicy of the early-modern philosopher Gottfried Leibniz, according to which God could only have created "the best of all possible worlds."

[ix] Lord Morley re-echoes and re-affirms Mr Morley's convictions of 1890. 'I hold firmly that all this idea of an election *ad hoc,* of a Referendum, a *plébiscite*, and a mandate is a complete departure from the wholesome usages of this country.' ('The Lords' Debate on the Finance Bill, 1909,' 'Times' ed., p. 107.)

[x] 'Contemporary Review,' April 1890, pp. 510, 511. [This is Chapter 3 here.]

in the party system have now become a patent disease which threatens to destroy the healthiness of English public life and the welfare of England. Such observers are no worshippers of democracy, but they acknowledge the existence of popular government and the democratic spirit. They hold that the worst form of popular government is democracy corrupted by the party system. They know as well as any one that the more or less mechanical devices of Constitution makers, or Constitution menders, can, however ingenious, never accomplish as much good as is always expected by its inventors from political machinery. But these critics of the English party system are convinced that the heart of England is sound, and hope that the veto of the nation may, if once constituted and honestly used, rescue the Constitution from the perils with which it is threatened.

8

The Parliament Act, 1911, and the Destruction of All Constitutional Safeguards (1912)

My readers may reasonably ask what is meant by a "constitutional safeguard"? My answer is this: A constitutional safeguard means, under any form of popular and parliamentary government (such as exists, e.g. in England, in the United States, or in France), any law, or received custom, which secures that no change in the constitution or the fundamental laws of the country shall take place until it has obtained the permanent assent of the nation.

So much may well be said as to the meaning of an expression which may cause some perplexity. With this explanation it is easy for me to state the object with which I have written this chapter. My aim is to impress upon my readers three important truths: The first truth is that the Parliament Act has destroyed our last effective constitutional safeguard.[1] The second truth is that the whole experience of every country, which enjoys popular government, proves that the absence of constitutional safeguards imperils the prosperity of the State. The last truth is that the absence of constitutional safeguards is full of danger to England; for it enables a party, or a coalition of parties, to usurp the sovereignty of the nation.

(A) The Parliament Act, 1911, has destroyed our last effective constitutional safeguard.

---

[1] Following the Lords' rejection of the Liberal government's "People's Budget" after its passage by the Commons, the Parliament Act became law on 18 August 1911. As with the First Reform Act, the Lords only relented after the issuance of a royal threat to create hundreds of Liberal peers.

(I) The nature of these safeguards.—The different safeguards which have from time to time protected the rights of the nation may be brought under three heads:—

(i.) The so-called Veto of the King.—Down at least to the accession of George I (1714) the King was the real head of the Government. He took an active, sometimes a predominant, part in Parliamentary legislation. No man disputed the King's right to refuse his assent to a Bill which had been passed by the two Houses of Parliament. This right in theory still exists: it is not touched by the Parliament Act, but it has never (for any political object) been made use of for at least 200 years.[i] The veto of the King, though its existence is of importance, is all but obsolete. It is not in the twentieth century an effective safeguard of the Constitution.

(ii.) The Constitution of the House of Commons up to the full development of Household Suffrage in 1884.—Everybody now acknowledges, what even thirty years ago educated men were slow to admit, that Parliament (by which term a lawyer must always mean the King and the two Houses) has constitutionally a right to make any new law it pleases, to repeal any law, or to change or abolish any law or institution whatever.[2] But every one also knows that this doctrine of Parliamentary omnipotence has, during long periods of history, been combined with a strong public opinion that though the constitution and the more important laws of the realm could be changed, yet the constitution and such laws should be treated as practically unchangeable, unless their amendment were unmistakably demanded by the voice of the nation, or, in other words, of the electors.

The existence of this feeling was, down from the Revolution of 1688 to very near the great Reform Act of 1832, an adequate constitutional safeguard, and sometimes too strong a safeguard, against sudden change not approved of by the nation. I do not deny for a moment that the

---

[2] Dicey was himself partly responsible for this change, given that the *Law of the Constitution* immediately raised the profile of the doctrine of parliamentary sovereignty upon its publication in 1885.

[i] Burke has pointed out that the veto and other latent rights of the Crown may, under unforeseen circumstances, be of great utility to the country. As regards the King's veto, experience has fully proved Burke's foresight. The royal veto is the foundation of the right of the British Cabinet to disallow a Bill passed by the legislature of a self-governing colony, when such Bill is clearly opposed to the legislation of the Imperial Parliament and to the interest of the Empire (see Dicey, *Law of the Constitution*, 7th ed., pp. 98–116).

constitution of the unreformed Parliament did exhibit serious defects. All I do maintain, and maintain with absolute confidence is, that if reforms were, as I admit, at times unduly delayed—the Catholic Emancipation Act, for example, might have been with great advantage to the country passed in 1820 or 1825 instead of in 1829[3]—yet the character of the unreformed House of Commons and the opinion of the day provided an ample safeguard against the danger of usurpation of the national sovereignty by a party which had obtained a temporary majority in the House of Commons. Oddly enough the great Reform Act produced less immediate change of public sentiment than was expected by either the opponents or the authors of the Act. The Whig leaders themselves insisted on the finality of the Reform Act.[4] Peel advocated administrative improvements instead of constitutional changes. Palmerston, after the middle of the nineteenth century, was in reality a Liberal-Conservative in domestic affairs.[5] The few reforms in which he personally took an interest often did not command public support. At the height of his popularity (1857) he with great sagacity proposed to revive the habitual creation of life peerages; but this most statesmanlike idea was not heartily supported by the people.

All these things, which some men still living can remember, are sure signs that till 1867, or rather till 1884, Englishmen and Parliament on the whole practically accepted the unchangeableness of the constitution.[6] The experience of the last 25 or 28 years proves that the change in the constitution of the House of Commons, and the change in public opinion has so weakened this second constitutional guarantee, that it can no longer be relied upon to protect the rights of the nation.

---

[3] Catholic Emancipation was another name for the aforementioned Catholic Relief Act.

[4] E.g. Lord John Russell, whose insistence in 1837 that the Reform Act was to be considered a "final measure" without further adjustments to the franchise earned him the moniker "Finality Jack."

[5] Palmerston's centrist premierships of the mid-1850s to 1860s, when there was a low degree of party discipline, helped to popularize the idea of "Liberal-Conservative" as a political identity, a label which had originally been applied to the Peelites, the followers of Robert Peel who broke away from the Conservatives in 1846 after he accepted free trade.

[6] 1884 was the year of the Third Reform Act, which extended the franchise so that it reached 60 percent of adult males, established a uniform criterion for the suffrage across the United Kingdom, and converted almost all constituencies into single-member districts.

(iii.) The legislative authority of the House of Lords.—Till last year it was universally admitted that (except in respect of Money Bills) the House of Lords possessed the same right as the House of Commons to reject any Bill whatever. Of course no man of sense had since 1832 ever supposed that the Upper House could reject or ought in fact to reject permanently any Bill passed by the House of Commons as the undoubted representatives of the nation.[7] The legislative authority of the House of Lords meant, and was up to 1911 understood to mean, that the House had the power, and was under the obligation to reject any Bill of first rate importance which the House reasonably and *bonâ fide* believed to be opposed to the permanent will of the country. This doctrine, like every other constitutional doctrine, must of course, as most Englishmen have always felt, be construed in accordance with common sense. The nation's assent to a Bill may be given in several different manners. It may be made manifest by the clear absence of any vigorous opposition to a particular measure. It may again be signified by the whole character of a proposed measure (e.g. Gladstone's plan for the Disestablishment of the Church in Ireland), having been laid before the electors and been the main object of debate at a General Election. If under such circumstances the electors should, by their votes, ratify, as they did, Mr. Gladstone's policy, it was surely right to treat such ratification as the deliberate approval by the nation.[8] But no one till 1910 and 1911 seriously disputed the doctrine that the House of Lords in modern times had the right to demand an appeal to the people whenever on any great subject of legislation the will of the electorate was uncertain or unknown.

The House of Lords has, of very recent days, used its authority to safeguard the rights of the nation. Any one may feel well assured that in 1869 the Bill for the Disestablishment of the Irish Church would have been rejected, and rightly rejected, by the Lords had not the question of Disestablishment been clearly and undoubtedly placed before the people at the General Election of 1868. The Lords again in 1893 rejected the

---

[7] Dicey is recalling the circumstances of the passage of the First Reform Act: the bill had been rejected by the Lords in the prior session, yielding overwhelming demonstrations in its favor, a massive general election victory for the Whigs, and the threat that the King would pack the Lords with new Whig peers to overcome any further resistance from the Upper House.

[8] See page 125, note 23.

Home Rule Bill of 1893, which had been passed by a small but unwavering, majority of the House of Commons. The Ministry of the day, after their defeat, held office unconstitutionally till 1895. The appeal to the people which ought to have been made at once was, when it took place, decisive. The return of a large Unionist majority was the approval by the people of the rejection by the House of Lords of the Home Rule Bill of 1893. It was the solemn condemnation by the people of the United Kingdom of the whole policy of Home Rule. This condemnation should never be forgotten; it is of infinite significance, it means that at a great crisis in the fortunes of England, the hereditary House of Lords represented, whilst the elected House of Commons misrepresented, the will of the nation.

Nor was the authority of the House of Lords, as protector of the Constitution, seen only in the cases in which the House came openly into conflict with the House of Commons. The legislative power of the Lords was seen sometimes in the modification of Bills passed by the House of Commons and even more frequently in preventing a Bill from being brought into the House of Commons.

The source of this power was, however, always one and the same, namely the doubt, and the reasonable doubt, whether the House of Lords in modifying or rejecting a Bill, might not be found at the next General Election to be the true representative of the will of the nation.[ii]

Its authority supplied a true, though imperfect, constitutional safeguard; and it was, in 1910, our last effective safeguard.

(II) The Parliament Act, 1911, destroys the last of our constitutional safeguards, for it indubitably produces the following effects:[iii]

The House of Lords retains no power whatever in regard to any Money Bill, and a Money Bill means, under the Parliament Act, any

---

[ii] The true defect of the House of Lords as a constitutional safeguard is not that it rejected Bills too often, but that it did not reject them often enough. It represented too much, not the conservatism of the nation, but a quite different thing, the interest of the Conservative Party. Its weakness was that it did not criticise with sufficient severity Bills proposed when Conservatives were in office. It is now admitted on all sides that the remedy for this weakness is a reform in the Constitution of the House of Lords. The so-called Liberals of the day have refused to apply this admitted remedy. [The membership of the House of Lords was overwhelmingly Tory and had rejected many lesser Liberal bills as well. It did not, on the other hand, reject bills passed by Conservative-Unionist majorities.]

[iii] See "Thoughts on the Parliament Act," iii and iv, *Times*, Tuesday, September 12th, and Saturday, September 23rd, 1911. [These articles were written by Dicey. He wrote several more in *The Times* on the subject.]

Bill which the Speaker of the House of Commons for the time being pleases to endorse as a Money Bill. The House of Commons, on the other hand, has absolute and uncontrolled power over every such Money Bill.

With regard to Public Bills (which are not Money Bills) the House of Lords has, under the Parliament Act, no final veto. The House of Lords may, however, exercise a suspensive veto which may delay such Bill (e.g., a Bill for the total abolition of the House of Lords or for changing the succession to the Crown, or giving to every woman of 21 years of age a vote for Parliament or the right to be elected to a seat in Parliament) from passing into an Act for a little more than two years.

But what is now the legislative power of the House of Commons in regard to any public Bill which is not a Money Bill? It is the answer to this question which I wish to force upon the careful attention of every one of my readers. The Parliament Act gives to the House of Commons, or in truth, to the majority thereof for the time being, power to pass into law any public Bill whatever,[iv] in spite of the rejection thereof by the House of Lords. Every Statute, past, present or to come, and every law, whether contained in the Statute Book or not, is now rendered subject to the sole and despotic authority of the present coalition or of any other faction which may attain a majority by whatever means in the House of Commons.

Upon the present House of Commons and every subsequent House of Commons, has been conferred an absolute legislative dictatorship. England is now governed by one Chamber alone. The House of Commons can repeal the Magna Charta; it can alter the Act of Settlement; it can enact that the Crown may descend to a Roman Catholic; it can extend the already enormous privileges conceded to Trade Unions under the Trades Disputes Act, 1906; it can dissolve the Union between Great Britain and Ireland, and between England and Scotland; it can establish universal suffrage in the strictest sense of that term, so as to include woman suffrage; it can pass an Act giving an old-age pension to every man or woman of 50.[9] All this may be done though

---

[9] The Liberal Government's Old Age Pensions Act of 1908 had for the first time implemented a (small) pension for those over 70. The Trades Disputes Act, also passed by the Liberals, reduced the legal liability of trades unions for acts committed during a strike. Dicey objected to both laws on "classical liberal" grounds: to him the former was imprudent, enlarged the scope of state activity, and contravened sound political economy, and the latter made the trades union a "privileged" entity in the state like an *ancien régime* corporation, exempt from ordinary notions of legal responsibility.

[iv] Except a Bill to extend the maximum duration of Parliament beyond five years.

the House of Lords may have rejected every one of these Acts; all this and much more can be done without any necessity whatever for an appeal to the electorate. This statement is no delusion of a fanatical Unionist. The world knows that one motive at least, for the passing of the Parliament Act by the House of Commons, and forcing it by means of a ministerial misuse of the prerogative through the House of Lords, was that the Act makes it possible to pass a Home Rule Bill and a Woman Suffrage Bill without an appeal to the nation. Nor does the matter end here. The Parliament Act, as we shall see, must continue in force for at least two years, but otherwise the Parliament Act can itself be repealed and modified by the House of Commons. The Parliament Act indeed places two limits on the exercise by a House of Commons majority of unlimited legislative power.

The one limit is that any Bill which is to be passed in spite of the dissent of the House of Lords, must be passed three times in three successive Sessions by the House of Commons. Note, however, that "three Sessions" is not the same as three years; two Sessions are often now held in one year. Note, too, that successive Sessions are a totally different thing from successive Parliaments. If the House of Commons would have substituted "Parliaments" for "Sessions" the inherent vice of the Bill would have disappeared. For such a change would have made it certain that no Bill rejected by the Lords could have passed into an Act without an appeal to the people. The first so-called restriction is worth little; its real effect, and in truth its real object, is not to restrain but to increase the power of a dominant party. It enables a House of Commons majority to pass Bills, say a Welsh Disestablishment Bill, which the party in power suspects to be opposed by the will of the nation.[10]

The second limit or restriction is that no Bill can, without the assent of the Peers, be passed into law "unless" two years have elapsed between the date of the second reading [of a Bill] in the first of [three successive] Sessions of the Bill[v] in the House of Commons and the date on which it

---

[10] Disestablishment of the Church of England in Wales, which had long been sought by Liberals in Wales where Nonconformity was dominant, was a leading campaign topic in elections in the early 1900s and was finally passed in 1914 against the will of the Lords by invoking the Parliament Act itself.

[v] "Sessions of the Bill" are the words of the Parliament Act. This language is dubious English. It apparently means "the three successive Sessions during which any Bill intended to pass into law, though rejected by the House of Lords, must be brought into, and passed by the House of Commons."

passes the House of Commons in the third of those Sessions."[vi] The meaning of these words is best made clear by an illustration. The second reading in the House of Commons of the present Home Rule Bill took place on May 9th, 1912. The Bill cannot, without the assent of the Lords, become an Act of Parliament till May 10th, 1914. This restriction is a real one. It means something, but it does not mean much. It gives to the Lords a suspensive veto for two years. But the importance of this suspensive veto is diminished by one material fact. A House of Commons majority may, under the Parliament Act, cut down the suspensive veto of the Peers to one year or to six months, or indeed may abolish it altogether. Under the Parliament Act then, any party which has obtained, by whatever means, a House of Commons majority, can arrogate to itself that legislative omnipotence which of right belongs to the nation.

(B) The experience of all countries, where popular and Parliamentary government exists or has existed proves the necessity for constitutional safeguards.

Many most respectable persons think that the House of Commons will never misuse its now exorbitant power to defy the will of the country. Every advocate of the Parliament Act relies upon this argument. It is utterly unfounded, it is confuted by universal experience.

The inhabitants of every country where popular and Parliamentary government exists or has existed have acknowledged the necessity of having two legislative Chambers or, as we should say, two Houses of Parliament. No country, except England, now dreams of placing itself under the rule of a single elected House. The most democratic of existing Governments, further, are not content with the safeguard provided by the existence of two Houses. They have generally instituted many other safeguards against Parliamentary despotism. To illustrate this truth, consider for a moment the Constitution of the United States—of the Swiss Confederacy—of the Third French Republic—of Norway—and of the Australian Commonwealth—and the annals of the English Commonwealth.[11]

---

[11] The following reflections are typical of Dicey's writing and teaching; he has a strong claim to be considered a founding father of comparative constitutionalism.

[vi] Parliament Act, 1911, S. 2, sub-s. (1).

The United States.—The Constitution of the American Commonwealth is based from top to bottom on the principle that no legislature can be entrusted with anything like unlimited power. Congress can alone legislate for the whole federation. It consists of two Houses: the Senate, which represents each of the States, and the House of Representatives, which represents in proportion to their numbers the citizens of each State. The two Houses have each real and effective power. The Senate may amend or reject any Bill passed by the House of Representatives; it has been through most periods of American history a more powerful body than the House of Representatives. The President again has a real, and an often exerted, veto on any Bill which has passed the two Houses; no Bill can be passed against his will, unless, after it has been returned (i.e., vetoed) by the President, it is supported by two-thirds of each of the Houses of Congress. The power of Congress itself is confined within narrow limits by the terms of the Constitution. The Constitution cannot be changed by Congress. Any alteration needs the assent of at least three-fourths of the forty-eight States which make up the United States. The Courts further, and ultimately the Supreme Court of the United States, can treat any Act passed by Congress in excess of its powers as invalid. Note also that any power not conferred upon Congress resides in the people of each State.

Every State of the Union (except one) has itself a Legislature of two Houses. The Constitution of the Union cuts down in some respects the power of the State legislatures. What is of even more importance, each State has its separate Constitution. This Constitution always limits the power of the State legislature, and, speaking broadly, in every State the principle is recognized that amendments of the Constitution cannot be passed and become part thereof until they have been submitted to and approved by the vote of the people. This appeal to the people is really what we now call in Europe a Referendum. It is recognized and practised in almost all the States of the American Commonwealth. Add to this that the Courts treat as invalid any law passed by the legislature of a State, e.g., New York, which is inconsistent with any article of the State Constitution. Thus, throughout the Constitutions of the American Commonwealth and of the States thereof, you find the strictest restrictions on the legislative power of elected Parliaments. The idea of giving in effect unlimited power to one House of any Parliament would be laughed down by all American citizens.

The Swiss Confederacy.—Switzerland is the most democratic of Republics; Switzerland is a well-governed country, and an economically governed country; Switzerland is a country of small extent and a comparatively small population; Switzerland is surrounded by huge military States, but Switzerland knows how to hold her own and to maintain both her dignity and her independence. This democratic Republic, however, repudiates the dogma of Parliamentary omnipotence. The legislature of the Confederacy is made up of two Houses—the Council of States, representing the cantons—the National Council, representing the people. This Two-House Parliament, or Federal Assembly, can pass Bills which change the Constitution, but these Bills cannot become law until they have been referred to the nation, and have received the assent both of the people and of the cantons. Here we have the celebrated Referendum.[vii]

The Third French Republic.—France has during a period of some 120 years made trial of at least twelve Constitutions. Her experience has very peculiar value. Thrice she has at crises of her fate felt the practical and disastrous result of government by one Chamber. She has found it also extremely difficult to constitute a Second Chamber or, as we should say, an Upper House, which should be different from the Lower House and yet exercise real power without obstructing the course of government. The Third Republic has already outlasted by a considerable number of years every French Constitution created since 1789. It shows signs of strength and life; it is accepted by every Republican, and apparently by the mass of the people. Yet the Third Republic is the condemnation of government by a single and omnipotent Chamber. The Senate or Upper House is, like the Chamber of Deputies, or, as we should say, the Lower House, a wholly elected body, but it is a Second Chamber of real dignity and power. A modern French statesman—I have been informed on good authority —prefers a seat in the Senate to a seat in the Chamber of Deputies. Then, too, no constitutional law can be changed unless by the vote of the two Chambers sitting and voting together at what is called a Congress. Modern France is assuredly not prepared to hazard the despotism either of Parliament or of one House of Parliament.

[vii] I have purposely omitted all details as to the working of the Referendum in respect either of federal laws which do not touch the Federal Constitution or in respect of cantonal legislation.

The Kingdom of Norway.—You may be surprised that I direct attention to the Norwegian Constitution. I do so because it has a peculiar interest of its own. Norway is (if the expression may be allowed) a monarchical democracy. It is based like other democracies on universal suffrage. The Norwegian Parliament is elected by every Norwegian man of 25 years of age. It consists in one sense of one House, the Parliament, or Storthing containing 123 members. But from the moment the Storthing meets, 30 of such members are elected by the Storthing to form an Upper House or Lagthing, whilst the remaining 93 constitute the Lower House, or Odelsthing. The powers of the Upper House are real. That House may reject or send back any Bill twice, but after the second rejection both Houses vote together as one, though in that case a majority of two-thirds is required for carrying the Bill. Add to this that the King's signature makes a Bill law. But if he refuses to sign and the Bill is passed in three successive Parliaments (not Sessions) it becomes law in spite of the King's veto. The experience of this little but thoroughly democratic State is worth notice. It affords an exceptional example of a One-House Parliament. But here, if ever, the exception not only proves but supports the rule. The sagacity of the Norwegian democracy has detected and corrected the defects of a Constitution devoid of Constitutional safeguards.

The Australian Commonwealth.—Australia possesses one of the latest and most elaborate of our Colonial Constitutions. She is a typical self-governing colony, and has as much of independence as can be given to any land forming part of the British Empire. The Constitution was drafted by Australian statesmen. I will call attention to two facts only. The Parliament of the Commonwealth is elected by strictly universal suffrage, for women no less than men, are entitled to vote as electors. This Parliament consists of two Houses—a Senate representing the separate States, a House of Commons representing the people of the States. No Australian dreams of a One-House Parliament. The Commonwealth Parliament, though created by an Act of the Imperial Parliament, can change most of the articles of the Constitution, but the alteration of the Constitution is surrounded by special safeguards. A Bill which is to alter the Constitution, must be passed by an absolute majority of each House. It cannot become an Act until it has been submitted to, and obtained the approval both of the majority of the States and of the electors who actually vote with regard to the proposed amendment.

The Commonwealth has accepted and practised with success the Referendum, or Poll of the People.

From the examination of modern democratic Constitutions we obtain two undeniable and important results. The first is that every country where popular government exists has recognized the necessity of constitutional safeguards. No country has the folly to place absolute sovereignty to one omnipotent House of Parliament. The absurdity of the Parliament Act, 1911, does not find a parallel in any country whatever outside the United Kingdom.[viii] The second conclusion is that during the last fifty or sixty years the sensible and wise men of every country have recognized the fact that even a fairly elected legislature made up of members who intend to do their duty may misrepresent the permanent wish of their country. This possibility was hardly recognized by reformers during the first half of the nineteenth century, yet the experience of Switzerland is conclusive. The Referendum often reveals the incapacity of sensible and well-meaning members of Parliament to understand on some one topic the will of the nation. This is so well understood in Switzerland that the Swiss electors constantly return again to Parliament the very men who have on a particular point mistaken the wishes of the nation but loyally accept the formally expressed will of the country.

I am not pleading for any servile and pedantic theory of what is called a "mandate." This dogma may no doubt be so interpreted as to forbid to members of Parliament the fair exercise of their common sense and discretion. I fully admit that "to follow not to force the public inclination; to give a direction, a form, a technical dress, and a specific sanction, to the general sense of the community, is the true end of legislature."[ix] But I confidently assert that the special danger of to-day in England is that a House of Commons majority, especially when it is a coalition of factions, should, in obedience to a policy of partisanship, defy the general sense of the community.

The English Commonwealth.—For eleven years (1649–1660), though most people have forgotten the fact, England was a Commonwealth.

[viii] Except it be Greece, and if Greece can afford any lesson to England the lesson is a warning against a One-House Parliament.

[ix] Burke, "Works: Letter to Sheriffs of Bristol," vol. iii. p 180. [Burke, "A Letter from Mr. Burke, to the Sheriffs of Bristol, on the Affairs of America," in *The Works of the Right Honourable Edmund Burke*, 12 vols. (London, 1808–13), vol. 3, 133–206].

During these years she had a Parliament consisting of only a House of Commons. For four years (1649–1653) this One-House Parliament was supreme. It at once abolished the monarchy and the House of Lords. It claimed to establish the rule of the people of England as a Commonwealth or Free State. This unlimited authority of the House of Commons was for these four years no mere form. The House stretched its power to the utmost. It usurped judicial functions. It was accused, not without reason, of corruption. It had neither the strength to restrain nor the wisdom to conciliate the Army. When in 1653 Cromwell and his soldiers put an end to the Parliament, they did an act which was popular with the country.[12] One lesson Englishmen, and especially English reformers and democrats had taken to heart—the despotism of a House of Commons which was legally under no restraint, might become a combination of incapacity and tyranny. Any one who doubts this should study the Constitution of 1653. It expresses in every line thereof the determination that the power of Parliament should be placed under strict restraints. That Constitution, known as the Instrument of Government, was a very rigid Constitution. It contained certain principles which Parliament had not the right to touch. According to the views of most historians the Articles of the Constitution were not changeable by Parliament. The legislative power of Parliament was in one shape or another controlled by the Protector. A strong Council of State went a good way towards supplying the lack of a Second Chamber. It is not my object in this article to give historical details of the change in the constitution effected or attempted during the Protectorate; but to one or two general considerations it is worthwhile calling attention.[13]

Cromwell was assuredly anxious to carry on Parliamentary government in England as he and his contemporaries understood it; yet with Parliamentarians filled with the idea of the unlimited authority of the

---

[12] Frustrated with the "Rump" Parliament's failure to pass reforms that suited the army, come up with a new constitution, or dissolve itself, Cromwell had the army disperse it. He then instituted a "Barebones" Parliament hand-picked by the army, and by the end of the year had been declared Lord Protector under the new Instrument of Government, which to this day remains the only republican constitution England has had.

[13] Dicey gave a much fuller discussion of the Commonwealth's political institutions which he saw as importantly prefiguring aspects of modern democratic arrangements and understandings, in his *Lectures on Comparative Constitutionalism*.

House of Commons he found it impossible to act. He and the reformers of his day had no belief in a House of Commons of unrestrained power. In the last year of his life he issued writs summoning to Parliament a newly created House of Lords. Many historians now perceive that if Cromwell's life had lasted, he would in all probability have accepted the Crown which had been pressed upon him and have re-established with some great reforms the old Parliament of England. He certainly would have kept alive and given force to the Parliamentary Union already created between England, Scotland, and Ireland. There is assuredly nothing in the failure of the experiment of a One-House Parliament during the seventeenth century[x] which supports the idea that a like experiment, though concealed under an absurd form, will be a success in the twentieth century.

(C) The Special Danger of the Absence of Constitutional Safeguards.

The Parliament Act gives, as I have shown, unrestricted powers of passing laws to a House of Commons majority. This power may assuredly be misused. Two new circumstances make this misuse certain. During the last fifty years, and especially during the last thirty years, the strength and the rigidity of the party system (or, as Americans would say, the machine) has been increased to an almost unlimited extent. This is an undeniable fact. There must still be alive some old men who, like myself, remember Palmerston and his immense popularity. In 1857 he had defeated a most unpopular coalition. At a general election he had obtained the support of what was then considered a huge majority. He was the people's hero. Yet before two years had elapsed, he was defeated in his own House of Commons and resigned the Premiership. This defeat means a great deal. It means that a good number of Palmerstonians, though elected as Palmerston's followers, felt free to withdraw their support. They were assuredly not under the pressure of the machine. Palmerston's return to power and his retention of office till his death (1859–1865) bear witness to the same laxity of party discipline. His authority arose from the fact that many men of both parties

---

[x] See Marriott, "Second Chambers," for the Unicameral Experiment, p. 26. [J.A.R. Marriott, *Second Chambers: An Inductive Study in Political Science* (Oxford, 1910). Marriott was then Dicey's colleague at Oxford, where he was a fellow of history at Worcester College. He was later a Conservative MP.]

preferred the government of Palmerston either to the government of the Radicals, as represented by Bright, or to the government of the Conservatives, as represented by Disraeli. Any man who keeps his eyes well open will see that neither Palmerston's overthrow in 1858 nor his subsequent tenure of office from 1859 to 1865, could find a parallel in the public life of to-day.

The second new circumstance to which I direct my reader's attention is the growth of Parliamentary groups or factions. A Parliamentary group is a body of members who are regularly organized and act together mainly for the promotion of some particular object. Such are, for example, the Irish Nationalists, the Labour Party, the Temperance Party, or the political Nonconformists.[14] The degree in which each of these groups may be organized of course differs, but they notoriously each act with a view to some one or more political objects. They may or they may not be allied with one of the two great parties which, under the varying name of Whigs and Tories, Liberals and Conservatives, and the like, have for generations divided the political life of England. But a group always exists primarily for the attainment of its own special object. Now the existence of each of these two new circumstances, viz., the rigidity of the party machine and the existence of organized groups, does, it will easily be seen, immensely increase the easiness with which the Parliament Act may be misused.

Let us suppose that the two large parties, whom we may call the Ministerialists and the Opposition, each command between two and three hundred votes in the House of Commons. Neither party can be

---

[14] Complaints about "crotchets" and "fads" disrupting the functioning of parliamentary government were common at the time. Typically given Dicey's alignment with the Unionists, all four of the groups listed fell on the "liberal" side: the fate of Labour, which then had 40 seats in the House, was uncertain, and Dicey seems to have been among those who imagined it would remain a pressure-group dependent on a "progressive alliance" with the Liberals; the Irish Nationalists (71 seats in this parliament) supported the Liberals in exchange for Home Rule, and temperance and nonconformity were causes with substantial single-issue backing that went Liberal. Dicey reflected at length on the existential threat to parliamentary government posed by the weakening of the two-party system; for more, see "Memorandum on English Party System of Government" and "Memorandum on Party Government," in Dicey, *General Characteristics of English Constitutionalism: Six Unpublished Lectures*, ed. Peter Raina (Berne, 2009), 37–58, 141–62.

at all sure of retaining office, for its opponents may always obtain a majority from having gained the votes of one or more of the groups or factions—say of the Irish Nationalists or of the Labour Party. It may even occur to some ingenious intriguer at the head, say, of the so-called Ministerialists, that he can obtain the permanent support of all or most of the groups by promising to each of them that if it will support his general policy, i.e., keep him in office, he will under the Parliament Act obtain for each group in turn the object for which it cares most, e.g., Home Rule for the Irish Nationalists, an extension of Trade Union privileges for the Labour Party, and an absolute prohibition of all traffic in liquor for the Temperance Party.

A moment's reflection will show that a coalition formed on this basis may represent neither the deliberate will of the nation nor even the true judgment of a majority of the House of Commons. A homely illustration will make my point clear. A business firm consists, we will say, of Brown, Jones and Robinson. Brown contributes a lot of money to the concern, and he therefore is entitled to four votes. Jones contributes little money, but, though a dull and cautious man, has a good deal of business experience. Robinson also contributes little money, but brings into the firm much cleverness and originality, though also no small amount of rashness. Each of these two partners has only three votes. Brown, the predominant partner, imagines that his position is safe enough. He believes that the prudence of Jones and the daring of Robinson will balance one another, and that if Jones's caution degenerates into timidity, Brown may rely on the votes of Robinson, and if Robinson tries to embark on a rash venture, Brown may rely on the votes of the prudent Jones. All turns out as Brown wishes until one fine day Robinson suggests to Jones that the perpetual predominance of Brown is tiresome, and proposes to remove it by a tacit arrangement that alternately on a difference of opinion arising with Brown, Robinson shall support the proposal of Jones, and Jones the proposal of Robinson. Under this arrangement the wealthy Brown will find himself nowhere. There are always six votes against his four. But note the following circumstance. The coalition against Brown succeeds because the votes of the majority, though they obtain satisfaction for some of the private objects of each partner, do not represent the real judgment of the majority. Robinson supports the caution of Jones when both he and Brown agree in thinking it unwise. Jones supports the rashness of Robinson though he really agrees with Brown in thinking that it involves considerable risks. The private agreement between Robinson and Jones would be looked upon with very unfavourable eyes by any court of justice. Common sense shows that it may lead the partnership to ruin.

The rules of private life are in this case applicable to political life. A Parliamentary coalition based on elaborate log-rolling, even though free from any taint of personal corruption, vitiates our whole Parliamentary system and is opposed both to the authority and to the interest of the nation. I confidently assert, as does every Unionist, that such a coalition exists. I appeal, not to secret documents, which probably do not exist, but to notorious facts. A Government which came into existence on the plea of protecting Free Trade is more and more inclining towards Socialism, and has entered upon a course of reckless extravagance foreign to every doctrine of Free Traders. Ministers who but a few years ago talked of Home Rule as a bogey invented by Tories, are now carrying through the House of Commons a Home Rule Bill far more injurious to England and far less likely to secure amity between England and Ireland than either of the Gladstonian Home Rule Bills. Their Irish allies have voted, consistently enough from their own point of view, for [such] measures as, for example, the Old Age Pensions Act and the National Insurance Act, which they did not think desirable for Ireland.[15] English Nonconformists have been induced, not one suspects without qualms, to turn, in Parliament at least, a deaf ear to the bitter cry of all Protestants, whether Nonconformists or not, in Ireland. The abolition of the Church Establishment in Wales has been carried through the House of Commons by the aid of Irish Roman Catholics, who are certainly not hostile to the State endowment of religion and who will have comparatively little to say—or rather ought to have little to say—when the Home Rule Bill has passed into law, to any matter regarding the government of any part of Great Britain.[16] At any moment when it

---

[15] The National Insurance Act, 1911, the great achievement of Lloyd George and (to a lesser extent) Winston Churchill, established compulsory national health insurance and targeted unemployment benefits. Again, Dicey was skeptical.

[16] Dicey's accusation that British dissenters were selling out their Protestant brethren in Ireland by supporting Home Rule to achieve their own anti-state-Church agenda was a common refrain from Unionists.

suits the Government Mr. Asquith may, as Prime Minister, be advocating the proposal of Parliamentary votes for women which he as a private man avowedly condemns.

I have said that political log-rolling has hitherto been free from any element of personal corruption. But a desire to be fair to opponents may have led me to express myself with some rashness. Personal corruption, thank Heaven, does not yet exist in the Imperial Parliament, but the corruption of classes has already begun. When an election in a country district is to be won at all costs, the candidate, backed by the Premier, boldly advocates, we are told, a policy of land reform which he sums up in the cry of "the land for the people" and thus assuredly holds out hopes which must sound to agricultural labourers very like promises for the distribution of land. The National Insurance Act was certainly meant to gain votes though it has not exactly attained its end. What shall we say about the payment to every member of Parliament who has not got a lucrative office under the Government of a nice little sum of £400 a year, which to the astonishment of many plain men outside Parliament, is being paid for services which members had undertaken to perform gratuitously?[17] And this £400 a year which imposes a tax of about a quarter of a million upon the overburdened taxpayer of the United Kingdom, is full, to members of Parliament, not only of comfort, but of hope. The originally modest payment of members of the French Parliament has risen from about £300 to £600 a year. The payment of members of Congress has at last reached the sum of at least £1500 a year, and, as some people say, comes by force of certain allowances up to near £2000 a year. Who shall say that ten years hence our excellent M.P.'s who, we know rise so much above members of Congress, will not be each blessed with a comfortable income of £1500?

Let me conclude with a question which it concerns every Englishman to answer; let me also give to it the plainest of replies. Why is it that the revolutionary proposals of the Government fill men of sense, who understand what the plans of the Ministry mean, with intense fear? My reply may be given in a very few words: The fear is caused by the

---

[17] Payment of members was introduced as part of the Parliament Act.

existence of the Parliament Act. This Act, and this Act alone, makes it possible, nay, even probable, that ministers who have lost, or are rapidly losing, the confidence even of their own followers, may pass into law without any appeal to the people proposals which ministers themselves dare not submit to the judgment of the nation.

9

Development during the Last Thirty Years of New Constitutional Ideas (Extract from the Introduction to the Eighth Edition of *Introduction to the Study of the Law of the Constitution*, 1915)

From the *Preface to the Eighth Edition*

The body of this work is the eighth edition, or rather a reprint of the seventh edition, of the *Law of the Constitution* first published in 1885. It is, however, accompanied by a new Introduction. This Introduction is written with two objects. The first object is to trace and comment upon the way in which the main principles of our constitution as expounded by me may have been affected either by changes of law or by changes of the working of the constitution which have occurred during the last thirty years (1884–1914). The second object of this Introduction is to state and analyse the main constitutional ideas which may fairly be called new, either because they have come into existence during the last thirty years, or because (what is much more frequently the case) they have in England during that period begun to exert a new and noticeable influence...

*****

From *Introduction to the Eighth Edition:* Development during the Last Thirty Years of New Constitutional Ideas

These ideas are (1) Woman Suffrage, (2) Proportional Representation, (3) Federalism, (4) The Referendum.

Two General Observations

The brief criticism of each of these new ideas which alone in this Introduction it is possible to give, will be facilitated by attending to two general observations which apply more or less to each of the four proposed reforms or innovations.

First observation.—Political inventiveness has in general fallen far short of the originality displayed in other fields than politics by the citizens of progressive or civilised States. The immense importance attached by modern thinkers to representative government is partly accounted for by its being almost the sole constitutional discovery or invention unknown to the citizens of Athens or of Rome.[i] It is well also to note that neither representative government nor Roman Imperialism, nor indeed most of the important constitutional changes which the world has witnessed, can be strictly described as an invention or a discovery. When they did not result from imitation they have generally grown rather than been made; each was the production of men who were not aiming at giving effect to any novel political ideal, but were trying to meet in practice the difficulties and wants of their time. In no part of English history is the tardy development of new constitutional ideas more noteworthy or more paradoxical than during the whole Victorian era (1837 to 1901). It was an age full of intellectual activity and achievement; it was an age rich in works of imagination and of science; it was an age which extended in every direction the field of historical knowledge; but it was an age which added little to the world's scanty store of political or constitutional ideas. The same remark in one sense applies to the years which have passed since the opening of the twentieth century. What I have ventured to term new constitutional ideas are for the most part not original; their novelty consists in the new interest which during the last fourteen years they have come to command.

Second observation.—These new ideas take very little, one might almost say no account, of one of the ends which good legislation ought, if possible, to attain. But this observation requires explanatory comment.

---

[i] It is hardly an exaggeration to say that there exist very few other modern political conceptions (except the idea of representative government) which were not criticised by the genius of Aristotle. Note however that the immense administrative system known as the Roman Empire lay beyond, or at any rate outside, the conceptions of any Greek philosopher.

Under every form of popular government, and certainly under the more or less democratic constitution now existing in England, legislation must always aim at the attainment of at least two different ends, which, though both of importance, are entirely distinct from one another. One of these ends is the passing or the maintaining of good or wise laws, that is laws which, if carried out, would really promote the happiness or welfare of a given country, and therefore which are desirable in themselves and are in conformity with the nature of things. That such legislation is a thing to be desired, no sane man can dispute. If, for example, the freedom of trade facilitates the acquisition of good and cheap food by the people of England, and does not produce any grave counterbalancing evil, no man of ordinary sense would deny that the repeal of the corn laws was an act of wise legislation. If vaccination banishes small-pox from the country and does not produce any tremendous counterbalancing evil, the public opinion even of Leicester would hold that a law enforcing vaccination is a wise law. The second of these two different ends is to ensure that no law should be passed or maintained in a given country, *e.g.* in England, which is condemned by the public opinion of the English people. That this where possible is desirable will be admitted by every thoughtful man. A law utterly opposed to the wishes and feelings entertained by the inhabitants of a country, a rule which every one dislikes and no one will obey, is a nullity, or in truth no law at all; and, even in cases where, owing to the power of the monarch who enacts a law opposed to the wishes of his subjects, such a law can to a certain extent be enforced, the evils of the enforcement may far overbalance the good effects of legislation in itself wise. This thought fully justifies an English Government in tolerating throughout India institutions, such as caste, supported by Indian opinion though condemned by the public opinion and probably by the wise opinion of England. The same line of thought explained, palliated, and may even have justified the hesitation of English statesmen to prohibit suttee.[1] Most persons, then, will acknowledge that sound legislation should be in conformity with the nature of things, or, to express the matter shortly, be "wise," and also be in conformity with the demands of public opinion, or, in other words, be "popular," or at any rate not unpopular. But there are few Englishmen who sufficiently realise that both of these two ends

---

[1] Suttee was the custom of widows burning themselves on their deceased husbands' funeral pyres. It was banned by the British in 1829.

cannot always be attained, and that it very rarely happens that they are each equally attainable. Yet the history of English legislation abounds with illustrations of the difficulty on which it is necessary here to insist. Thus the Reform Act, 1832,[ii] is in the judgment of most English historians and thinkers a wise law; it also was at the time of its enactment a popular law. The Whigs probably underrated the amount and the strength of the opposition to the Act raised by Tories, but that the passing of the Reform Act was hailed with general favour is one of the best attested facts of modern history. The Act of Union passed in 1707 was proved by its results to be one of the wisest Acts ever placed on the statute-book. It conferred great benefits upon the inhabitants both of England and of Scotland. It created Great Britain and gave to the united country the power to resist in one age the threatened predominance of Louis XIV., and in another age to withstand and overthrow the tremendous power of Napoleon. The complete success of the Act is sufficiently proved by the absence in 1832 of any demand by either Whigs, Tories, or Radicals for its repeal. But the Act of Union, when passed, was unpopular in Scotland, and did not command any decided popularity among the electors of England. The New Poor Law of 1834 saved the country districts from ruin; its passing was the wisest and the most patriotic achievement of the Whigs, but the Act itself was unpopular and hated by the country labourers on whom it conferred the most real benefit.[2] Within two years from the passing of the Reform Act it robbed reformers of a popularity which they had hoped might be lasting. Indeed the wisdom of legislation has little to do with its popularity. Now all the ideas which are most dear to constitutional reformers or innovators in 1914 lead to schemes of more or less merit for giving full expression in the matter of legislation to public opinion, *i.e.* for ensuring that any law passed by Parliament shall be popular, or at lowest not unpopular. But these schemes make in general little provision for increasing the chance that legislation shall also be wise, or in other words that it shall increase the real welfare of the country. The singular superstition embodied in the maxim *vox populi vox Dei* has experienced in this miscalled scientific

---

[2] On the poor law, see Chapter 3, note 10. Dicey's certainty about the beneficial character of this legislation despite its unpopularity recalls the attitude of an earlier generation of liberal reformer epitomized by J.S. Mill.

[ii] See J.R.M. Butler, *The Passing of the Great Reform Bill* (Longmans, Green & Co., 1914). This is an excellent piece of historical narrative and inquiry.

age an unexpected revival. This renewed faith in the pre-eminent wisdom of the people has probably acquired new force from its congeniality with democratic sentiment. May we not conjecture that the new life given to a popular error is in part and indirectly due to the decline in the influence of utilitarianism? Faith in the voice of the people is closely connected with the doctrine of "natural rights." This dogma of natural rights was in England contemned and confuted by Bentham and his disciples.[iii] The declining influence of the utilitarian school appears therefore to give new strength to this doctrine. People forget that the dogma of natural rights was confuted not only by Benthamites but by powerful thinkers of the eighteenth and of the nineteenth century who had no sympathy with utilitarianism.

Criticism of each of the Four New Constitutional Ideas[iv]

I. *Woman Suffrage.*—The claim for women of the right to vote for members of Parliament, or, as now urged, to be placed in a position of absolute political equality with men, is no new demand. It was made in England before the end of the eighteenth century,[v] but no systematic, or at any rate noticeable, movement to obtain for Englishwomen the right to vote for members of Parliament can be carried back much earlier than 1866–67, when it was supported in the House of Commons by J.S. Mill.[3]

---

[3] See Mill's speeches of 17 July 1866 and 20 May 1867.

[iii] See *Law and Opinion*, pp. 309, 171, 172. [Dicey, *Lectures on the Relation between Law and Public Opinion in the Nineteenth Century*, second edition (London, 1914).]

[iv] It would be impossible, and it is not my aim in this Introduction, to state or even summarise all the arguments for or against each of these ideas; my sole object is to bring into light the leading thoughts or feelings which underlie the advocacy of, or the opposition to, each of these new ideas. See p. lviii, *ante.* [The line cross-referenced here is not included in this collection. This and all similar cross-references in the notes to this chapter can be found in Dicey, *Introduction to the Study of the Law of the Constitution*, eighth edition (London, 1915).]

[v] See the *Vindication of the Rights of Women*, by Mary Wollstonecraft, published 1792. Little was heard about such rights during the great French Revolution. There is no reason to suppose that Madame Roland ever claimed parliamentary votes for herself or for her sex. [Wollstonecraft, *A Vindication of the Rights of Men and a Vindication of the Rights of Woman and Hints*, ed. Sylvana Tomaselli (Cambridge, 2012). Marie-Jeanne Roland hosted an influential salon and was a leader of the Girondins, for which she lost her life in the Terror. Although many Girondin figures of both sexes supported political rights for women, Roland did not.]

Let my readers consider for a moment first the *causes* which have added strength to a movement which in 1866 attracted comparatively little public attention, and next the *main lines of argument* or of feeling which really tell on the one hand with the advocates and on the other with the opponents of the claim to votes for women.[vi]

The Causes.—These may be thus summarised. Since the beginning of the nineteenth century the number in the United Kingdom of self-supporting and also of unmarried women has greatly increased; and this class has by success in literature, as well as in other fields, acquired year by year greater influence. In the United Kingdom there exists among the actual population an excess of women over men, and this excess is increased by the emigration of Englishmen to our colonies and elsewhere. The low rate of payment received by women as compared with men, for services of any kind in which men and women enter into competition, has excited much notice. The spreading belief, or, as it used to be considered, the delusion, that wages can be raised by legislation, has naturally suggested the inference that want of a parliamentary vote inflicts severe pecuniary loss upon women. The extension of the power of the state and the enormous outgrowth of social legislation results in the daily enactment of laws which affect the very matters in which every woman has a personal interest. In an era of peace and of social reform the electors themselves constantly claim the sympathy and the active co-operation of women on behalf of causes which are treated, at any rate by partisans, as raising grave moral or religious controversy. Hence the agitation in favour of Woman Suffrage often commends itself to ministers of religion and notably to the English clergy, who believe, whether rightly or not, that the political power of women would practically add to the authority in the political world of the Church of England.[4] These circumstances, and others which may be suggested by the memory or the ingenuity of my readers, are enough to explain the prominence and weight acquired for the movement in favour of giving the parliamentary franchise to women.

The Main Lines of Argument.—These may be brought under two heads; they are most clearly and briefly exhibited if under each head is

---

[4] The fear that women's greater religiosity would lead to a risk of clerical domination if they were enfranchised was expressed by many liberal opponents of women's suffrage.

[vi] For an examination of all the main arguments alleged on either side see Dicey, *Letters to a Friend on Votes for Women* [(London, 1909)].

stated the argument of the Suffragist and the answer or reasoning in reply of the Anti-Suffragist.

First argument.—Every citizen, or, as the point is generally put, every person who pays taxes under the law of the United Kingdom, is entitled as a matter of right to a vote for a member of Parliament. Hence the obvious conclusion that as every Englishwoman pays taxes under the law of the United Kingdom, every Englishwoman is at any rate *prima facie* entitled to a vote.

Answer.—This line of reasoning proves too much. It inevitably leads to the conclusion that any form of popular government ought to be based on the existence of strictly universal suffrage. An extreme suffragette will say that this result is not a *reductio ad absurdum.* But there are thousands of sensible Englishmen and Englishwomen who, while they doubt the advisability of introducing into England even manhood suffrage, refuse to admit the cogency of reasoning which leads to the result that every Englishman and Englishwoman of full age must have a right to vote for a member of Parliament. But the full strength of an anti-suffragist's reply cannot be shown by any man who does not go a little further into the nature of things. A fair-minded man prepared to do this will, in the first place, admit that many democratic formulas, *e.g.* the dictum that "liability to taxation involves the right to representation," do verbally cover a woman's claim to a parliamentary vote. His true answer is that many so-called democratic principles, as also many so-called conservative principles, are in reality not principles at all but war-cries, or shibboleths which may contain a good deal of temporary or relative truth but are mixed up with a vast amount of error. The idea, he will ultimately say, that the possession of a vote is a personal right is a delusion. It is in truth the obligation to discharge a public duty, and whether this miscalled right should be conferred upon or withheld from Englishwomen can be decided only by determining whether their possession of the parliamentary vote will conduce to the welfare of England.

Second argument.—The difference of sex presents no apparent or necessary reason for denying to Englishwomen the same political rights as are conferred upon Englishmen. It is found by experience, as suffragists will add, that some women have in many ways even greater capacity for the exercise of government than have some men. This argument may best be put in its full strength if it be placed, as it often is, in the form of a question: Was it reasonable that Florence Nightingale should not have possessed the right to vote for a member of Parliament when even in her day her footman or her coachman, if he had happened to be a ten-pound householder, or a forty-shilling freeholder, might have exercised a right denied to a lady who, as appears from her biography, possessed many statesmanlike qualities, who did in fact in some lines of action exert more political power than most M.P.s, and who always exercised power disinterestedly, and generally exercised it with admitted benefit to the country? There is not the remotest doubt that the argument involved in this inquiry (in whatever form it is stated) seems to many women, to a great number of parliamentary electors, and also to a considerable number of M.P.s, to afford an unanswerable and conclusive reason in favour of giving parliamentary votes to women.

Answer.—The claim of parliamentary votes for women as now put forward in England is in reality a claim for the absolute political equality of the two sexes. Whether its advocates are conscious of the fact or not, it is a demand on behalf of women for seats in Parliament and in the Cabinet. It means that Englishwomen should share the jury box and should sit on the judicial bench. It treats as insignificant for most purposes that difference of sex which, after all, disguise the matter as you will, is one of the most fundamental and far-reaching differences which can distinguish one body of human beings from another. It is idle to repeat again and again reasoning which, for the last thirty years and more, has been pressed upon the attention of every English reader and elector. One thing is certain: the real strength (and it is great) of the whole conservative argument against the demand of votes for women lies in the fact that this line of reasoning, on the face thereof, conforms to the nature of things. The anti-suffragists can re-echo the words of Burke whilst adapting them to a controversy unknown to him and practically unknown to his age: "The principles that guide us, in public and in private, as they are not of our devising, but moulded into the nature and the essence of things, will endure with the sun and moon—long, very long after whig and tory, Stuart and Brunswick [suffragist, suffragette, and anti-suffragist], and all such miserable bubbles and playthings of the hour, are vanished from existence and from memory."[vii]

[vii] Burke, *Correspondence,* i. pp, 332, 333. [Edmund Burke, Draft Letter of 1771 in *The Works and Correspondence of the Right Honourable Edmund Burke*, 8 vols. (London, 1852), vol. 1, 166.]

II. *Proportional Representation.*[viii] — The case in favour of the introduction of proportional representation into England rests on the truth of
three propositions.

First proposition.—The House of Commons often fails to represent
with precision or accuracy the state of opinion, *e.g.* as to woman suffrage,
existing among the electorate of England. In other words, the House of
Commons often fails to be, as it is sometimes expressed, "the mirror of
the national mind," or to exactly reflect the will of the electors.

Second proposition.—It is quite possible by some system of proportional representation to frame a House of Commons which would reflect
much more nearly than at present the opinion of the nation, or, in other
words, of the electorate.

Third proposition.—It is pre-eminently desirable that every opinion
bonâ fide existing among the electors should be represented in the House
of Commons in as nearly as possible the same proportion in which it
exists among the electors, or, to use popular language, among the nation.

Now of these three propositions the substantial truth of the first and
second must, in my judgment, be admitted. No one can doubt the
possibility, and even the high probability, that, for example, the cause
of woman suffrage may, at the present moment, obtain more than half
the votes of the House of Commons while it would not obtain as many as
half the votes of the electorate. Nor again is it at all inconceivable that at
some other period the cause of woman suffrage should, while receiving
the support of half the electorate, fail to obtain the votes of half the
House of Commons. No one, in the second place, can, I think, with
reason dispute that, among the numerous plans for proportional representation thrust upon the attention of the public, some one, and probably
several, would tend to make the House of Commons a more complete
mirror of what is called the mind of the nation than the House is at
present; and this concession, it may with advantage be noted, does not
involve the belief that under any system of popular government whatever, a representative body can be created which at every moment will

---

[viii] See Humphreys, *Proportional Representation*; Fischer Williams, *Proportional
Representation and British Politics*; Lowell, *Public Opinion and Popular Government*,
pp. 122–124. [John H. Humphreys, *Proportional Representation: A Study in Methods of
Election* (London, 1911); J. Fischer Williams, *Proportional Representation and British
Politics* (London, 1914); A. Lawrence Lowell, *Public Opinion and Popular Government*
(New York, 1913). Lowell's is an especially rich work of democratic theory.]

absolutely and with complete accuracy reflect the opinions held by various classes of the people of England. Now my belief in the substantial truth of the first and the second of our three propositions makes it needless for me, at any rate for the purpose of this Introduction, to consider the reservations with which their absolute accuracy ought to be assumed. For the sake of argument, at any rate, I treat them as true. My essential objection to the system of proportional representation consists in my grave doubt as to the truth of the third of the above three propositions, namely, that it is desirable that any opinion existing among any large body of electors should be represented in the House of Commons as nearly as possible in the same proportion in which it exists among such electors.

Before, however, any attempt is made to state the specific objections which in my judgment lie against the introduction of proportional representation into the parliamentary constitution of England, it is essential to discriminate between two different ideas which are confused together under the one demand for proportional representation. The one of these ideas is the desirability that every opinion entertained by a substantial body of Englishmen should obtain utterance in the House of Commons, or, to use a vulgar but effective piece of political slang, "be voiced by" some member or members of that House. Thus it has been laid down by the leader of the Liberal party that "it was infinitely to the advantage of the House of Commons, if it was to be a real reflection and mirror of the national mind, that there should be no strain of opinion honestly entertained by any substantial body of the King's subjects which should not find there representation and speech."[ix] To this doctrine any person who has been influenced by the teaching of Locke, Bentham, and Mill will find it easy to assent, for it is well known that in any country, and especially in any country where popular government exists, the thoughts, even the bad or the foolish thoughts, of the people should be known to the national legislature. An extreme example will best show my meaning. If among the people of any land the hatred of the Jews or of Judaism should exist, it would certainly be desirable that this odious prejudice should find some exponent or advocate in the Parliament of such country, for the knowledge of popular errors or delusions may well be essential to the carrying out of just government

---

[ix] See Mr. Asquith's speech at St. Andrews, Feb. 19, 1906, cited by J. Fischer Williams, *Proportional Representation,* p. 17.

or wise administration. Ignorance is never in truth the source of wisdom or of justice. The other idea or meaning attached by Proportionalists to proportional representation is that every influential opinion should not only find utterance in the House of Commons, but, further, and above all, be represented in the House of Commons by the same proportionate number of votes which it obtains from the voters at an election. Thus the eminent man who advocated the desirability of every opinion obtaining a hearing in the House of Commons, used on another occasion the following words: "It is an essential and integral feature of our policy that we shall go forward with the task of making the House of Commons not only the mouthpiece but the mirror of the national mind."[x] Now the doctrine of proportional representation thus interpreted is a dogma to which a fair-minded man may well refuse his assent. It is by no means obviously true; it is open to the following (among other) objections that admit of clear statement.

Objections to the Third Proposition

First objection.— The more complicated any system of popular election is made, the more power is thrown into the hands of election agents or wire-pullers. This of itself increases the power and lowers the character of the party machine; but the greatest political danger with which England is now threatened is the inordinate influence of party mechanism. This objection was long ago insisted upon by Bagehot.[xi] It explains, if it does not wholly justify, John Bright's denunciation of fancy franchises.[5]

Second objection.—The House of Commons is no mere debating society. It is an assembly entrusted with great though indirect executive authority; it is, or ought to be, concerned with the appointment and the criticism of the Cabinet. Grant, for the sake of argument, that every influential opinion should in the House of Commons gain a hearing. This result would be obtained if two men, or only one man, were to be

---

[5] "Fancy franchises" was a derogatory term for a category of proposed electoral regulations, such as the bestowal of votes on those who had reached a certain threshold in savings deposits, meant to enable a "safe" expansion of the suffrage that excluded the unworthy and avoided the tyranny of the poor majority.

[x] Mr. Asquith at Burnley, Dec. 5, 1910, cited by J. Fischer Williams, *Proportional Representation,* p. 17.

[xi] Bagehot, *English Constitution,* pp. 148–159. [Bagehot, *The English Constitution,* ed. Paul Smith (Cambridge, 2001), 105–11.]

found in the House who could ensure a hearing whenever he spoke in favour of some peculiar opinion. The argument for woman suffrage was never stated with more force in Parliament than when John Mill represented Westminster. The reasons in its favour would not, as far as argument went, have commanded more attention if a hundred members had been present who shared Mill's opinions but were not endowed with his logical power and his lucidity of expression. But where a body of men such as constitute the House of Commons are at all concerned with government, unity of action is of more consequence than variety of opinion. The idea, indeed, of representation may be, and often is, carried much too far. A Cabinet which represented all shades of opinion would be a Ministry which could not act at all. No one really supposes that a Government could in ordinary circumstances be formed in which two opposite parties balanced one another. Nor can it often be desirable that an opinion held by, say, a third of a ministerial party should necessarily be represented by a third of the Cabinet. It may well be doubted whether even on commissions appointed partly, at any rate, for the purpose of inquiry, it is at all desirable that distinctly opposite views should obtain recognition. The Commission which laid down the leading lines of Poor Law Reform in 1834 rendered an immense service to England. Would there have been any real advantage in placing on that Commission men who condemned any change in the existing poor law?

Third objection.—Proportional representation, just because it aims at the representation of opinions rather than of persons, tends to promote the existence in the House of Commons of numerous party groups and also fosters the admitted evil of log-rolling. The working of English parliamentary government has owed half of its success to the existence of two leading and opposed parties, and of two such parties only. Using somewhat antiquated but still intelligible terms, let me call them by the name of Tories and Whigs.[xii] These two parties have, if one may speak in very broad terms, tended, the one to uphold the rule of the well-born, the well-to-do, and therefore, on the whole, of the more educated members of the community; the other has promoted the power of numbers, and has therefore aimed at increasing the political authority of the comparatively poor, that is, of the comparatively ignorant. Each tendency has obviously

---

[xii] I choose these old expressions which have been in use, at any rate from 1689 till the present day, because they make it easier to keep somewhat apart from the burning controversies of 1914.

some good and some bad effects. If, for a moment, one may adopt modern expressions while divesting them of any implied blame or praise, one may say that Conservatism and Liberalism each play their part in promoting the welfare of any country where popular government exists. Now, that the existence of two leading parties, and of two such parties only, in England has favoured the development of English constitutionalism is past denial. It is also certain that during the nineteenth century there has been a notable tendency in English public life to produce in the House of Commons separate groups or parties which stood more or less apart from Tories and Whigs, and were all but wholly devoted to the attainment of some one definite change or reform. The Repealers, as led by O'Connell, and still more the Free Traders, as led by Cobden,[xiii] are early examples of such groups. These groups avowedly held the success of the cause for which they fought of greater consequence than the maintenance in office either of Tories or of Whigs. Even in 1845 they had perplexed the working of our constitution; they had gone far to limit the operation of the very valuable rule that a party, which persuades Parliament to adopt the party's policy, should be prepared to take office and carry that policy into effect. The Free Traders, in fact, give the best, if not the earliest, example of an English group organised to enforce the adoption by the English Parliament of an opinion, doctrine, or theory to which that group was devoted. Now an observer of the course of events during the last sixty years will at once note the increasing number of such groups in the House of Commons. To-day we have Ministerialists and Unionists (corresponding roughly with the old Whigs and Tories), we have also Irish Nationalists and the Labour Party. These parties have each separate organisations. But one can easily observe the existence of smaller bodies each devoted to its own movement or cause, such, for example, as the temperance reformers, as the advocates of woman suffrage, or as the

---

[xiii] Cobden would have supported any Premier, whether a Tory or a Whig, who undertook to repeal the Corn Laws. O'Connell would have supported any Premier who had pledged himself to repeal the Act of Union with Ireland; but O'Connell's position was peculiar. He took an active interest in English politics, he was a Benthamite Liberal, and during a part of his career acted in alliance with the Whigs. [Richard Cobden was a radical-liberal MP and the most famous crusader for free trade of the mid-century. Dicey wrote about him (often not positively) in his journalism. Daniel O'Connell was the leader of the Irish reform movement in the first half of the century, as well as a champion of other liberal causes. He founded the Repeal Association in 1830 which sought to undo the 1800 Act of Union and which was in many ways a forerunner of the Home Rule positions which Dicey combated.]

members who hold that the question of the day is the disestablishment of the Church. This state of things already invalidates our constitutional customs. Nor is it easy to doubt that any fair system of proportional representation must increase the number of groups existing in Parliament, for the very object of Proportionalists is to ensure that every opinion which exists among an appreciable number of British electors shall have an amount of votes in Parliament proportionate to the number of votes it obtains among the electors. If, for example, a tenth of the electors should be anti-vaccinators, the anti-vaccinators ought, under a perfect scheme of representation, to command sixty-seven votes in the House of Commons. Sixty-seven anti-vaccinators who might accidentally obtain seats in the House of Commons, *e.g.* as Conservatives or Liberals, would, be it noted, constitute a very different body from sixty-seven members sent to the House of Commons to represent the cause of anti-vaccination. The difference is this: In the first case each anti-vaccinator would often perceive that there were matters of more pressing importance than anti-vaccination; but the sixty-seven men elected under a system of proportional representation to obtain the total repeal of the vaccination laws would, one may almost say must, make that repeal the one dominant object of their parliamentary action. That the multiplication of groups might weaken the whole system of our parliamentary government is a probable conjecture. That proportional representation might tend to extend the vicious system of log-rolling is all but demonstrable. Let me suppose the sixty-seven anti-vaccinators to be already in existence; let me suppose, as would probably be the case, that they are elected because of their firm faith in anti-vaccination, and that, both from their position and from their creed, they feel that to destroy the vaccination laws is the supreme object at which every good man should aim. They will soon find that their sixty-seven votes, though of high importance, are not enough to save the country. The course which these patriots must follow is obvious. They are comparatively indifferent about Home Rule, about Disestablishment, about the objects of the Labour Party. Let them promise their support to each of the groups advocating each of these objects in return for the help in repealing legislation which originates, say our anti-vaccinators, in the delusions of Jenner.[6] A political miracle will have been performed. A majority in favour of anti-vaccination will have been

---

[6] Edward Jenner developed the first smallpox vaccine at the end of the eighteenth century.

obtained; the voice of fanatics will have defeated the common sense of the nation. Let me, as an illustration of my contention, recall to public attention a forgotten fact. Some forty years ago the Claimant, now barely remembered as Arthur Orton, was a popular hero.[7] His condemnation to imprisonment for fourteen or fifteen years excited much indignation. He obtained one representative, and one representative only, of his grievances in the House of Commons. Under a properly organised system of proportional representation, combined with our present household suffrage, he might well have obtained twenty. Does any one doubt that these twenty votes would have weighed with the Whips of any party in power? Is it at all certain that the Claimant might not, thus supported, have obtained a mitigation of his punishment, if not a re-trial of his case? This is an extreme illustration of popular folly. For this very reason it is a good test of a logical theory. I do not contend that proportional representation cannot be defended by weighty considerations; my contention is that it is open to some grave objections which have not received an adequate answer.[xiv]

III. *Federalism.*[xv]—In 1884 the peculiarities and the merits of federal government had not attracted the attention of the English public. Here and there a statesman whose mind was turned towards the relation of England and her colonies had perceived that some of the self-governing colonies might with advantage adopt federal constitutions. In 1867 Parliament had readily assented to the creation of the Canadian Dominion and thereby transformed the colonies possessed by England on the continent of America into a federal state. In truth it may be said that the success of the Northern States of the American Commonwealth in the War of Secession had, for the first time, impressed upon Englishmen the belief that a democratic and a federal state might come

---

[7] Dicey is referring to a dramatic legal episode from the 1860s–70s that sparked a populist groundswell in which an unidentified man came out of the blue claiming to be the presumptively dead heir to the Tichborne baronetcy.

[xiv] Proportional representation was in Mill's day known as minority representation. The change of name is not without significance. In 1870 the demand for minority representation was put forward mainly as the means for obtaining a hearing for intelligent minorities whose whisper might easily be drowned by the shouts of an unintelligent majority. In 1914 minority representation is recommended mainly as the means of ensuring that the true voice of the nation shall be heard. It was once considered a check upon democracy; it is now supported as the best method for giving effect to the true will of the democracy.

[xv] Compare especially as to federal government, Chap. III. p. 134, *post*. [Not included in this collection.]

with success through a civil war, carried on against states which asserted their right to secede from the Republic of which they were a part. Still in 1884 hardly a statesman whose name carried weight with Englishmen advocated the formation of a federal system as a remedy for the defects, whatever they were, of the English constitution, or as the means for uniting the widely scattered countries which make up the British Empire. Walter Bagehot was in his day, as he still is, the most eminent of modern English constitutionalists. He compared the constitution of England with the constitution of the United States. But the result of such comparison was, in almost every case, to illustrate some hitherto unnoted merit of the English constitution which was not to be found in the constitution of the great American Republic. Sir Henry Maine was in his time the most brilliant of the writers who had incidentally turned their thoughts towards constitutional problems. Maine's *Popular Government*, published in 1885, expressed his admiration for the rigidity or the conservatism of American federalism. But he never hinted at the conviction, which he probably never entertained, that either the United Kingdom or the British Empire would gain by transformation into a federal state. Thirty years ago the nature of federalism had received in England very inadequate investigation.[xvi] In this, as in other matters, 1914 strangely contrasts with 1884. The notion is now current that federalism contains the solution of every constitutional problem which perplexes British statesmanship. Why not, we are told, draw closer the bonds which maintain peace and goodwill between the United Kingdom and all her colonies, by constructing a new and grand Imperial federation governed by a truly Imperial Parliament, which shall represent every state, including England, which is subject to the government of the King? Why not, we are asked, establish a permanent reconciliation between England and Ireland by the conversion of the United Kingdom into a federalised kingdom whereof England, Scotland, Ireland, and Wales, and, for aught I know, the Channel Islands and the Isle of Man, shall form separate states? This new constitutional idea of the inherent excellence of federalism is a new faith or delusion which deserves examination. My purpose, therefore, is to consider two different matters—namely, first, the general characteristics of federalism;

[xvi] In Chap. III., *post*, federalism was analysed (1885) as illustrating, by way of contrast, that sovereignty of the English Parliament which makes England one of the best examples of a unitary state.

secondly, the bearing of these characteristics on the proposal popularly known as Imperial federalism, for including England[xvii] and the five self-governing colonies in a federal constitution, and also the proposal (popularly known as Home Rule all round) for federalising the United Kingdom.[8]

Leading Characteristics of Federal Government[xviii]

Federalism is a natural constitution for a body of states which desire union and do not desire unity. Take as countries which exhibit this state of feeling the United States, the English federated colonies, the Swiss Confederation, and the German Empire, and contrast with this special condition of opinion the deliberate rejection by all Italian patriots of federalism, which in the case of Italy presented many apparent advantages, and the failure of union between Sweden and Norway to produce any desire for unity or even for a continued political connection, though these Scandinavian lands differ little from each other in race, in religion, in language, or in their common interest to maintain their independence against neighbouring and powerful countries.

The physical contiguity, further, of countries which are to form a confederated state is certainly a favourable, and possibly a necessary, condition for the success of federal government.

The success of federal government is greatly favoured by, if it does not absolutely require, approximate equality in the wealth, in the population, and in the historical position of the different countries which make up a confederation. The reason for this is pretty obvious. The idea which lies at the bottom of federalism is that each of the separate states should have approximately equal political rights and should thereby be

---

[8] The self-governing colonies or "dominions" at this time were Canada, Australia, New Zealand, Newfoundland, and South Africa.

[xvii] In treating of Imperial federalism, as often in other parts of this book, I purposely and frequently, in accordance with popular language, use "England" as equivalent to the United Kingdom.

[xviii] See especially Chap. III. p. 134, *post.* [Not included in this edition.] It is worth observing that the substance of this chapter was published before the production by Gladstone of his first Home Rule Bill for Ireland. [That is, Dicey had not substantially revised that chapter since the first edition of *Law of the Constitution* in 1885, all of the Home Rule Bills having been produced subsequently.]

able to maintain the "limited independence" (if the term may be used) meant to be secured by the terms of federal union. Hence the provision contained in the constitution of the United States under which two Senators, and no more, are given to each state, though one be as populous, as large, and as wealthy as is New York, and another be as small in area and contain as few citizens as Rhode Island. Bagehot, indeed, points out that the equal power in the Senate of a small state and of a large state is from some points of view an evil. It is, however, an arrangement obviously congenial to federal sentiment. If one state of a federation greatly exceed in its numbers and in its resources the power of each of the other states, and still more if such "dominant partner," to use a current expression, greatly exceed the whole of the other Confederated States in population and in wealth, the confederacy will be threatened with two dangers. The dominant partner may exercise an authority almost inconsistent with federal equality. But, on the other hand, the other states, if they should possess under the constitution rights equal to the rights or the political power left to the dominant partner, may easily combine to increase unduly the burdens, in the way of taxation or otherwise, imposed upon the one most powerful state.

Federalism, when successful, has generally been a stage towards unitary government. In other words, federalism tends to pass into nationalism. This has certainly been the result of the two most successful of federal experiments. The United States, at any rate as they now exist, have been well described as a nation concealed under the form of a federation. The same expression might with considerable truth be applied to Switzerland. Never was there a country in which it seemed more difficult to produce national unity. The Swiss cantons are divided by difference of race, by difference of language, by difference of religion. These distinctions till nearly the middle of the nineteenth century produced a kind of disunion among the Swiss people which in 1914 seems almost incredible. They forbade the existence of a common coinage; they allowed any one canton to protect the financial interest of its citizens against competition by the inhabitants of every other canton. In 1847 the Sonderbund threatened to destroy the very idea of Swiss unity, Swiss nationality, and Swiss independence. Patriots had indeed for generations perceived that the federal union of Switzerland afforded the one possible guarantee for the continued existence of their country. But attempt after attempt to secure the unity of Switzerland had ended in failure. The victory of the Swiss federalists in the Sonderbund war gave new life to Switzerland: this was the one indubitable success directly due to the movements of 1847–48. It is indeed happy that the victory of the federal armies took place before the fall of the French Monarchy, and that the Revolution of February, combined with other movements which distracted Europe, left the Swiss free to manage their own affairs in their own way.[9] Swiss patriotism and moderation met with their reward. Switzerland became master of her own fate. Each step in the subsequent progress of the new federal state has been a step along the path leading from confederate union to national unity.

A federal constitution is, as compared with a unitary constitution, a weak form of government. Few were the thinkers who in 1884 would have denied the truth of this proposition. In 1914 language is constantly used which implies that a federal government is in itself superior to a unitary constitution such as that of France or of England. Yet the comparative weakness of federalism is no accident. A true federal government is based on the division of powers. It means the constant effort of statesmanship to balance one state of the confederacy against another. No one can rate more highly than myself the success with which a complicated system is worked by the members of the Swiss Council or, to use expressions familiar to Englishmen, by the Swiss Cabinet. Yet everywhere throughout Swiss arrangements you may observe the desire to keep up a sort of balance of advantages between different states. The members of the Council are seven in number; each member must, of necessity, belong to a different canton. The federal Parliament meets at Bern; the federal Court sits at Lausanne in the canton of Vaud; the federal university is allotted to a third canton, namely Zurich. Now rules or practices of this kind must inevitably restrict the power of bringing into a Swiss Cabinet all the best political talent to be found in Switzerland. Such a system applied to an English or to a French Cabinet would be found almost unworkable. Federalism again would mean, in any country where English ideas prevail, the predominance of legalism or, in other words, a general willingness to yield to the authority of the law courts. Nothing is more remarkable, and in the eyes of any impartial critic more praiseworthy, than the reverence paid on the whole by American opinion to the Supreme Court of the United States. Nor must one forget that the respect paid to the opinion of their own judges,

---

[9] On the Sonderbund War and the birth of modern democratic Switzerland therefrom, see page 21, note 5.

even when deciding questions on which political feeling runs high, is, on the whole, characteristic of the citizens of each particular state. The Supreme Court, *e.g.*, of Massachusetts may be called upon to determine in effect whether a law passed by the legislature of Massachusetts is, or is not, constitutional; and the decision of the Court will certainly meet with obedience. Now, what it is necessary to insist upon is that this legalism which fosters and supports the rule of law is not equally displayed in every country. No French court has ever definitely pronounced a law passed by the French legislature invalid, nor, it is said, has any Belgian court ever pronounced invalid a law passed by the Belgian Parliament. Whether English electors are now strongly disposed to confide to the decision of judges questions which excite strong political feeling is doubtful. Yet—and this is no insignificant matter—under every federal system there must almost of necessity exist some body of persons who can decide whether the terms of the federal compact have been observed.[10] But if this power be placed in the hands of the Executive, the law will, it may be feared, be made subservient to the will of any political party which is for the moment supreme. If it be placed in the hands of judges, who profess and probably desire to practise judicial impartiality, it may be very difficult to ensure general respect for any decision which contradicts the interests and the principles of a dominant party. Federalism, lastly, creates divided allegiance. This is the most serious and the most inevitable of the weaknesses attaching to a form of government under which loyalty to a citizen's native state may conflict with his loyalty to the whole federated nation. Englishmen, Scotsmen, and Irishmen have always, as soldiers, been true to the common flag. The whole history of the Sonderbund in Switzerland and of Secession in the United States bears witness to the agonised perplexity of the noblest among soldiers when called upon to choose between loyalty to their country and loyalty to their canton or state. One example of this difficulty is amply sufficient for my purpose. General Scott and General Lee alike had been trained as officers of the American Army; each was a Virginian; each of them was determined from the outbreak of the Civil

[10] Dicey's theory that federalism required the supremacy of constitutional courts was influential in its time, and he expounded it repeatedly. In the eighth edition of the *Law of the Constitution* the relevant discussions occur in ch. 3 and appendices 2, 8, and 9. Dicey's comments here on the lack of judicial review in many countries highlight the fact that the judicialization of European politics is in many ways quite a recent phenomenon.

War to follow the dictates of his own conscience; each was placed in a position as painful as could be occupied by a soldier of bravery and honour; each was a victim of that double allegiance which is all but inherent in federalism. General Scott followed the impulse of loyalty to the Union. General Lee felt that as a matter of duty he must obey the sentiment of loyalty to Virginia.[11]

In any estimate of the strength or the weakness of federal government it is absolutely necessary not to confound, though the confusion is a very common one, federalism with nationalism. A truly federal government is the denial of national independence to every state of the federation. No single state of the American Commonwealth is a separate nation; no state, it may be added, *e.g.* the State of New York, has anything like as much of local independence as is possessed by New Zealand or by any other of the five Dominions.[xix] There is of course a sense, and a very real sense, in which national tradition and national feeling may be cultivated in a state which forms part of a confederacy. The French inhabitants of Quebec are Frenchmen to the core. But their loyalty to the British Empire is certain. One indisputable source of their Imperial loyalty is that the break-up of the Empire might, as things now stand, result to Canada in union with the United States. But Frenchmen would with more difficulty maintain their French character if Quebec became a state of the Union and ceased to be a province of the Dominion. In truth national character in one sense of that term has less necessary connection than Englishmen generally suppose with political arrangements. It would be simple folly to assert that Sir Walter Scott did not share the sentiment of Scottish nationalism; yet the influence of Scott's genius throughout Europe was favoured by, and in a sense was the fruit of, the union with England.[12] But the aspiration and the effort towards actual national independence is at least as inconsistent with the conditions of a federal as with the conditions of a unitary government. Any one will see that this is so who considers how patent would have been the folly of the attempt

---

[11] Winfield Scott and Robert E. Lee had both been at the top of the army ranks prior to the American Civil War. Scott's service for the Union was brief, whereas Lee led the Confederate military throughout the war.

[12] Walter Scott was one of the most important poets and novelists of the Romantic period. Like many of the great Romantics he was a political conservative and had nationalist sympathies.

[xix] As to the meaning of "Dominions" see p. xxiv, note 1 *ante*. [Not included in this collection.]

to establish a confederacy which should have left Italy a state of the Austrian Empire. Nor does historical experience countenance the idea that federalism, which may certainly be a step towards closer national unity, can be used as a method for gradually bringing political unity to an end.

The Characteristics of Federal Government in Relation to Imperial Federalism

Many Englishmen of to-day advocate the building up of some grand federal constitution which would include the United Kingdom (or, to use popular language, England) and at any rate the five Dominions. This splendid vision of the advantages to be obtained by increased unity of action between England and her self-governing colonies is suggested by obvious and important facts. The wisdom of every step which may increase the reciprocal goodwill, strong as it now is, of England and her Dominions is proved by the success of each Imperial Conference. It is perfectly plain already, and will become every day plainer both to Englishmen and to the inhabitants of the British Empire outside England, that the existence of the Empire ought to secure both England and her colonies against even the possibility of attack by any foreign power. It to-day in reality secures the maintenance of internal peace and order in every country inhabited by British subjects. It is further most desirable, it may probably become in no long time an absolute necessity, that every country throughout the Empire should contribute in due measure to the cost of Imperial defence. To this it should be added that the material advantages accruing to millions of British subjects from the Imperial power of England may more and more tend to produce that growth of loyalty and goodwill towards the Empire which in 1914 is a characteristic and splendid feature both of England and of her colonies. Any man may feel pride in an Imperial patriotism grounded on the legitimate belief that the Empire built up by England furthers the prosperity and the happiness of the whole body of British subjects.[xx] But, when every admission which the most ardent of

---

[xx] "But this Empire of ours is distinguished from [other Empires] by special and dominating characteristics. From the external point of view it is made up of countries which are not geographically conterminous or even contiguous, which present every variety of climate, soil, people, and religion, and, even in those communities which have attained to complete self-government, and which are represented in this room to-day, does not draw

192

Imperialists can ask for, is made of the benefits conferred in every quarter of the world upon the inhabitants of different countries, by the existence of England's Imperial power, it is quite possible for a calm observer to doubt whether the so-called federalisation of the British Empire is an object which ought to be aimed at by the statesmen either of England or of the Dominions. The objections to the creed of federalism, in so far as it means the building up of a federal constitution for the Empire, or rather for England and her Dominions, may be summed up in the statement that this belief in a new-fangled federalism is at bottom a delusion, and a delusion perilous not only to England but to the whole British Empire. But this general statement may be best justified by the working out of two criticisms.

First.—The attempt to form a federal constitution for the Empire is at this moment full of peril to England, to the Dominions, and, it may well be, to the maintenance of the British Empire. The task imposed upon British and upon colonial statesmanship is one of infinite difficulty. As we all know, the creation of the United States was for the thirteen independent colonies a matter of absolute necessity. But the highest statesmanship of the ablest leaders whom a country ever possessed was hardly sufficient for the transformation of thirteen different states into one confederated nation. Even among countries differing little in race, religion, and

---

its unifying and cohesive force solely from identity of race or of language. Yet you have here a political organisation which, by its mere existence, rules out the possibility of war between populations numbering something like a third of the human race. There is, as there must be among communities so differently situated and circumstanced, a vast variety of constitutional methods, and of social and political institutions and ideals. But to speak for a moment for that part of the Empire which is represented here to-day, what is it that we have in common, which amidst every diversity of external and material conditions, makes us and keeps us one? There are two things in the self-governing British Empire which are unique in the history of great political aggregations. The first is the reign of Law: wherever the King's writ runs, it is the symbol and messenger not of an arbitrary authority, but of rights shared by every citizen, and capable of being asserted and made effective by the tribunals of the land. The second is the combination of local autonomy—absolute, unfettered, complete—with loyalty to a common head, co-operation, spontaneous and unforced, for common interests and purposes, and, I may add, a common trusteeship, whether it be in India or in the Crown Colonies, or in the Protectorates, or within our own borders, of the interests and fortunes of fellow-subjects who have not yet attained, or perhaps in some cases may never attain, to the full stature of self-government."—See speech of the Right Hon. H. H. Asquith (President of the Conference), Minutes of Proceedings of the Imperial Conference, 1911 [Cd. 5745], p. 22. [For the full speech, see "Opening Meeting: Address by the President" in *Minutes of Proceedings of the Imperial Conference, 1911* (London, 1911), 21–8.]

history, it was found all but impossible to reconcile the existence of state rights with the creation of a strong central and national power. If any one considers the infinite diversity of the countries which make up the British Empire, if he reflects that they are occupied by different races whose customs and whose civilisation are the product of absolutely different histories, that the different countries of the Empire are in no case contiguous, and in many instances are separated from England and from each other by seas extending over thousands of miles, he will rather wonder at the boldness of the dreams entertained by the votaries of federal Imperialism, than believe that the hopes of federalising the Empire are likely to meet with fulfilment. I shall be reminded, however, and with truth, that Imperial federalism, as planned by even its most sanguine advocates, means something very different from the attempt to frame a constitution of which the United Kingdom, the Dominions, the Crown colonies, and British India shall constitute different states.[13] Our Imperialists really aim, and the fact must be constantly borne in mind, at federalising the relation not between England and the rest of the Empire, but between England and the five self-governing Dominions. But then this admission, while it does away with some of the difficulties besetting the policy which is miscalled *Imperial* federalism, raises a whole body of difficult and all but unanswerable questions. Take a few of the inquiries to which sanguine reformers, who talk with easy confidence of federalism being the solution of all the most pressing constitutional problems, must find a reply. What is to be the relation between the new federated state (consisting of England and the five Dominions) and British India? Will the millions who inhabit India readily obey a new and strange sovereign, or will the states of the new confederacy agree that the rest of the Empire shall be ruled by the Parliament and Government of England alone? Is the whole expense of Imperial defence to be borne by the federated states, or will the new federation of its own authority impose taxes upon India and the Crown colonies for the advantage of the federated state? Is it certain, after all, that the mutual goodwill entertained between England and the Dominions really points towards federalism? No doubt England and the states represented at the Imperial Conferences entertain a genuine and ardent wish that the British Empire should be strong and be able, as against foreigners, and even in resistance to secession, to use

[13] "Crown Colony" was a classification that included all colonies that were not self-governing except India.

all the resources of the whole Empire for its defence and maintenance. But then each one of the Dominions desires rather the increase than the lessening of its own independence. Is there the remotest sign that, for example, New Zealand, though thoroughly loyal to the Empire, would tolerate interference by any Imperial Parliament or Congress with the internal affairs of New Zealand which even faintly resembled the authority exerted by Congress in New York, or the authority exerted by the Parliament of the Canadian Dominion in Quebec? But if the Dominions would not tolerate the interference with their own affairs by any Parliament, whatever its title, sitting at Westminster, is there the remotest reason to suppose that the existing Imperial Parliament will consent to become a Parliament of the Empire in which England, or rather the United Kingdom, and each of the five Dominions shall be fairly represented? But here we come to a further inquiry, to which our new federalists hardly seem to have given a thought: What are they going to do with the old Imperial Parliament which has, throughout the whole history of England, inherited the traditions and often exerted the reality of sovereign power? Under our new federation is the Imperial Parliament to become a Federal Congress wherein every state is to have due representation? Is this Federal Congress to be for Englishmen the English Parliament, or is there to be in addition to or instead of the ancient Parliament of England a new local English Parliament controlling the affairs of England alone? This question itself is one of unbounded difficulty. It embraces two or three inquiries the answers whereto may trouble the thoughts of theorists, and these replies, if they are ever discovered, may give rise throughout England and the British Empire to infinite discord. Is it not one example of the perplexities involved in any plan of Imperial federalism, and of the intellectual levity with which they are met, that our Federalists never have given a clear and, so to speak, intelligible idea of what is to be under a federal government the real position not of the United Kingdom but of that small country limited in size, but still of immense power, which is specifically known by the august name of England? The traditional feuds of Ireland and the ecclesiastical grievances of Wales, the demand of some further recognition of that Scottish nationality, for which no sensible Englishman shows or is tempted to show the least disrespect, all deserve and receive exaggerated attention. But England and English interests, just because Englishmen have identified the greatness of England with the prosperity of the United Kingdom and the greatness and good government of the

Empire, are for the moment overlooked. I venture to assure all my readers that this forgetfulness of England—and by England I here mean the country known, and famous, as England before the legal creation either of Great Britain or of the United Kingdom—is a fashion opposed both to common sense and to common justice, and, like all opposition to the nature of things, will ultimately come to nothing.[xxi] The questions I have mentioned are numerous and full of complexity. The present time, we must add, is intensely unfavourable to the creation of a new federalised and Imperial constitution. The Parliament and the Government of the United Kingdom may be chargeable with grave errors: they have fallen into many blunders. But they have never forgotten—they will never, one trusts, forget—that they hold "a common trusteeship, whether it be in India or in the Crown Colonies, or in the Protectorates, or within our own borders, of the interests and fortunes of fellow-subjects who have not yet attained, or perhaps in some cases may never attain, to the full stature of self-government."[xxii] Is it credible that, for instance, the peoples of India will see with indifference this trusteeship pass from the hands of an Imperial Parliament (which has more or less learned to think imperially, and in England has maintained the equal political rights of all British subjects) into the hands of a new-made Imperial Congress which will consist in part of representatives of Dominions which, it may be of necessity, cannot give effect to this enlarged conception of British citizenship?[xxiii]

Secondly.—The unity of the Empire does not require the formation of a federal or of any other brand-new constitution.—I yield to no man in my

---

[xxi] Sir Joseph Ward is an eminent colonial statesman; he is also an ardent Imperialist of the colonial type. In his plan for an Imperial Council, or in other words for an Imperial Parliament representing the United Kingdom, or rather the countries which now make it up, and also the Dominions, he calmly assumes that Englishmen will without difficulty allow the United Kingdom to be broken up into four countries ruled by four local Parliaments. He supposes, that is to say, as a matter of course, that Englishmen will to a radical change in the government of England which no sane English Premier would have thought of pressing upon the Parliaments of the self-governing colonies which now constitute the Dominion of Canada or which now constitute the Commonwealth of Australia. See Minutes of Proceedings of the Imperial Conference, 1911 [Cd. 5745], pp. 59–61. ["Imperial Council, 25 May," in *Minutes of Proceedings of the Imperial Conference, 1911*, 46–75. Ward was twice Prime Minister of New Zealand and an advocate of a liberal vision of Imperial unity.]

[xxii] See Mr. Asquith's address, cited p. lxxxi, note 1, *ante*. [This is note xx on pages 192–3.]

[xxiii] See p. xxxvii, and note 1, *ante*. [Not included in this collection.]

passion for the greatness, the strength, the glory, and the moral unity of the British Empire.[xxiv] I am one of the thousands of Englishmen who approved, and still approve, of the war in South Africa because it forbade secession. But I am a student of the British constitution; my unhesitating conviction is that the constitution of the Empire ought to develop, as it is actually developing, in the same way in which grew up the constitution of England.[xxv] The relation between England and the Dominions, and, as far as possible, between England and the colonies which are not as yet self-governing countries, need not be developed by arduous feats of legislation. It should grow under the influence of reasonable understandings and of fair customs. There are, as I have intimated,[xxvi] two objects on which every Imperialist should fix his eyes. The one is the contribution by every country within the Empire towards the cost of defending the Empire. The second object is the constant consultation between England and the Dominions. The English taxpayer will not, and ought not to, continue for ever paying the whole cost of Imperial defence. The Dominions cannot for an indefinite period bear the risks of Imperial wars without having a voice in determining if such wars should begin, and when and on what terms they should be brought to an end. Imperial statesmanship is rapidly advancing in the right direction. The system of Imperial Conferences[xxvii] and other modes of inter-communication between England and the Dominions will, we may hope, result in regulating both the contribution which the Dominions ought to make towards the defence of the Empire, and the best method for collecting colonial opinion on the policy of any war which may assume an Imperial character. My full belief is that an Imperial constitution based on goodwill and fairness may within a few years come into real existence, before most Englishmen have realised that the essential foundations of

[xxiv] See *A Fool's Paradise*, p. 24. [Dicey, *A Fool's Paradise: Being a Constitutionalist's Criticism on the Home Rule Bill of 1912* (London, 1913).]
[xxv] This conviction is strengthened by the facts now daily passing before our eyes (Sept. 1914). [Dicey is here referring to the early days of the First World War.]
[xxvi] See pp. lxxx, lxxxi, *ante*. [This is at pages 192–3 above.]; and see *A Fool's Paradise*, p. 25.
[xxvii] Consider the gradual, the most hopeful, and the most successful development of these conferences from 1887 to the last conference in 1911. A sort of conference was held in 1887, and the conferences of 1897 and 1902 were held in connection with some other celebration. The first regular conference for no other purpose than consultation was held in 1907, in which the Imperial Conference received by resolution a definite constitution. The conference of 1911 was held under the scheme thus agreed upon in 1907.

Imperial unity have already been firmly laid. The ground of my assurance is that the constitution of the Empire may, like the constitution of England, be found to rest far less on parliamentary statutes than on the growth of gradual and often unnoted customs.

Characteristics of Federal Government in Relation to Home Rule all Round

Advocates of the so-called "federal solution" apparently believe that the United Kingdom as a whole will gain by exchanging our present unitary constitution for some unspecified form of federal government. To an Englishman who still holds, as was universally held by every English statesman till at the very earliest 1880, that the union between England and Scotland was the wisest and most fortunate among the achievements of British statesmanship, there is great difficulty in understanding the new belief that the federalisation of the United Kingdom will confer benefit upon any of the inhabitants of Great Britain.[xxviii] A candid critic may be able to account for the existence of a political creed which he does not affect to share.

The faith in Home Rule all round has been stimulated, if not mainly created, by the controversy, lasting for thirty years and more, over the policy of Home Rule for Ireland. British Home Rulers have always been anxious to conceal from themselves that the creation of a separate Irish Parliament, and a separate Irish Cabinet depending for its existence on such Parliament, is a real repeal of the Act of Union between Great Britain and Ireland. This refusal to look an obvious fact in the face is

---

[xxviii] The omission of reference to the policy of Home Rule for Ireland as embodied in the Government of Ireland Act, 1914, is intentional. The true character and effect of that Act cannot become apparent until some years have passed. The Act itself stands in a position never before occupied by any statute of immense and far-reaching importance. It may not come into operation for an indefinite period. Its very authors contemplate its amendment before it shall begin to operate. The Act is at the moment detested by the Protestants of Ulster, and a binding though ambiguous pledge has been given that the Act will not be forced upon Ulster against her will. The people of Great Britain will insist on this pledge being held sacred. To a constitutionalist the Act at present affords better ground for wonder than for criticism. If any reader should be curious to know my views on Home Rule he will find them in a general form in *England's Case against Home Rule,* published in 1887; and as applied to the last Home Rule Bill, in *A Fool's Paradise,* published in 1913. [Dicey, *England's Case against Home Rule* (London, 1887). The Government of Ireland Act, or Third Irish Home Rule Bill, was finally passed in 1914 over the rejection of the Lords via the Parliament Act but did not go into effect because of the outbreak of the Great War.]

facilitated by the use of that most ambiguous phrase, "Home Rule all round." Federalism has, no doubt, during the last thirty, or one may say fifty, years acquired a good deal of new prestige. The prosperity of the United States, the military authority of the German Empire, may by federalists be put down to the credit of federal government, though in matter of fact no two constitutions can, either in their details or in their spirit, bear less real resemblance than the democratic and, on the whole, unmilitary constitution of the United States and the autocratic Imperial and, above all, military government of Germany. Federal government has also turned out to be the form of government suitable for some of the British Dominions. It has been an undoubted success in the Canadian Dominion. It has not been long tried but has not been a failure in the Australian Commonwealth. It may become, Englishmen are inclined to think it is, the best form of government for the states included in the Union of South Africa. Little reflection, however, is required in order to see that none of these federations resemble the constitution of England either in their historical development or in their actual circumstances. Then, too, it is thought that whereas English statesmen find it difficult to regulate the relation between Great Britain and Ireland, the task will become easier if the same statesmen undertake to transform, by some hocus-pocus of political legerdemain, the whole United Kingdom into a federal government consisting of at least four different states. It is supposed, lastly, though the grounds for the supposition are not very evident, that the federalisation of the United Kingdom is necessary for, or conducive to, the development of Imperial federalism.

Federalism, in short, has at present the vague, and therefore the strong and imaginative, charm which has been possessed at one time throughout Europe by the parliamentary constitutionalism of England and at another by the revolutionary republicanism of France. It may be well, therefore, to state with some precision why, to one who has studied the characteristics of federal government, it must seem in the highest degree improbable that Home Rule all round, or the federal solution, will be of any benefit whatever to any part of the United Kingdom.

(1) There is no trace whatever of the existence of the federal spirit throughout the United Kingdom. In England, which is after all by far the most important part of the kingdom, the idea of federalism has hitherto been totally unknown. Politicians may have talked of it when it happened to suit their party interest, but to the mass of the people the

idea of federation has always been, and I venture to assert at this moment is, unknown and all but incomprehensible. Scotsmen sometimes complain that Great Britain is often called England. They sometimes talk as though they were in some mysterious manner precluded from a fair share in the benefits accruing from the unity of Great Britain. To any one who investigates the actual course of British politics, and still more of British social life since the beginning of the nineteenth century, these complaints appear to be utterly groundless. The prejudices which, say, in the time of Dr. Johnson, kept Scotsmen and Englishmen apart, have in reality vanished.[14] To take one example of disappearing differences, we may note that while many leading Englishmen fill in Parliament Scottish seats many Scotsmen fill English seats. What is true is that the course of events, and the way in which the steam-engine and the telegraph bring the world everywhere closer together, are unfavourable to that prominence in any country which at one time was attainable by particular localities, or by small bodies of persons living somewhat apart from the general course of national life. This change has, like all other alterations, its weak side. It is quite possible honestly to regret the time when Edinburgh possessed the most intellectual society to be found in Great Britain or Ireland. It is also possible honestly to wish that Lichfield and Norwich might still have, as they had at the beginning of the nineteenth century, a little and not unfamous literary coterie of their own. There is a sense in which the growth of large states is injurious to the individual life of smaller communities. The Roman Republic and the Roman Empire did not produce thinkers or writers who did as much for the progress of mankind as was done by the philosophers, the historians, and the poets of Greece, and the fruits of Greek genius were mainly due to the intellectual achievements of Athens during not much more than a century. Ireland is, as regards most of its inhabitants, discontented with the Union. But it is idle to pretend that Ireland has ever desired federalism in the sense in which it was desired by the colonies which originally formed the United States, or by the inhabitants of what are now the provinces of the Canadian Dominion. O'Connell for a very short time exhibited a

---

[14] Samuel Johnson was the archetypal English man of letters of the eighteenth century. He was notably lacking in fondness for the Scots.

tendency to substitute federalism for repeal. He discovered his mistake and reverted to repeal, which with his more revolutionary followers meant nationalism. No one who reads the last and the strangest of the biographies of Parnell can doubt that "Ireland a Nation" was the cry which met his own instinctive feeling no less than the wishes of his followers, except in so far as their desires pointed towards a revolutionary change in the tenure of land rather than towards the claim for national independence.

(2) There is good reason to fear that the federalisation of the United Kingdom, stimulating as it would the disruptive force of local nationalism, might well arouse a feeling of divided allegiance. This topic is one on which I have no wish to dwell, but it cannot be forgotten by any sensible observer who reflects upon the history of secession in the United States, or of the Sonderbund in Switzerland, or who refuses to forget the preeminently uneasy connection between the different parts of the Austrian Empire and the deliberate determination of Norway to sever at all costs the union with Sweden.[15] Nor is it possible to see how the federalisation of the United Kingdom should facilitate the growth of Imperial federalism.

(3) Federalism, as the dissolution of the United Kingdom, is absolutely foreign to the historical and, so to speak, instinctive policy of English constitutionalists. Each successive generation from the reign of Edward I. onwards has laboured to produce that complete political unity which is represented by the absolute sovereignty of the Parliament now sitting at Westminster. Let it be remembered that no constitutional arrangements or fictions could get rid of the fact that England would, after as before the establishment of Home Rule all round, continue, in virtue of her resources and her population, the predominant partner throughout the United Kingdom, and the partner on whom sovereignty had been conferred, not by the language of any statute or other document, but by the nature of things. It would be hard indeed to prevent the English Parliament sitting at Westminster from not only claiming but exercising sovereign authority; and to all these difficulties must be added one ominous and significant reflection. To every foreign country, whether it were numbered among our allies or among our rivals, the

---

[15] Norway separated from Sweden in 1905, after a referendum in which Norwegians voted overwhelmingly for dissolution of the union of the kingdoms.

federalisation of Great Britain would be treated as a proof of the declining power alike of England and of the British Empire.[xxix]

IV. *The Referendum.*[xxx]—The word Referendum is a foreign expression derived from Switzerland. Thirty years ago it was almost unknown to Englishmen, even though they were interested in political theories. Twenty years ago it was quite unknown to British electors. The word has now obtained popular currency but is often misunderstood. It may be well, therefore, to define, or rather describe, the meaning of the "referendum" as used in this Introduction and as applied to England. The referendum is used by me as meaning the principle that Bills, even when passed both by the House of Commons and by the House of Lords,[xxxi] should not become Acts of Parliament until they have been submitted to the vote of the electors and have received the sanction or approval of the majority of the electors voting on the matter. The referendum is sometimes described, and for general purposes well described, as "the people's veto." This name is a good one; it reminds us that the main use of the referendum is to prevent the passing of any important Act which does not command the sanction of the electors. The expression

[xxix] Any great change in the form of the constitution of England, *e.g.* the substitution of an English republic for a limited monarchy, might deeply affect the loyalty of all the British colonies. Can any one be certain that New Zealand or Canada would, at the bidding of the Parliament of the United Kingdom, transfer their loyalty from George V. to a President chosen by the electorate of the United Kingdom, and this even though the revolution were carried out with every legal formality including the assent of the King himself, and even though the King were elected the first President of the new Commonwealth? Is it certain that a federated union of England, Ireland, Scotland, and Wales would command in our colonies the respect paid to the present United Kingdom? These questions may well seem strange: they are not unimportant. The King is what the Imperial Parliament has never been, the typical representative of Imperial unity throughout every part of the Empire.

[xxx] Lowell, *Public Opinion and Popular Government*, part iii. chaps, xi. –xv., especially chaps, xii. and xiii. (best thing on the subject); Lowell, *Government of England*, i. p. 411; "The Referendum and its Critics," by A.V. Dicey, *Quarterly Review*, No. 423, April 1910; *The Crisis of Liberalism*, by J.A. Hobson; Low, *The Governance of England*, Intro, p. xvii; "Ought the Referendum to be introduced into England?" by A. V. Dicey, *Contemporary Review*, 1890, and *National Review*, 1894. [J.A. Hobson, *The Crisis of Liberalism: New Issues of Democracy* (London, 1909); Sidney Low, *The Governance of England* (London, 1904). Hobson was a formative theorist of "New Liberalism" and an important critic of aspects of capitalism and imperialism. Low was a prolific journalist and historian. The essays by Dicey himself are Chapters 7, 3, and 5 of this volume, respectively.]

[xxxi] And *a fortiori* when passed under the Parliament Act, without the consent of the House of Lords.

"veto" reminds us also that those who advocate the introduction of the referendum into England in fact demand that the electors, who are now admittedly the political sovereign of England, should be allowed to play the part in legislation which was really played, and with popular approval, by *e.g.* Queen Elizabeth at a time when the King or Queen of England was not indeed the absolute sovereign of the country, but was certainly the most important part of the sovereign power, namely Parliament.[xxxii] In this Introduction the referendum, or the people's veto, is considered simply with reference to Bills passed by the Houses of Parliament but which have not received the royal assent. The subject is dealt with by no means exhaustively, but with a view in the first place to bring out the causes of the demand in England for the referendum; and in the next place to consider carefully and examine in turn first by far the strongest argument against, and secondly the strongest argument in favour of introducing the referendum into the constitution of England.

The causes.—During forty years faith in parliamentary government has suffered an extraordinary decline or, as some would say, a temporary eclipse.[xxxiii] This change is visible in every civilised country. Depreciation of, or contempt for, representative legislatures clearly exists under the parliamentary and republican government of France, under the federal and republican constitution of the Swiss Confederacy, or of the United States, under the essential militarism and the superficial parliamentarism of the German Empire, and even under the monarchical and historical constitutionalism of the British Empire. This condition, whether temporary or permanent, of public opinion greatly puzzles the now small body of surviving constitutionalists old enough to remember the sentiment of the mid-Victorian era, with its prevalent belief that to imitate the forms, or at

---

[xxxii] The referendum, it should be noted, can be applied to legislation for different purposes and in different ways. It may, for instance, be applied only to a Bill affecting fundamental changes in the constitution, *e.g.* to a Bill affecting the existence of the monarchy, or to any Bill which would in popular language be called a Reform Bill, and to such Bill after it has been passed by the two Houses. In this case the object of the referendum would be to ensure that no Act of transcendent importance shall be passed without the undoubted assent of the electors. The referendum may again be applied, as it is applied in the Commonwealth of Australia, for preventing "deadlocks," as they are called, arising from the fact of one House of Parliament having carried repeatedly, and the other having repeatedly rejected, a given Bill.

[xxxiii] Compare *Law and Opinion* (2nd ed.), pp. 440–443.

any rate to adopt the spirit of the English constitution, was the best method whereby to confer upon the people of any civilised country the combined blessings of order and of progress. To explain in any substantial degree the alteration in popular opinion it would be necessary to produce a treatise probably longer and certainly of more profound thought than the book for which I am writing a new Introduction. Yet one or two facts may be noted which, though they do not solve the problem before us, do to some slight extent suggest the line in which its solution must be sought for. Parliamentary government may under favourable circumstances go a great way towards securing such blessings as the prevalence of personal liberty and the free expression of opinion. But neither parliamentary government nor any form of constitution, either which has been invented or may be discovered, will ever of itself remove all or half the sufferings of human beings. Utopias lead to disappointment just because they are utopias. The very extension of constitutional government has itself led to the frustration of high hopes; for constitutions have by force of imitation been set up in states unsuited to popular government. What is even more important, parliamentary government has by its continued existence betrayed two defects hardly suspected by the Liberals or reformers of Europe, or at any rate of England, between 1832 and 1880. We now know for certain that while popular government may be under wise leadership a good machine for simply destroying existing evils, it may turn out a very poor instrument for the construction of new institutions or the realisation of new ideals. We know further that party government, which to many among the wisest of modern constitutionalists appears to be the essence of England's far-famed constitution, inevitably gives rise to partisanship, and at last produces a machine which may well lead to political corruption and may, when this evil is escaped, lead to the strange but acknowledged result that a not unfairly elected legislature may misrepresent the permanent will of the electors. This fact has made much impression on the political opinion both of England and of the United States. The above considerations taken as a whole afford some explanation of a demand for that referendum which, though it originates in Switzerland, flourishes in reality, though not in name, in almost every state of the American Commonwealth.

The main argument against the referendum.—To almost all Englishmen the chief objection to the referendum is so obvious, and seems to many fair-minded men so conclusive, that it ought to be put forward in its full strength and to be carefully examined before the reader is called upon to consider the possible advantages of a great change in our constitution. This objection may be thus stated:

In England the introduction of the referendum means, it is urged, the transfer of political power from knowledge to ignorance. Let us put this point in a concrete form. The 670 members of the House of Commons together with the 600 and odd members of the House of Lords[xxxiv] contain a far greater proportion of educated men endowed with marked intellectual power and trained in the exercise of some high political virtues than would generally be found among, say, 1270 electors collected merely by chance from an electorate of more than 8,000,000. The truth of this allegation can hardly be disputed; the inference is drawn therefrom that to substitute the authority of the electorate for the authority of the House of Commons and the House of Lords is to transfer the government of the country from the rule of intelligence to the rule of ignorance. This line of argument can be put in various shapes. It is, in whatever form it appears, the reasoning on which the most capable censors of the referendum rely. Oddly enough (though the matter admits of explanation) this line of reasoning is adopted at once by a thoughtful conservative, such as Maine, and by revolutionists who wish to force upon England, through the use of authoritative legislation, the ideals of socialism. Maine saw in the referendum a bar to all reasonable reforms. He impresses upon his readers that democracy is not in itself a progressive form of government, and expresses this view in words which deserve quotation and attention: "The delusion that democracy," he writes, "when it has once had all things put under its feet, is a progressive form of government, lies deep in the convictions of a particular political school; but there can be no delusion grosser. . . . All that has made England famous, and all that has made England wealthy, has been the work of minorities, sometimes very small ones. It seems to me quite certain that, if for four centuries there had been a very widely extended franchise and a very large electoral body in this country, there would have been no reformation of religion, no change of dynasty, no toleration of Dissent, not even an accurate Calendar. The threshing-machine, the power-loom, the spinning-jenny, and possibly the steam-engine, would have been prohibited. Even in our day, vaccination is in the utmost danger, and we may say generally that the gradual establishment of the masses in power is

---

[xxxiv] Strictly, 638 members. See *Whitaker's Almanack,* 1914, p. 124.

of the blackest omen for all legislation founded on scientific opinion, which requires tension of mind to understand it, and self-denial to submit to it."[xxxv] And he thence practically infers that democracy as it now exists in England would, combined with the referendum, be probably a death-blow to all reasonable reform.[xxxvi] To Maine, in short, the referendum is the last step in the development of democracy, and his censure of the referendum is part of a powerful attack by an intellectual conservative on democratic government which he distrusted and abhorred. Now revolutionists who probably think themselves democrats have of recent years attacked the referendum on grounds which might have been suggested by Maine's pages. The referendum, we are told by socialistic writers, will work steadily to the disadvantage of the Liberal Party.[xxxvii] Would not, we are asked, the anti-reforming press exhaust itself in malignant falsehoods calculated to deceive the people? Such suggestions and others of the same quality may be summed up in an argument which from a socialistic point of view has considerable force. The people, it is said, are too stupid to be entrusted with the referendum; the questions on which the electors are nominally called upon to decide must never be put before them with such clearness that they may understand the true issues submitted to their arbitrament. The party machine, think our new democrats, may be made the instrument for foisting upon the people of England changes which revolutionary radicals or enthusiasts know to be reforms, but which the majority of the electorate, if they understood what was being done, might condemn as revolution or confiscation. The attacks of conservatives and the attacks of socialistic democrats to a certain extent balance one another, but they contain a common element of truth. The referendum is a mere veto. It may indeed often stand in the way of salutary reforms, but it may on the other hand delay or forbid innovations condemned by the weight both of the uneducated and of the educated opinion of England. Thus it is, to say the least, highly probable that, if the demand of votes for women were submitted to the present electorate by means of a referendum, a negative answer would be returned, and an answer of such decision as to check for years the progress or success of the movement in favour of woman

---

[xxxv] Maine, *Popular Government*, pp. 97–98. [Quoted earlier on pages 131–2. This was clearly the articulation of the anti-democratic viewpoint which Dicey regarded as most compelling.]

[xxxvi] See ibid. pp. 96–97.

[xxxvii] See *Against the Referendum* and *Quarterly Review*, April 1910, No. 423, pp. 551, 552.

suffrage. It must, in short, be admitted that a veto on legislation, whether placed in the hands of the King, or in the hands of the House of Lords, or of the House of Commons, or of the 8,000,000 electors, would necessarily work sometimes well and sometimes ill. It might, for example, in England forbid the enforcement or extension of the vaccination laws; it might forbid the grant of parliamentary votes to Englishwomen; it might have forbidden the passing of the Government of Ireland Act, 1911; it might certainly have forbidden the putting of any tax whatever on the importation of corn into the United Kingdom. Now observe that if you take any person, whether an Englishman or Englishwoman, he or she will probably hold that in some one or more of these instances the referendum would have worked ill, and that in some one or more of these instances it would have worked well. All, therefore, that can be conclusively inferred from the argument against the referendum is that the people's veto, like any other veto, may sometimes be ill, and sometimes be well employed. Still it certainly would be urged by a fair-minded opponent of the referendum that there exists a presumption that the Houses of Parliament acting together will exhibit something more of legislative intelligence than would the mass of the electorate when returning their answer to a question put to them by the referendum. But a reasonable supporter of the referendum, while admitting that such a presumption may exist, will however maintain that it is of very slight weight. The Parliament Act gives unlimited authority to a parliamentary or rather House of Commons majority. The wisdom or experience of the House of Lords is in matters of permanent legislation thereby deprived of all influence. A House of Commons majority acts more and more exclusively under the influence of party interests. It is more than possible that the referendum might, if introduced into England, increase the authority of voters not deeply pledged to the dogmas of any party. The referendum, as I have dealt with it, cannot, be it always borne in mind, enforce any law to which at any rate the House of Commons has not consented. It has the merits as also the weaknesses of a veto. Its strongest recommendation is that it may keep in check the inordinate power now bestowed on the party machine.

The main argument in favour of the referendum.—The referendum is an institution which, if introduced into England, would be *strong* enough to curb the absolutism of a party possessed of a parliamentary majority. The referendum is also an institution which in England promises some *considerable diminution* in the most patent defects of party government. Consider first the *strength* of the referendum. It lies in the fact that the people's veto is at once a democratic institution, and, owing to its merely negative character, may be a strictly conservative institution. It is democratic, for it is in reality, as also on the face thereof, an appeal to the people. It is conservative since it ensures the maintenance of any law or institution which the majority of the electors effectively wish to preserve. Nor can any one who studies the present condition of English society seriously believe that, under any system whatever, an institution deliberately condemned by the voice of the people can for a long time be kept in existence. The referendum is, in short, merely the clear recognition in its negative form of that sovereignty of the nation of which under a system of popular government every leading statesman admits the existence. But the mere consonance of a given arrangement with some received doctrine, such as "the sovereignty of the people," must with a thoughtful man carry little weight, except in so far as this harmony with prevalent ideas promises permanence to some suggested reform or beneficial institution. Let us then consider next the *tendency* of the referendum to *lessen the evils* of the party system. An elected legislature may well misrepresent the will of the nation. This is proved by the constant experience of Switzerland and of each of the States which make up the American Commonwealth. This danger of misrepresenting the will of the nation may exist even in the case of an honest and a fairly-elected legislative body. This misrepresentation is likely or even certain to arise where, as in England, a general election comes more and more to resemble the election of a given man or a given party to hold office for five years. Partisanship must, under such a system, have more weight than patriotism. The issues further to be determined by the electors will year by year become, in the absence of the referendum, more complicated and confused. But in the world of politics confusion naturally begets intrigue, sometimes coming near to fraud. Trust in elected legislative bodies is, as already noted, dying out under every form of popular government. The party machine is regarded with suspicion, and often with detestation, by public-spirited citizens of the United States. Coalitions, log-rolling, and parliamentary intrigue are in England diminishing the moral and political faith in the House of Commons. Some means must, many Englishmen believe, be found for the diminution of evils which are under a large electorate the natural, if not the necessary, outcome of our party system. The obvious corrective is to confer upon the people a veto which may restrict the unbounded power of a parliamentary majority. No doubt the referendum must be used with vigilance and with sagacity. Perpetual watchfulness on the part of all honest citizens is the unavoidable price to be paid for the maintenance of sound popular government. The referendum further will promote or tend to promote among the electors a kind of intellectual honesty which, as our constitution now works, is being rapidly destroyed. For the referendum will make it possible to detach the question, whether a particular law, *e.g.* a law introducing some system of so-called tariff reform, shall be passed, from the totally different question, whether Mr. A or Mr. B shall be elected for five years Prime Minister of England. Under the referendum an elector may begin to find it possible to vote for or against a given law in accordance with his real view as to its merits or demerits, without being harassed through the knowledge that if he votes against a law which his conscience and his judgment condemns, he will also be voting that A, whom he deems the fittest man in England to be Prime Minister, shall cease to hold office, and that B, whom the elector happens to distrust, shall at once become Prime Minister. And no doubt the referendum, if ever established in England, may have the effect, which it already has in Switzerland, of making it possible that a minister or a Cabinet, supported on the whole by the electorate, shall retain office honestly and openly, though some proposal made by the Prime Minister and his colleagues and assented to by both Houses of Parliament is, through the referendum, condemned by the electorate. These possible results are undoubtedly repulsive to men who see nothing to censure in our party system. But, as I have throughout insisted, the great recommendation of the referendum is that it tends to correct, or at lowest greatly to diminish, the worst and the most patent evils of party government.

No effort has been made by me to exhaust the arguments against or in favour of the referendum. My aim in this Introduction has been to place before my readers the strongest argument against and also the strongest argument in favour of the introduction of the referendum into the constitution of England. It is certain that no man, who is really satisfied with the working of our party system, will ever look with favour on an institution which aims at correcting the vices of party government. It is probable, if not certain, that any one, who realises the extent to which parliamentary government itself is losing credit from its too close connection with the increasing power of the party machine, will hold with myself that the referendum judiciously used may, at any rate in the case of England, by checking the omnipotence of partisanship, revive faith in that parliamentary government which has been the glory of English constitutional history.

Index

Aberdeen, Lord, George Hamilton-Gordon, 86

Act of Mediation (1803), 22

Act of Settlement (1701), 143, 157

Act of Toleration (1689), 114

Adams, Francis, 16–19, 27, 31, 34, 39–40, 45, 50, 53–4, 76

American Commonwealth, xli, 28, 36, 127, 139

ancien régime, xx, 20–1, 117, 125, 157

Anglicanism. *See* Church of England

Anglo-Irish War, xlii

Anne, Queen of Great Britain, 42

Appenzell, 23

Aristotle and Aristotelianism, 6, 172

Arnold, Matthew, xlv

Asquith, Lord, Henry Herbert, xxvii, 136, 169, 180–1, 193, 196

Athens, 172, 200

Australia, xxvii, 42, 128, 145, 159, 162–3, 187, 196, 199, 203

Austria, 118, 192, 201

Bagehot, Walter, x, 27, 67, 124, 133, 181, 186, 188

Balfour, Lord, Arthur James, 88, 91, 103, 136

Basle (Basel), 23

Belgium, xxviii, 20, 97, 118, 190

Bentham, Jeremy, x, xv–xviii, 4, 109, 175, 180

Benthamism and Benthamites, xii, 125, 175, 183

Bern, 16–18, 21–2, 47, 189

Birmingham, 19, 111

Bonaparte, Napoleon. *See* Napoleon Bonaparte

Bonapartism, xxxv

Bonham-Carter, Elinor Mary, xli

Borgeaud, Charles, 103

Boston, 19

Boulanger, George Ernest, 25

Bourbons (France), 25

boycott, xxix, 84–7, 106

Bright, John, 4, 9, 123, 166, 181

Bryce, James, x, xli, 16, 24, 28, 32, 36, 84, 127, 139

Burke, Edmund, x, xiv, xxiii, 45, 67–8, 72, 101, 153, 163, 178

Cabinet, 27, 32, 34, 36, 38, 40, 50, 115, 189, 198

England, xxxviii, 29, 32, 37, 39, 60, 64, 86, 149, 178, 181, 189, 209

France, 27, 189

Caesarism, xxxiv–xxxv, xxxix

Cairns, Hugh, 3–6, 10–11, 14–15

Calvin, John, 30

Canada, 113, 185, 191, 195, 199–200. *See also* Newfoundland

Carnot, Sadi, 32, 37

Catholic Emancipation (Roman Catholic Relief Act), 46, 65, 74, 125, 154

Catholicism, xiv, 21, 25, 28, 114, 125, 157, 168

Cavour, Count, Camilo Benso, 120, 122

Cecil, Robert (1864–1958), 139

Chamberlain, Joseph, 88, 111

210

Index

Channel Islands, 186
Charles I, King of England, 116, 125
Charles II, King of England, 116
Charles X, King of France, 25
Charter of 1814 (France), 43
Chatham, Earl, William Pitt the Elder, 38, 138
Christian Socialists, xli
Church of England, 7, 13, 63, 65, 70, 74, 77, 89, 158, 176, 184
Church of Ireland. *See* Ireland, Church of
Churchill, Winston, 168
Civil War (England), 116, 125
Clavière, Étienne, 30
Cobden, Richard, 183
Commons, House of. *See* Parliament, Commons, House of
Commonwealth, The (England), 115, 164
Comte, Auguste, xiii
Conservative (Party), xix, xxvi, 3, 14, 44, 76, 88, 90, 93, 106, 109, 129, 140, 142, 166, 184
Constant, Benjamin, xvi
Cork, 111
Corn Laws, 8, 10, 51, 125, 173, 183
Cox, Harold, 139
Cromwell, Oliver, 115–16, 164–5
Crown (Institution), xxii–xxiii, xxxiii, xxxv, 47–50, 63–6, 72–4, 94, 106–7, 113–18, 143, 157–8
Cunningham, C.D., 16, 34

Davitt, Michael, 84, 86, 90
de Lolme, Jean-Louis, x
debate. *See* discussion (in government)
deliberation, xiv, xxxii, xxxv–xxxvi, 57
democracy, xi, xiii, xv–xviii, xx, xxiii–xxiv, xxvi–xxxiii, xxxvi, xxxviii–xxxix, 4, 14, 30, 32–3, 45–9, 52, 61, 71, 74–5, 79, 82, 88, 91, 93–5, 97, 108, 127–8, 130–5, 142, 147, 150–1, 159, 163, 175, 177, 179, 181, 185, 208
  American, xxx, 28, 52, 93, 104, 185, 199
  anti-democracy, xiii, xvii, 127–8, 132, 134, 205–6
  democratic age, xix, xxiv, xxxiv, xxxvii, xxxix, 72, 91
  democratization, xvii, xxiii, xxxviii
democrats, xiv, xvii–xviii, xxvi–xxvii, xxx–xxxii, 6, 44, 75, 95, 101, 141, 147, 150, 164, 206
  direct democracy, xxxii, xxxiv, xxxviii
  English, ix, xxx, 75, 93, 107, 133, 173
  French, 25–7, 52
  Hungarian, 120
  liberal democracy, xi, xix, xxv, xxxii, xxxix
  monarchical, 162
  Norwegian, 162
  parliamentary, xx, 53, 71, 98
  representative democracy, xxxvi
  Swiss, xxxii, 16, 19, 23–4, 29, 31–2, 40–4, 48, 52–3, 62, 80, 93, 104, 135, 161, 189
Democrat (US Party), 26, 90
Denmark, 117
Derby, Lord, Edward Smith-Stanley, 51, 78
despotism, 22, 57, 114, 118, 122, 142, 148, 159, 161, 164
Devonshire, Duke, Spencer Compton Cavendish, Lord Hartington, 88
Dicey, Albert Venn (references from editor's introduction and notes only)
  against corporatist representation, xv
  against socialism, xvi, 142
  against the *plébiscite*, xxxiv
  and A. Lawrence Lowell, 129
  and Abraham Lincoln, 38
  and Australia, 128
  and Carl Schmitt, xxxix
  and Catholic emancipation, 125
  and conservatism, xix
  and Corn Laws, 51, 125
  and federalism, xi, xv, 190
  and France, xxxiv, 114
  and Henry Labouchere, 101
  and Henry Maine, 18, 71, 133, 206
  and Home Rule, xii, xix, xxiv–xxvi, xxviii, 82, 168, 183, 187, 198
  and Ireland, 87, 90, 125
  and J.A.R. Marriott, 165
  and James Bryce, 28
  and John Henry Maden, 84
  and John Morley, 79
  and judicial review, 190
  and Lord Salisbury, 37
  and Max Weber, xxxix
  and mob rule, xxviii
  and Montesquieu, 67

Index

Dicey, Albert Venn (references from editor's
introduction and notes only) (cont.)
  and national insurance, 168
  and parliamentarism, 52, 120, 166
  and partisanship, xxxi, xxxvi–xxxvii, xxxix
  and political decline, xxvii, xxix, xxxi
  and Poor Laws, 174
  and Richard Cobden, 183
  and Scotland, 113
  and sentimentalism, xxx
  and social contract theory, xxix
  and Switzerland, xix, xxxii, 21, 32
  and the American Civil War, 86
  and the Commonwealth, 116
  and the eight-hour workday, 91
  and the First Reform Act, 155
  and the House of Lords, xxvi
  and the intellectual aristocracy, xiii
  and the need for expertise, xxxvii
  and the *Oxford English Dictionary*, 120
  and the referendum, xxxii–xxxvii, 21, 202
  and the Tichborne pretender, 185
  and W.E.H. Lecky, 128
  and Walter Bagehot, 123
  and Whiggery, xxiii
  and William Gladstone, 59, 81
  and World War I, 197
  as a "loser" of history, xi
  as a disillusioned liberal, xix, xxi
  as a lawyer, viii
  as a liberal democrat, xxxii
  as a political theorist, xi
  as a theorist of history, xv
  as constitutional theorist, xxvii, xxxiii
  as democratic theorist, xiii, xvi–xvii, xx,
    xxiv, xxviii, xxx, xxxiii, xxxvi, xxxviii
  as egalitarian, xxxvii
  as legal theorist, xxix–xxx, 144
  as liberal theorist, xiv, xviii, xxxviii, 157
  as theorist of sovereignty, xxi–xxiii, xxxiii,
    xxxv
  as theorist of the state, xxxiii
  between liberalism and democracy, xxxix
  between old and new liberalism, xi
  Law of the Constitution, xx, 153
  *Lectures on the Relation of Law and Public
    Opinion*, 125
  trajectory of his thought, xii
Dicey, Anne Mary, xl

Dicey, Thomas Edward, xl
Dillon, John, 86, 90
discussion (in government), xxxv, 33, 35, 44,
  46, 57, 61, 69–70, 82, 118, 122, 124, 129,
  133, 146
disestablishment (religion), 58, 63, 70, 77, 89,
  125, 155, 158, 168, 184
Disraeli, Benjamin, 9–10, 130, 166
dissent (religion), 132, 134, 205
divine right of kings, xxiii, 48
Droz, Numa, 18
Dublin, xii, 82, 84, 86, 140
Dubs, Jakob, 18, 31
Dufour, Guillaume Henri, 30

East India Company, 133
education, xiii, xxxiii, 19, 36, 45, 49–50, 55,
  68, 78
Edward I, King of England, 112, 201
Eight Hours Bill, 64, 91, 110
Eldon, Lord, John Scott, 130
Elizabeth I, Queen of England, xxxiv, 42, 47,
  50, 69, 79, 203
Empire (British), xv, xix, xxv, 113, 116, 143,
  162, 186–7, 191–2, 202–3
Enlightenment, x
equality, xv–xvi, xxix, xxxvi, 19, 105, 175, 178,
  187–8
Evangelicalism, viii, xl

Fabians, 142
federalism, xi, xv, xxxvii, 117, 171, 185–202
  American, 23, 186, 191, 199
  and Ireland, 200
  Canadian, 185
  German, 199
  Imperial, 187, 192–9
  Italian, 187
  of the United Kingdom, xv, xxv, 186,
    192–202
  Swiss, 22–3, 30–1, 40, 52, 68, 188–9, 203
Fenians, xxix
Ford, Patrick, 90
Fox, Charles James, 101
France, 26, 32, 37, 39, 46, 50, 52, 56, 70–1, 90,
  96, 104, 114, 117–18, 146, 152, 161, 189,
  199, 203
  Chamber of Deputies, 28, 33, 146, 161
  Consulate, 43

Directory, 22
Estates General, 29, 117
First Empire, 43, 57, 114
National Assembly, 28–9, 37, 125
Restoration, 22, 25, 43
Revolution of 1789. *See* French Revolution
Second Empire, xxviii, xxxiv, 24, 57, 118
Second Republic, xxxiv, 24, 118
Senate, 43, 49, 75, 145, 161
Third Republic, xxiv, xxviii, 25, 37, 146, 161
Franco-Prussian War, xxxiv
free speech, xxxi
free trade, xiii, 4, 8, 51, 74, 78, 90, 108, 136–7, 139, 154, 168, 173, 183
Freeman, Edward Augustus, 30, 124
French Revolution, xx, 22, 29, 67, 74, 114, 118, 125, 129–30, 175
fundamental laws, xxvi, 48, 71–5, 93–4, 107–8, 152

Galway, 95
Garibaldi, Giuseppe, 30, 122
Gatton (rotten borough), 11
Geneva, 23, 30
George I, King of Great Britain, 153
George III, King of Great Britain, 9, 73, 102, 113
George V, King of the United Kingdom, 202
Germany, 20, 32, 36, 39, 104, 114, 187, 199, 203
Girondins, 175
Gladstone, William Ewart, xii, xix–xx, xxiv–xxvi, xxviii, 3, 76, 82–9, 99, 105–8, 119, 130, 133, 155
Gladstonianism, 59, 73–4, 81–8, 90, 92, 96, 98–100, 108, 111, 168
Glorious Revolution (1688), 29, 38, 42, 114, 116, 153
Greece, 163, 172, 200
Grégoire, Louis, 28, 43
Grévy, Jules, 37
Guizot, François, 27

Hallam, Henry, x, 124
Hanoverians, 114, 143
Hapsburgs, 118
Harcourt, William, 101, 103
Harrison, Benjamin, 32
Harvard University, xlii, 125, 129

Healy, Timothy, 84, 86, 111
Hearn, William Edward, 42
Herodotus, 17
Herschell, Farrer, 84
Hill, Frank, 64
Hobson, J.A., 127, 202
Holland. *See* Netherlands, The
Home Rule, xiii, xix–xxi, xxiv–xxvi, xxviii, 28, 53, 59, 64, 74, 79, 81–7, 89–90, 93–101, 105, 109–11, 130, 136, 140, 152, 156, 158, 167–9, 184, 187, 198–9, 201
    First Home Rule Bill (1886), xii, xli, 58–9, 84, 99, 187
    Fourth Home Rule Act (1920), xlii
    Second Home Rule Bill (1893), xli, 99, 130, 156
    Third Home Rule Bill (1914), xlii, 159, 198
Horace, 68
household suffrage, 5, 14, 130, 153, 178, 185
Humphreys, John H., 179
Hungary, 119–20

India, 113, 133, 173, 194, 196
Ireland, viii, xii, xiv, 12, 20, 53, 59, 74, 82, 86, 92, 95, 98–100, 109, 146, 168, 186, 195, 200, 202, 207. *See also* Home Rule
    Church of, 58, 65, 74, 125, 155
    Irish nationalism, xviii, xxvi, xxviii, 81, 83–4, 87, 89, 96, 111, 137, 166–7, 183
    North of, xlii, 95, 198
    proposed parliament for, 83, 85, 93, 100, 105, 108, 111, 146, 198
    South of, xlii
    union with Great Britain, 65, 74, 77, 87, 100, 104–5, 112, 140, 143–4, 157, 165, 198
Isle of Man, 186
Italy, 30, 117–18, 120–2, 187, 192

Jacobinism and Jacobins, 57, 91, 114
James I, King of England, 42
James II, King of England, 114
James VI, King of Scotland. *See* James I, King of England
Japan, 16, 18, 115, 117
Johnson, Samuel, 200
Judaism, 180
judicial review, xi, xxxvii, 190
July Monarchy. *See* Louis Philippe, King of France

Kilkenny, 95
Kossuth, Lajos, 120

Labouchere, Henry, 101
Labour (Party), 166–7, 183–4
Lamartine, Alphonse de, 120
Lamennais, Félicité de, 29
Lancashire, 20, 95
Land Purchase Act, 87, 91
land reform, 169
Land War, xxix
Lausanne, 189
Lecky, W.E.H., 128
Lee, Robert E., 190–1
legal positivism, ix, xxiv
Leicestershire, xl
Leopold II, King of the Belgians, xxviii
Leviathan, xi
Liberal (Party), xii, xix, xxv, 4, 76, 82–5, 88,
    90, 106, 130, 140–1, 166, 180, 184, 204,
    206
Liberal Unionist (Party), xix, 59, 73
Liberalism, xi, xiii, xv, xix, xxxii, xxxix, 183
Lichfield, 200
Lincoln, Abraham, 38
Lloyd George, David, 137, 168
Local Option, 110
Locke, John, xxix, 180
London, xl, 20, 68, 95, 117
Lords, House of. *See* Parliament, Lords,
    House of
Lorimer, James, 11
Louis Philippe, King of France, 24–6, 29
Louis XIV, King of France, 117, 174
Louis XVI, King of France, 117
Louis XVIII, King of France, 43
Louis-Napoleon. *See* Napoleon III
Low, Sidney, 202
Lowell, A. Lawrence, 129, 179, 202
Lowell, James Russell, x
Lucerne, 21

Macaulay, Thomas Babington, x, xxiii, 119
Maden, John Henry, 84
Magna Carta, 157
Maine, Henry, 18–19, 24, 46, 56, 71, 127–8,
    131–5, 186, 205–6
Mallet du Pan, Jacques, 23, 30
Manin, Daniele, 122

Marriott, J.A.R., 165
Mary II, Queen of England, 114
Massachusetts, 190
Mazzini, Giuseppe, 120, 122
Meiji Constitution, 115
Mexico, 117
Mill, John Stuart, ix–x, xiii, xviii, 4, 10, 13, 27,
    133, 174–5, 180, 182, 185
Montesquieu, Baron, Charles Louis de
    Secondat, 67
Morley, John, 79, 86, 101, 150
Moses, Bernard, 44
Murray, James, 120

Napoleon Bonaparte, 22, 43, 57, 118, 174
Napoleon III, xxxiv, xl, 24, 43, 57, 118
National Insurance Act (1911), 168–9
natural rights, 175
Necker, Jacques, 30
Netherlands, The, 20, 42
New York, 9, 26–7, 160, 188, 191, 195
New Zealand, 187, 191, 195–6, 202
Newcastle Programme, 105, 110
Newfoundland, 187
Newry, 95
Nightingale, Florence, 177
nonconformism, 49, 141, 158, 166, 168
Norway, 159, 162, 187, 201
Norwich, 200

O'Brien, William, 86, 90
O'Connell, Daniel, 183, 200
Oberholtzer, Ellis, 97, 103
Old Age Pensions Act (1908), 157, 168
Old Sarum (rotten borough), 11, 73
opposition (government), 34, 50, 60, 82–3, 89,
    98–100, 115, 166
Orelli, Aloys von, 16, 31, 40, 54
Ostrogorski, Moisei, x
Oxford, xiii, xl, 28, 30, 120, 165

Paley, William, x
Palmerston, Viscount, John Henry Temple,
    119, 123, 129, 133, 138, 154, 165–6
Paris, 22, 25, 56, 117
Parliament
    as a mirror, xiii, xv, 3–4, 15, 179–81
    Commons, House of, xiv, xx, xxiii,
        xxv–xxvi, xxxiii, xxxvi, xlii, 3, 44, 47, 58,

63–4, 66, 69, 72, 77, 82, 85–6, 94–102, 104, 107–8, 110, 112, 122–4, 129–32, 136–40, 145, 147, 153–9, 163–8, 175, 179–85, 202, 205, 207–8

Lords, House of, xxii, xxvi, xxxiii, xlii, 44, 58, 63, 66, 69, 73, 75, 77, 94, 97–9, 101, 108, 111, 125, 136–7, 141, 145–7, 155–9, 164–5, 202, 205, 207

Parliament Act of 1911 xxvi, 137, 152–3, 156–9, 163, 165–7, 170, 207

Parliamentarism, xviii, xxxviii, xlviii, 32, 52, 107, 120, 203

parliamentary sovereignty. *See* sovereignty, parliamentary

Parnell, Charles, xxix, 201

Parnellites, 96

Peel, Robert, 51, 78–9, 108, 114, 129, 138, 154

Peelites, 154

People's Budget, xxvi, 137

Piedmont, 118

Pitt, William (the elder). *See* Chatham, Earl, William Pitt the Elder

Pitt, William (the younger), 9, 102, 148

Plantagenets, 112

plébiscite, xxviii, xxxiv–xxxv, xl, 43–4, 56–8, 118

Plutocracy, 11

Poor Laws, 69, 174, 182

popular sovereignty. *See* sovereignty, popular

proportional representation, 120, 128, 147, 171, 179–85

protectionism, 90, 108

Protestantism, 21, 74, 106, 114, 128, 143, 168, 198

Quebec, 191, 195

Radical (Party), 14, 62, 67, 76, 128, 166, 174

Redmond, John, 84

referendum, xi, xviii, xxviii, xxxii–xxxix, 47–51, 97, 103–4, 127–30, 135, 160, 171, 202–3

American, xxxiv, 97, 103, 120, 160, 204

and general elections, 58–9, 63, 135–9

and *plébiscite*, 43–4, 56–8

Australian, xxvii, 128, 145, 163

Belgian, xxviii

criticism of, 44–7, 131–42, 150, 204–7

French, xxviii

Norwegian, 201

proposal for England, 53, 63, 65–73, 75–80, 97, 107–11, 142–9, 207–9

Referendum Act. *See* Referendum Act

Swiss, xix, xxvii, xxxiii, xxxvii, xli, 18, 21, 29, 31, 40–2, 47–8, 51, 54–6, 61–2, 64, 66, 69, 120, 124, 130, 135, 144, 148, 161, 163

Referendum Act, xxxiii, 107, 143–4

reform, xiv, 4–5, 10–11, 13–15, 41–2, 49, 55, 74, 78, 143, 206

First Reform Act of 1832, xii, 10, 50–1, 58, 60, 73, 78–9, 108, 129, 133, 135, 153, 174

Second Reform Act of 1867, xiii, 10, 60, 133

Third Reform Act of 1884, xxiv

representative government, xx, xxii, xxiv–xxv, xxxiv, xxxix, 7, 47, 52, 112, 114, 119, 121–2, 124, 130, 172

Republican (US Party), 26, 90

Restoration, The (England), 116

revolutions of 1848, 7, 118–19

Rhode Island, 188

Rome, 12, 30, 43, 117, 122, 172, 200

Rosebery, Lord, Archibald Primrose, 131

rotten borough. *See* Gatton (rotten borough), Old Sarum (rotten borough)

Rousseau, Jean-Jacques, 30, 44, 129

Ruchonnet, Louis, 18

Russell, Lord, John, 133, 154

Russia, 90, 115

Russian Revolution, xii

Salisbury, Lord, Robert Gascoyne-Cecil, 37, 76, 88, 105

Schmitt, Carl, xxxix

Scotland, 12, 20, 68, 99, 109, 186, 191, 195, 200, 202

union with England, 112, 143, 157, 165, 174, 191, 198

Scott, Walter, 191

Scott, Winfield, 190

sentimentalism, xxx, 72

Separatism (Ireland), 82–4, 86–7, 96, 109

Septennial Act, 45

Sidgwick, Henry, x, xix, 88

Socialism, xvi, 28, 128, 131, 135, 140, 146, 168, 205–6

Sonderbund, 21, 23, 30, 188, 190, 201

South Africa, 187, 197, 199

sovereignty, xvi, 7, 23, 31, 55, 62, 64, 93, 108, 163, 195, 201, 203
  legal, xxi, 70
  monarchical, xxiii
  national, xx, 66, 98, 103, 152, 154, 208
  parliamentary, x, xxi–xxiv, xxxv, 42, 46–7, 62, 70, 104, 144, 153, 186, 201, 203
  political, xxii, 70
  popular, xxiii, xxix, xxxiii–xxxv, xxxvii, 44, 46, 50, 62, 71, 75, 79, 94, 140, 150, 208
Spain, 117–18
Spencer, 5th Earl, John, 86
Spencer, Herbert, x
Stephen, James Fitzjames, x, xxix, xlv
Stephen, Leslie, x, xxii, 16
Strachey, John St. Loe, 95
Stuarts, 42, 114
Sweden, 20, 117, 187, 201
Swiss Council, 18, 27, 29, 32, 38, 40, 50, 62, 79, 189
Switzerland
  Conspiracy of Davel, 21
  constitutional revision of 1874, 21, 29, 41, 44, 54
  Federal Assembly, 27, 29, 33, 35, 38–40, 44–5, 47, 51, 54, 56, 58, 62, 66, 70, 124, 134, 161
  Peasant War of 1653, 21

Taine, Hippolyte, 56
technocracy, xxxviii, 142
temperance, 89, 166–7, 183
Thiers, Adolphe, 27, 43
Tocqueville, Alexis de, ix–x, xix, xxiv, xxxi, 23, 28
toleration, 46, 114, 132, 134, 205
trades unions, 157, 167
Trevelyan, George, 86, 95, 101
Tudors, 42, 62, 113
Turkey, 115

Ulster. *See* Ireland, North of
Unionism, 81–5, 87–93, 109–11, 137, 156, 168
United States of America, xxx, xxxiv, 9, 20, 23–5, 30–1, 34, 52, 75, 93–4, 113, 117, 146, 185, 187–8, 191, 193, 199–200, 203, 208
  Civil War, xl, 23, 38, 86, 90, 185, 190–1, 201
  Congress of, 27, 29, 33, 36, 52, 77, 122, 160, 169, 195

constitution of, 26, 29, 31, 75, 104, 133, 152, 159, 186, 188
  Constitutional Convention, 80, 124
  foreign policy of, 26
  House of Representatives, 33, 86, 122, 160
  President of, 26, 29, 31–2, 36, 38
  Senate, 31, 33, 160, 188
  state constitutions and rights, xv, xxvii, 13, 97, 103, 120, 124, 128, 160, 190–1, 204, 208
  Supreme Court, 160, 189
  War of Independence, 102
universal suffrage, xiv, 5, 7, 15, 25, 157, 162, 177
Unterwald, 23
utilitarianism, 175

vaccination, xxxi, 132, 134–5, 173, 184–5, 205, 207
Vaud, 22, 189
Virginia, 191
Voltaire, x, 150
vox populi, xvii, 43, 48, 140, 174
Vulliemin, Louis, 21

Wales, 95, 99, 168, 186, 195
  union with England, 112
Walpole, Robert, 38, 114
Walsh, William, Archbishop, 86
Wandsworth, 95
War of the Roses, 113
Ward, Joseph, 196
Washington, George, 38
Weber, Max, xi, xxxix
Westminster, 70, 82, 84, 96, 99, 123, 150, 182, 195, 201
Whig, x, xiv, xxiii, xl, 10, 38, 59, 102, 120, 124, 129, 133, 154–5, 166, 174, 182
Whiggery, xxiii
William III, King of England, 42, 114
Williams, J. Fischer, 179–80
Wilson, Woodrow, 129
Wollstonecraft, Mary, 175
women's suffrage, 63, 109, 140, 157, 171, 175–9, 182–3, 207
Wordsworth, William, x
World War I, xii, 197

Young, Arthur, 17

Zurich, 19, 21, 43, 54, 189

CAMBRIDGE TEXTS IN THE HISTORY OF POLITICAL THOUGHT

Titles published in the series thus far

Aquinas *Political Writings* (edited and translated by R.W. Dyson)

Aristotle *The Politics and The Constitution of Athens* (edited and translated by Stephen Everson)

Arnold *Culture and Anarchy and Other Writings* (edited by Stefan Collini)

Astell *Political Writings* (edited by Patricia Springborg)

Augustine *The City of God against the Pagans* (edited and translated by R. W. Dyson)

Augustine *Political Writings* (edited by E. M. Atkins and R. J. Dodaro)

Austin *The Province of Jurisprudence Determined* (edited by Wilfrid E. Rumble)

Bacon *The History of the Reign of King Henry VII* (edited by Brian Vickers)

Bagehot *The English Constitution* (edited by Paul Smith)

Bakunin *Statism and Anarchy* (edited and translated by Marshall Shatz)

Baxter *Holy Commonwealth* (edited by William Lamont)

Bayle *Political Writings* (edited by Sally L. Jenkinson)

Beccaria *On Crimes and Punishments and Other Writings* (edited by Richard Bellamy; translated by Richard Davies)

Bentham *A Fragment on Government* (edited by Ross Harrison)

Bernstein *The Preconditions of Socialism* (edited and translated by Henry Tudor)

Bodin *On Sovereignty* (edited and translated by Julian H. Franklin)

Bolingbroke *Political Writings* (edited by David Armitage)

Bossuet *Politics Drawn from the Very Words of Holy Scripture* (edited and translated by Patrick Riley)

Botero *The Reason of State* (edited and translated by Robert Bireley)

The British Idealists (edited by David Boucher)

Burke *Pre-Revolutionary Writings* (edited by Ian Harris)

Burke *Revolutionary Writings* (edited by Iain Hampsher-Monk)

Cavendish *Political Writings* (edited by Susan James)

Christine de Pizan *The Book of the Body Politic* (edited by Kate Langdon Forhan)

Cicero *On Duties* (edited by E. M. Atkins; edited and translated by M. T. Griffin)

Cicero *On the Commonwealth and On the Laws* (edited and translated by James E. G. Zetzel)

Comte *Early Political Writings* (edited and translated by H. S. Jones)

Comte *Conciliarism and Papalism* (edited by J. H. Burns and Thomas M. Izbicki)

Condorcet *Political Writings* (edited by Steven Lukes and Nadia Urbinati)

Constant *Political Writings* (edited and translated by Biancamaria Fontana)

Dante *Monarchy* (edited and translated by Prue Shaw)

Albert Venn Dicey *Writings on Democracy and the Referendum* (edited by Gregory Conti)

The Dutch Revolt (edited and translated by Martin van Gelderen)

Early Greek Political Thought from Homer to the Sophists (edited and translated by Michael Gagarin and Paul Woodruff)

The Early Political Writings of the German Romantics (edited and translated by Frederick C. Beiser)

Diderot *Political Writings* (edited and translated by John Hope Mason and Robert Wokler)

Emerson *Political Writings* (edited by Kenneth S. Sacks)

The English Levellers (edited by Andrew Sharp)

Erasmus *The Education of a Christian Prince with the Panegyric for Archduke Philip of Austria* (edited and translated by Lisa Jardine; translated by Neil M. Cheshire and Michael J. Heath)

Fénelon *Telemachus* (edited and translated by Patrick Riley)

Ferguson *An Essay on the History of Civil Society* (edited by Fania Oz-Salzberger)

Fichte *Addresses to the German Nation* (edited by Gregory Moore)

Filmer *Patriarcha and Other Writings* (edited by Johann P. Sommerville)

Fletcher *Political Works* (edited by John Robertson)

Sir John Fortescue *On the Laws and Governance of England* (edited by Shelley Lockwood)

Fourier *The Theory of the Four Movements* (edited by Gareth Stedman Jones; edited and translated by Ian Patterson)

Franklin *The Autobiography and Other Writings on Politics, Economics, and Virtue* (edited by Alan Houston)

Gramsci *Pre-Prison Writings* (edited by Richard Bellamy; translated by Virginia Cox)

Guicciardini *Dialogue on the Government of Florence* (edited and translated by Alison Brown)

Hamilton, Madison, and Jay (writing as 'Publius') *The Federalist with Letters of 'Brutus'* (edited by Terence Ball)

Harrington *The Commonwealth of Oceana and A System of Politics* (edited by J. G. A. Pocock)

Hegel *Elements of the Philosophy of Right* (edited , by Allen W. Wood,; translated by H. B. Nisbet)

Hegel *Political Writings* (edited by Laurence Dickey and H. B. Nisbet)

Hess *The Holy History of Mankind and Other Writings* (edited and translated by Shlomo Avineri)

Hobbes *On the Citizen* (edited and translated by Michael Silverthorne and Richard Tuck)

Hobbes *Leviathan* (edited by Richard Tuck)

Hobhouse *Liberalism and Other Writings* (edited by James Meadowcroft)

Hooker *Of the Laws of Ecclesiastical Polity* (edited by A. S. McGrade)

Hume *Political Essays* (edited by Knud Haakonssen)

Jefferson *Political Writings* (edited by Joyce Appleby and Terence Ball)

John of Salisbury *Policraticus* (edited by Cary J. Nederman)

Kant *Political Writings* (edited by H. S. Reiss; translated by H. B. Nisbet)

King James VI and I *Political Writings* (edited by Johann P. Sommerville)

Knox *On Rebellion* (edited by Roger A. Mason)

Kropotkin *The Conquest of Bread and Other Writings* (edited by Marshall Shatz)

Kumazawa Banzan *Governing the Realm and bringing Peace to All below Heaven* (edited and translated by John A. Tucker)

Lawson *Politica Sacra et Civilis* (edited by Conal Condren)

Leibniz *Political Writings* (edited and translated by Patrick Riley)

Lincoln *Political Writings and Speeches* (edited by Terence Ball)

Locke *Political Essays* (edited by Mark Goldie)

Locke *Two Treatises of Government* (edited by Peter Laslett)

Loyseau *A Treatise of Orders and Plain Dignities* (edited and translated by Howell A. Lloyd)

Luther and Calvin on Secular Authority (edited and translated by Harro Höpfl)

Catharine Macaulay *Political Writings* (edited by Max Skjönsberg)

Machiavelli *The Prince, Second Edition* (edited by Quentin Skinner and Russell Price)

Joseph de Maistre *Considerations on France* (edited and translated by Richard A. Lebrun)

Maitland *State, Trust and Corporation* (edited by David Runciman and Magnus Ryan)

Malthus *An Essay on the Principle of Population* (edited by Donald Winch)

Marsiglio of Padua *Defensor minor and De translatione Imperii* (edited by Cary J. Nederman)

Marsilius of Padua *The Defender of the Peace* (edited and translated by Annabel Brett)

Marx *Early Political Writings* (edited and translated by Joseph O'Malley)

Medieval Muslim Mirrors for Princes: An Anthology of Arabic, Persian and Turkish Political Advice (edited and translated by Louise Marlow)

James Mill *Political Writings* (edited by Terence Ball)

J. S. Mill *On Liberty and Other Writings* (edited by Stefan Collini)

Milton *Political Writings* (edited by Martin Dzelzainis; translated by Claire Gruzelier)

Montesquieu *The Spirit of the Laws* (edited and translated by Anne M. Cohler, Basia Carolyn Miller and Harold Samuel Stone)

More *Utopia* (edited by George M. Logan and Robert M. Adams)

Morris *News from Nowhere* (edited by Krishan Kumar)

Nicholas of Cusa *The Catholic Concordance* (edited and translated by Paul E. Sigmund)

Nietzsche *On the Genealogy of Morality* (edited by Keith Ansell-Pearson; translated by Carol Diethe)

Paine *Political Writings* (edited by Bruce Kuklick)

William Penn *Political Writings* (edited by Andrew R. Murphy)

Plato *Gorgias, Menexenus, Protagoras* (edited by Malcolm Schofield; translated by Tom Griffith)

Plato *Laws* (edited by Malcolm Schofield; translated by Tom Griffith)

Plato *The Republic* (edited by G. R. F. Ferrari; translated by Tom Griffith)

Plato *Statesman* (edited by Julia Annas; edited and translated by Robin Waterfield)

Political Thought in Portugal and its Empire, c.1500–1800 (edited by Pedro Cardim and Nuno Gonçalo Monteiro)

The Political Thought of the Irish Revolution (edited by Richard Bourke and Niamh Gallagher)

Price *Political Writings* (edited by D. O. Thomas)

Priestley *Political Writings* (edited by Peter Miller)

Proudhon *What is Property?* (edited and translated by Donald R. Kelley and Bonnie G. Smith)

Pufendorf *On the Duty of Man and Citizen according to Natural Law* (edited by James Tully; translated by Michael Silverthorne)

The Radical Reformation (edited and translated by Michael G. Baylor)

Rousseau *The Discourses and Other Early Political Writings* (edited and translated by Victor Gourevitch)

Rousseau *The Social Contract and Other Later Political Writings* (edited and translated by Victor Gourevitch)

Seneca *Moral and Political Essays* (edited and translated by John M. Cooper; edited by J. F. Procopé)

Sidney *Court Maxims* (edited by Hans W. Blom, Eco Haitsma Mulier and Ronald Janse)

Sorel *Reflections on Violence* (edited by Jeremy Jennings)

Spencer *Political Writings* (edited by John Offer)

Stirner *The Ego and Its Own* (edited by David Leopold)

Emperor Taizong and ministers *The Essentials of Governance* (compiled by Wu Jing; edited and translated by Hilde De Weerdt, Glen Dudbridge and Gabe van Beijeren)

Thoreau *Political Writings* (edited by Nancy L. Rosenblum)

Tönnies *Community and Civil Society* (edited and translated by Jose Harris; translated by Margaret Hollis)

Utopias of the British Enlightenment (edited by Gregory Claeys)

Vico *The First New Science* (edited and translated by Leon Pompa)

Vitoria *Political Writings* (edited by Anthony Pagden and Jeremy Lawrance)

Voltaire *Political Writings* (edited and translated by David Williams)

Weber *Political Writings* (edited by Peter Lassman; edited and translated by Ronald Speirs)

William of Ockham *A Short Discourse on Tyrannical Government* (edited by Arthur Stephen McGrade; translated by John Kilcullen)

William of Ockham *A Letter to the Friars Minor and Other Writings* (edited by Arthur Stephen McGrade; edited and translated by John Kilcullen)

Wollstonecraft *A Vindication of the Rights of Men and A Vindication of the Rights of Woman* (edited by Sylvana Tomaselli)